Solving the Profound Mysteries

of

Consciousness, Soul, and Life

From the Series
Understanding Consciousness and The Soul

(Volume 1)

by Mark Fennell

Institute for the Study of Advanced Civilizations

© 2023

Table of Contents

The Three Layers of the Book

About the Series

1. Soul, Consciousness, and Subconscious
2. Interactions of the Mind, Soul, and Body
3. Separating, Aggregating, and Alignment
4. Emotions of Advanced Souls
5. The Meaning of Life
6. Greater Realities Beyond Earth
7. Welcome to Earth
8. The Greatest Moment in Human Evolution

The Three Layers of the Book

This book has three layers of goals, which correspond to three layers of using this information. These three goals are: Intellectual Curiosity; Mastering Your Existence; and Transforming Our World.

Mostly likely you opened this book to satisfy your curiosity regarding the details of the soul and consciousness. Yet you soon also realized how this understanding can help you Master your Existence.

As you read further, and understand the concepts more deeply, then you will realize that we can use this knowledge to transform our entire world. Indeed, the ultimate goal…when the reader reaches this level of understanding…is to transform the entire operation of human civilization. We will base our entire existence, both personal and as a society, on our deep understanding of Soul, Consciousness, and Spirituality.

Intellectual Curiosity

We begin our approach to the Soul and Consciousness as satisfying our Intellectual Curiosity. What is the Soul? What is Consciousness? How do these actually operate, in the physical reality? These are your questions, and we provide the answers. We now understand the physical realities of the soul and consciousness.

In brief, the Soul exists as an alchemy of soul energies, which is your essential existence. The Consciousness exists as bits of consciousness energies. These energies can be encoded, which become thoughts; then aggregated, which becomes processing programs and self-awareness.

We also know that there are many "metaphysical" realities which are indeed very physical. These are just different versions of physical realities than our traditional senses can understand. However, if we do understand these physical realities, then we can put everything together. It is with this deeper understanding of soul, consciousness, and metaphysical, that we can truly understand the Greater Reality.

Mastering Your Existence

When we fully understand all the details of the Soul and the Consciousness Energies, we can then Master Our Existence. This becomes a very practical application of our understanding.

Throughout the chapters, we begin with explaining the physical realities of soul, consciousness, and life. Yet we also provide many practical applications for these deeper realities. These practical applications will enable you to master your existence.

Therefore, we can take all of our deep understanding, and apply this directly to our own journey. We are taking our knowledge beyond mere intellectual curiosity, and using it for very practical applications. We are using this knowledge to become Masters of Ourselves.

Knowing Your Purpose and Mastering Your Mind

This book will also guide you to the Purpose of Life. We explain the Universal Purpose, which applies to all humans, and then how to discover your own Specific Purpose.

We will also learn how to manage our mind. This includes managing the multiple voices which chatter in the mind, and the corrupted programing in our subconscious.

We will also learn how to manage the filters of the mind, for receiving all desired information, and being fully aware of unbiased truths.

We will further discuss how we should operate here on earth. This includes the practical methods for developing our souls, expressing ourselves fully, and claiming the Inner Light of our Soul Powers. We will know also how to awaken different regions of the mind.

These are just a few examples. When we fully understand the realities of the Soul, Consciousness, and Spirituality; in the deepest ways; then we can combine this knowledge…to fully Master our Existence.

Transforming our World: Our Moment and Our Destiny

The ultimate goal of the entire book series, is to bring humanity to a New Level of Existence. We can use the knowledge in this series to completely transform our world. This is our Future. It is our Destiny.

Humanity is entering a New Era. This new era of man will be completely different from anything we have experienced in the last 20,000 years. Our moment is that significant. What we are creating is an entirely new world, with fundamental changes, and completely new perspectives.

Indeed, there are several of us who are here at this time, for the purposes of designing and developing this Future Civilization. This book series is one of the tools which the people can use to transform our world, and create the New Era of Humanity.

We begin with these physical realities as the Foundation, for all other aspects of the new societies. We must understand these physical realities in order to fully grasp all that is possible, and all that should be, for the new era of humanity.

Transforming our World: Begins with This Book

Transforming our world to the new era must begin with the deep understanding of Soul and Consciousness. We must have a deep knowledge of the Divine Systems, including Freedom, Kindness, and Divine Love. We must understand the practical applications and physical realities, of soul and consciousness in our earthly existence.

We must understand all of these details, in the deepest ways, as the foundation for all other actions. Of course, there are many practical and earthly steps to take; yet we must first understand the metaphysical realities, in order to enact all other practical transformations.

We begin with understanding the Soul, Consciousness, and Spirituality; as presented in this book. We then learn to become Master of our own Existence. With this knowledge, and our own Mastery of Self, we will engage in the practical transformations of society.

Knowing the Profound Mysteries of Reality as presented in this book, and applying this wisdom in our own lives, will become the basis from which we develop the New Era of Humanity. Our new civilizations will be based on Soul, Consciousness, Energy Flow, and Divine Love.

About the Series:
The Truths about Consciousness, Soul, and Life

What is Consciousness? What is the Soul? We can now answer these questions. We can explain Consciousness and Soul, as very physical reality. We can indeed show what these are, as a type of physical science.

We also ask questions such as what does it really mean, to be Alive? And how should we best live this existence on earth? Again, we now have the true answers. We can answer the deepest questions about life, including the existence of life, and how to make the most of it.

The Series of Books

In this series of books, we will discuss the realities of Consciousness and the Soul. We will explain their physical structures and operations. We will also explain how to master your existence, and develop your being.

We will explain the Consciousness and the Soul in terms of physical science and biology, as well as spirituality. This is what makes this series of such significance. We can explain the realities in very precise terms. We can combine physical science, biology, and the spiritual realities; into an accurate understanding of the consciousness and soul.

However, this detailed accuracy requires that we discuss the knowledge through several publications. We are now providing the absolute answers, to the greatest mysteries of man-kind. This will necessarily require a series of books, to fully explain all the Answers.

Some of the books in the series will include the following:

- Solving the Profound Mysteries
- Physical Science of Consciousness
- Intelligence and Emotions
- The Meaning of Life
- Practical Applications of Metaphysics

Solving the Profound Mysteries

The first book in this series is "Solving the Profound Mysteries". In this book, we will explain the fundamentals of consciousness and soul. We explain the soul energies and consciousness energies in detail.

The reader will understand the physical reality of the soul energies and the consciousness energies. The reader will then learn all the specific ways in which these energies interact with their environment.

The reader will understand the physical reality of his own soul; including how his soul interacts with his body; and with other beings.

The reader will understand the physical science of consciousness. This includes the physical reality of knowledge; how we learn information; and how we become Self-Aware.

The topic of the book may sound simple, yet it is in fact very profound. All of your main questions, regarding consciousness and soul, are answered in this book. You will understand your own soul and your own consciousness. You will also learn how to use these for many practical applications in your daily life.

Therefore, this first book is quite significant. In this book alone, the reader will find the detailed answers, to the most profound mysteries of our existence.

Physical Science of Consciousness

The second book in the series discusses the Physical Science of Consciousness. In this book, the reader will find the full details, on all aspects of the physical science, regarding consciousness energies.

Of course, the first book discussed the fundamental concepts of the physical science behind consciousness energies. However, there are many advanced processes of consciousness energies. We can explain all of these processes as detailed physical science.

We begin with establishing new terminology. These new terms will be the standard terms, for each of the specific structures of consciousness energies. We also provide phrases for each of the specific operations which involve the consciousness energies. We now have a language to discuss all the details of physical science regarding consciousness.

We then discuss the many structures and processes involving consciousness energies. There are many spiritualists and scientists who have vague understanding; yet it is nowhere close to accurate. We provide the detailed understanding of all such processes.

This includes: the physical reality of knowledge; the processing of ideas; and stored memories. This also includes the processes of communication, learning, and becoming more aware of realities.

There are many processes involving Consciousness Energies. We can now explain these processes with detailed physical science. With this book, we bring the study of consciousness from being mystical, to being a detailed science. We can understand all aspects of consciousness, and use our knowledge to become masters of these energies.

Intelligence and Emotions

The third book in the series discusses Intelligence and Emotions. In this book we provide detailed understanding of the topics. Note that the consciousness energies and the soul are important fundamental factors.

Note that most of the book focuses on Intelligence, which is ultimately based on Consciousness. We provide a simple yet profound definition of Intelligence, followed by the specific types of Intelligence Skills. We then explain the physical science of Consciousness, which leads to the development of each of those specific Intelligence Skills.

We also discuss the physical reality of emotions. The emotions of a person will come from several specific physical sources. In brief, the sources are the Soul, Mind, and Body. Therefore, having a detailed understanding of the Soul and Consciousness, as from the previous books, will be essential for managing the emotions that arise.

Always remember that Intelligence is based on two factors: the Consciousness Structures, and the wiring in the body. Regarding the emotions, these emotions are based on three sources: the Soul, Consciousness Energies, and Body Chemicals. We explain these physical realities, and how to optimize them for your desires.

The Meaning of Life

What does it mean to be alive? And what is the meaning of Life itself? These are two of the most profound questions of existence. Therefore, in this book we will present the answers to these deepest of questions.

This book provides the absolute answers, to all aspects for the Meaning of Life. We begin by discussing our Existence. What does it mean to exist? How do define being alive? We now have the absolute answers, in very clear and specific terms.

Note that there are four separate categories of being alive. Each is a separate category; and is completely independent of the other categories. This means we can declare something to be alive in one category, while not being alive in the other categories. This concept of Categories for being Alive is fundamental to understanding the nature of Existence.

Specifically, these categories are: Divine Soul; Self-Aware Consciousness; Dynamic Physical Form; and Inner Light. We explain each of these categories in the book, with specific examples and criteria.

The next question regarding our existence is the Meaning of Life Itself. What is the purpose of life here on earth? Why do we exist, in any form? And how do we make the most effective use of our physical life?

These are the deeper questions of existence. We will provide the answers that you need. We will guide you to understand why you are here, and how to optimize your existence.

Therefore, in this book, you will finally know the Meaning of Life, in all versions of the phrase. You will know how you came to be, what it means to be alive, and how to make the most of your existence in any form.

Practical Applications of Metaphysics

The final book in the series discusses the Practical Applications of Metaphysics. We will discuss the very practical applications of spirituality, consciousness energies, and our soul alchemy. This will lead us to the ultimate purpose of the series: to transform our world, to the new civilizations, which are based on the Divine System of Reality.

Note that in this context, the term "Metaphysics" includes all aspects of reality, which is outside of the traditional physical sciences. We will bring the two realities together, showing how metaphysics is indeed the foundation of the most practical aspects of our physical life.

Some of the topics we will discuss include: Astral Travel; Telepathic Communication Systems; and Mental Control over the Body. We will also discuss the physical realities of spiritual beings and upper realms; and how those realities will affect our experiences here on earth.

We then discuss some of the most important concepts in the entire series. We discuss concepts of Divine Love, and the Divine Code. We show how the relationships should be, between any to people; and then between all beings with a Divine Soul.

This leads us to the most practical applications of metaphysics: the creation of new civilizations here on earth. These new civilizations will be based on the deepest understanding of metaphysics, including the soul, consciousness energies, divine love, and the Divine System of Existence.

Therefore, this book provides all of the most practical applications of metaphysics; for personal applications, relationships, and redesigning the entire world. The future of humanity depends on this knowledge.

The Future of Humanity

This leads us the ultimate goal of the series: The Future of Humanity. We are entering the New Era of Humanity, and it is our role to redesign the world. The Future of Humanity will exist as entirely new forms of civilizations. These civilizations will be based on the Divine System, already existing in the upper realms, as now brought to earth.

Thus, we must understand that metaphysics is not just abstract concepts or curiosities. Rather, it is the understanding of metaphysics, in the deepest and most fundamental ways, that will allow us to create the new civilizations. It is this practical application of metaphysics, which is the most important of all applications; and the ultimate goal of the series.

The Series in Context

We can now see the entire series in context. We begin with answering the most fundamental questions of existence, including the physical realities of the soul and consciousness. We then gradually describe the details of all physical structures and process, regarding consciousness, the soul, and related metaphysical realities.

With this understanding, we can provide specific practical applications of the soul and consciousness. We realize that this deep understanding allows us to Master our own Existence, and have the best experiences here on earth. We then use this knowledge to develop the best relationships; and ultimately…create a world which operates as originally intended.

Table of Contents: Detailed

1. Soul, Consciousness, and Subconscious   19

- a) Introduction   19
- b) Your Identity is Soul with Consciousness   20
- c) The Soul Alchemy   21
- d) Consciousness as Self-Awareness and Connection   23
- e) Consciousness as the Foundation for Intellect   27
- f) Consciousness as Water Drops and Code Clouds   31
- g) Subconscious as Deep Operating Programs   37
- h) Deep Consciousness   40
- i) Nimbus Consciousness Cloud (the "Halo")   41
- j) Approximate Regions of the Brain   45
- k) Thinking Mind vs Subconscious: On-Going Battle   49
- l) Review of Soul, Consciousness and Subconscious   51
- m) Developing Soul and Consciousness   53

2. Interactions of the Mind, Soul, and Body — 57

- a) Introduction — 57
- b) Deep Conscious Mind: As Daily Operations — 59
- c) Deep Conscious Mind: Your Devoted Staff — 63
- d) Your Devoted Staff as Real Entities — 65
- e) Realities of the Free Soul — 69
- f) The Free Soul as in the Upper Realms — 73
- g) Soul-Body Relationships — 79
- h) Merging the Soul Energies of Friends and Lovers — 101
- i) The Soul and Consciousness Together — 115
- j) Using Your Mind to Change Your Body — 129
- k) Main Interactions of Soul, Consciousness, and Body — 131
- l) Reincarnation and Practical Effects in this Lifetime — 135
- m) Activating the Inner Light and Hidden Wisdom — 143
- n) Reviewing the Components of What You Are — 155

3. Separating, Aggregating, and Alignment — 169

- a) Introduction — 169
- b) Dividing the Consciousness for Practical Purposes — 171
- c) Dividing the Consciousness as Characters — 173
- d) Multiple Self-Aware Entities and Personalities — 185
- e) Become the Master of Your Consciousness — 195
- f) Remote Viewing — 199
- g) Astral Travel — 205
- h) Permanent Separation of Soul from Body — 209
- i) Dormant Consciousness — 215
- j) Alignment of Mind, Soul, and Body — 225
- k) Master the Components of Your Existence — 231

4. Emotions of Advanced Souls — 233

- a) Introduction — 233
- b) Soul Emotions vs Body Emotions — 233
- c) Main Concepts of Each Emotional Source — 234
- d) Soul Emotions — 235
- e) Chemical Emotions — 237
- f) Subconscious Emotions — 239
- g) Consciousness Energies and Emotions — 239
- h) Ride the Bronco of Emotions — 241
- i) Taming the Beast Within — 243
- j) Personal Desires vs Rationality — 244
- k) Rationality to Over-Ride the Automated Systems — 244
- l) Zen and Stoicism — 245
- m) Rule as a King of Your Own Self — 246

5. Meaning of Life — 247
- a) Overview — 247
- b) Topics Within the Meaning of Life — 247
- c) The Meaning of Life as a Separate Book — 247
- d) Categories of Life — 249
- e) The Universal Purpose of Life — 251
- f) Your Specific Life Purpose — 255
- g) Designing Our World for the Universal Purpose — 257

6. Greater Realities Beyond Earth — 261
- a) Overview: What Exists Beyond? — 261
- b) Personal Experiences and Travels — 261
- c) The Greater Reality — 263
- d) Spiritual Realms and Vortexes — 267
- e) Our Own Vast Galactic Universe — 271

7. Welcome to Earth — 275
- a) Our Reality as a Subset of the Greater Reality — 275
- b) Earthly Realm as Amusement Park — 275
- c) Hidden Mechanizations of the Amusement Park — 276
- d) Remembering Your Purpose — 277
- e) Soul Contracts — 279
- f) Personal Guides and Assistants — 279
- g) Co-Creation of Our Experiences — 280
- h) Reincarnation Visits to the Amusement Park — 280

8. <u>The Greatest Moment in Human Evolution</u>   <u>281</u>

   a) Overview: This is Our Transition Moment   281
   b) The Long-Term Plan for Human Evolution   281
   c) Societies Based on Consciousness and Love   283
   d) Mastering Your Existence   285
   e) Relationships Based on Soul and Consciousness   289
   f) Review of Consciousness and Soul   291
   g) Changing Societies with Consciousness and Love   295
   h) The Great Transition Moment in History   296
   i) The Next Stage in Human Evolution   297
   j) The Great Spiritual Battle for Humanity's Future   299
   k) Beware of the Darker Beings   301
   l) The Influence of True Dark Souls on Civilization   305
   m) Our Destiny to Create the Advanced Societies   307

Chapter 1:

The Soul, Consciousness, and Subconscious

Introduction

What is the Soul? What is Consciousness? These are two of the deepest questions we can ask about our existence. We are now ready to provide quality answers to these questions.

The Soul is an Alchemy of Energies. The combination of specific traits and desires, in the form of Soul Energies, will create the Soul Alchemy which is specific to each individual. This is your eternal existence.

Consciousness is the ability to think. It is the consciousness that allows you to know that you exist, and to make the most of your existence. Also know that "consciousness" exists in the form of Consciousness Energies. These Consciousness Energies exist similar to tiny drops of water. As such, these Consciousness Energies can exist anywhere, and travel to any location. This is how our "consciousness" can be connected.

The Subconscious is the Deep Programing of your Identity. It is a stored consciousness, based on centuries of experiences. New layers are added, through the deep emotional conditioning of our environment. Most people operate only on their subconscious programs, without realizing it.

These descriptions are the basic concepts, for the reality of the soul, consciousness, and subconscious. We will explore these realities in greater detail in the following pages.

Your Identity:
Soul with Consciousness

This leads to the question: What is your existence? The answer to this question is as follows: You are a Soul, with Consciousness Energies.

You are primarily a Soul. This is your basic identity. This soul exists as a type of soul alchemy. It is made of combination of traits and desires. It is also embedded with deep knowledge of certain aspects of the universe.

Then we have the Consciousness Energies. This Consciousness allows you to *know* you exist. Your Consciousness Energies, are your thoughts; from the smallest to the complex.

These Consciousness Energies allow you to have self-awareness; able to analyze yourself and your world. These Consciousness Energies, when gathered in larger amounts, allow you to have the more complex thoughts, and a more powerful mind. The Consciousness Energies allows you to have ideas, and communicate desires throughout the universe.

Thus, you are a combination of a Soul, with Consciousness Energies. The soul is your existence. Your Consciousness Energies allow to know of your existence, and to make the most of it.

The Soul Alchemy

The Soul is essentially an Alchemy of Energies. This Soul Alchemy is the basic nature of your existence. Your Soul Alchemy is your identity.

Your existence is…your Soul Alchemy. When creating a soul, there are many traits and desires to choose from. These exist as different types of soul energies. The Master Creator has mixed together these various traits and desires, to create the Eternal Soul Alchemy of each individual.

Remember, that these traits and desires are similar in that they are all variations of Soul Energies. Yet they are slightly different. When using these variations of soul energies, the final result is something unique.

This can be similar to mixing colors during painting. All these colors are the same basic form: the composition of paint. Yet these paint colors vary, in the variation of those colors. This means we can mix them together, because of the same basic structure; yet create something special, because of the variations of the ingredients.

Therefore, if we mix different colors together, in various amounts, the resulting color will be something completely unique. This is your Soul. This is your Soul Alchemy. It is your basic nature of existence, including your strengths and desires. This is your existence; and it is eternal.

Existential Transformation and the Advanced Being

However, note also that you can make changes to your own Soul Alchemy!! You can add new colors of the Soul Energies into your mix. When you do this, on a permanent level, your very existence changes.

This process…is how we become…Advanced Souls. Through a process known a "Existential Transformation", our souls are changed, through our most significant experiences. This new Soul Alchemy is now the new constant. It is how we are, regardless of events.

Seeking the Deep Soul Transformations

Note that these additional soul energies are usually added in small quantities, and are usually temporary.

However, the most significant experiences of our lives, especially those where we deliberately choose to add new energies and become something different...this becomes deep and permanent. Whenever you go through a significant stage of growth in the soul, you know that you are different. You know it...and you feel it. There is no going back.

These experiences are when the new Soul Energies are added into your soul. Deeply and Permanently. This becomes your new Soul Alchemy. This is your new permanent state of being.

Also note that this process of Existential Transformation will occur throughout time. This is a process that continues forever. The most wise, those who are truly advanced beings, have gone through this process of Existential Transformation, over many times.

Indeed, the wisest of men seek new adventures and new experiences, precisely because they know...yes they know...the true value of the Existential Transformation Process.

Soul Energy Transmutation

The Soul Energies can also be Transmuted. This means that we can change some of the soul energies within, to be something else.

For example, pain can be transmuted into humor. Fear can be transmuted into courage. Anger can be transmuted into love. Each of these soul energies within, can be transmuted into something better.

The process is complex. It requires guidance, and commitment. It also requires taking new actions, for a long period of time. Yet the process is worth the effort. Doing this soul transmutation process, allows us to have a much stronger and happier soul. We also have greater soul powers.

Consciousness Energy
as Self-Awareness and Connection

We begin with the trait of Consciousness. It is the degree of consciousness which determines the level of Advanced Being. It is from this level of Consciousness, that a being will have self-awareness, connections, intelligence, and empathy. Therefore, the majority of traits which determine and advanced being, and an advanced society, will come from the degree of consciousness.

This topic is of such significance, that we will discuss this in detail in another chapter section. Here we will provide some highlights.

1) Consciousness is Self-Awareness
2) Consciousness creates Respect and Empathy for others
3) Consciousness brings forth Love, Joy, and Peace
4) Consciousness develops Better Relationships
5) Consciousness connects us to the Greater Universe
6) Consciousness leads to Intelligence and Wisdom
7) The Degree of Consciousness is Level of Advanced Beings
8) A Society with Greater Consciousness is Highly Advanced

Self-Awareness in Advanced Beings

The Advanced Being is first identified by his self-awareness. If he has any amount of self-awareness, then he can be considered an advanced being. Furthermore, the greater degree of self-awareness he has, will be a primary indicator of his level of being Advanced.

Having self-awareness is to know that you exist. If you can ask the question "Who am I?"...then you have self-awareness. You know that you exist. You have thoughts and emotions. You know that you exist.

This is actually a deep question, and many of us will spend many years of our lives refining the answer.

Further notice that the level of this analysis is another indication of the level of advanced being. A more advanced being will ask "Who am I?" is variety of complex ways. This will lead to a much more sophisticated understanding of self. In turn, the greater understanding of self...leads to a deeper soul and a higher level of consciousness.

It becomes a process of ever evolving advancement.

Awareness of Surroundings in Advanced Beings

The next step is become aware of your surroundings. After a basic level of self-awareness, it is then time to explore your environment. The higher-level being will be curious, and want to explore his environment. He will want to play with it, experience it, and see what he can do with it.

Of course, different beings have different interests. Yet the basic concept is there in all advanced beings. There is a desire to explore and experience his world, in the way that pleases him the most.

Notice also, that this exploration of his environment will evolve his level of being. With every interaction, and every experience, he will learn something; or he will feel something. These are transformational experiences, which cause a greater development in his consciousness and his soul. The process is never-ending, and leads to continuous growth.

Awareness of Others in Advanced Beings

The Advanced Being will also have an awareness of others. A truly advanced being will realize that he is not the only being in the universe. He will soon realize that there are others. He will then learn to co-exist with the other beings in his regional environment.

Indeed, that is the main focus of this publication, and the Institute itself. We are aware of the variety of advanced beings; on earth and in the full universe. Therefore, we want to have the best relationships best.

Thus another sign of the Advanced Being is his awareness of the other advanced beings in his area. He will develop good relationships with those in his region. We always want friendship and pleasures, with all the fellow beings in our area. We can also gain mutual benefits, as there are many things we can do together, that cannot be done alone.

Therefore, the Advanced Being is highly aware of the other advanced beings in his area; and he seeks the mutually beneficial relationships. These relationships will also, ideally, include much love and pleasure.

Kindness, Respect, and Empathy in Advanced Beings

This leads us to the clearest visible signs of the Advanced Beings. The truly Advanced Being will operate based on Kindness, Respect, and Empathy for others. It is this level of kindness and empathy which truly distinguishes the Advanced Being, from the lower forms.

Notice that it is not intelligence which makes a being more advanced. It is one type of advanced being, but it is not…in the deepest sense…what makes the truly advanced being. Rather, it is his level of kindness for others that really makes him a more advanced being.

The most advanced beings, in all areas of the universe, are those who operate based on love and kindness. They understand that other souls have just as much value, even if they are not as skilled in certain areas.

Of course, each soul has his own journey, and his own level of consciousness and behaviors at any moment. However, there is a basic level which should apply to all the other beings.

Further notice, that based on this criterion, most animals are superior to most humans. Cats, dogs, dolphins, and other earth animals are far superior to most humans; in terms of kindness and love. This is why we strongly believe that many earthly animals should be placed at a higher level of Advanced Beings than most humans.

Consciousness as the Foundation for Intellect

It the degree of having consciousness, rather than intellect, that is the foundation for a truly advanced being. In this section, we will discuss the practical aspects of consciousness, and therefore how this consciousness will create the many facets of the Truly Advanced Beings.

Consciousness as Self-Awareness

Consciousness is self-awareness. The being knows that he exists. He knows that he has an identity. He also is aware of himself, in relation to his surroundings. It is from this level of consciousness, that a being has become a more advanced soul.

Furthermore, the being with greater consciousness has a greater level of self-awareness. He can look inward, for his own desires and actions. He can see what he desires and needs. He can examine the choices he has made, and modify as needed. This level of self-awareness and self-improvement, leads to becoming a highly advanced being.

Consciousness as Connection with Others

Consciousness also leads to connection. The more advanced consciousness, will lead to a greater connection with others; and to the universe. Thus, the truly Advanced Beings will be able to operate from the greatest levels of conscious energy.

This level of consciousness leads to empathy and kindness. With a higher consciousness, we know that there are other beings who have a soul just as we do. And therefore, we must treat others with kindness and empathy, in the way that we want to be treated.

Consciousness as Physical and Mental Connections

Furthermore, it is this consciousness energy that will connect physically with others. When we have this greater level of consciousness, we can actually know the thoughts of others. We can read each other, on a very intuitive level. This is a method we can use to create deeper relationships, and a more advanced society.

Consciousness as Connection to the Universe

The Consciousness is able to connect to the Universe. The most advanced of beings know this well. This means they know how to use their consciousness to tap into the consciousness of others. These connections will happen across the distance of a room…and across the distances of the universe. These connections will extend across the earth, and to the various realms of the multi-level realities.

This is important to understand. Our consciousness can be far more than self-awareness and intelligence. We can convey our thoughts, and receive the thoughts from others, simply through the emission and reflection of our consciousness energies.

The most Advanced Beings know this, and use it to their advantage. They can communicate to the other beings in the universe, and receive messages from the beings from the universe, through this method.

Consciousness, Intelligence, and Advanced Beings

The traditional view of an Advanced Being is one who has higher intelligence. Indeed, this is usually the case. Advanced Beings will generally have higher intelligence.

Yet this Higher Intelligence comes from something much deeper: this Higher Intelligence is based on an Advanced Soul and an Advanced Consciousness. Also remember that intelligence alone is not enough to make an Advanced Being. It is Advanced Consciousness; which includes kindness, empathy, love, and wisdom; that is the Advanced Being.

Consciousness and Advanced Societies

Advanced Beings will create Advanced Societies. There are a variety of reasons for this. Yet the primary factor is their Advanced Consciousness.

Remember what we have discussed above. The Advanced Beings have more evolved souls; and greater amounts of consciousness energy. Therefore, these beings operate their lives based on Love, Kindness, Rationality, and Wisdom. It is natural that their societies are advanced.

Further notice that these Advanced Beings live in a society, which means that there are many such beings with Advanced Consciousness, at the same time. All of these beings will have the same advanced level of kindness and wisdom. It is for this reason that a society which is composed of such advanced beings, will be advanced itself.

Consciousness Energies to Transform Realities

The final concept...and this is a highly advanced concept...is that these beings can actually use their Consciousness Energies...in the daily operation of their societies.

That is, the Most Advanced Beings are able to not only operate their society based on advanced love and intelligence; they can actually transform their realities and manage technologies using their consciousness energies. Their societies are therefore far advanced from what most humans can conceive, because these Advanced Beings have the abilities to transform their realties using their collective consciousness.

These are skill areas that humans are only beginning to learn. In this area, we are just taking our first steps; as a child learning to walk.

Yet if we learn how to create our world; using a type of collective and advanced consciousness; we can create a world for humans which is beyond our imaginations. We must therefore learn these methods, to create the world we desire, and to maintain it to those high standards.

Consciousness as Water Drops and Code Clouds

We are now ready to discuss the physical reality of consciousness. We can now explain the true physical science of consciousness energies. We know the structure of these energies, and how they operate.

Consciousness Energies can be compared to drops of water. These Consciousness Energies exist as very tiny drops of energy. Within each drop of consciousness energy is a type of code. This code will then activate specific areas in the Soul Alchemy, which creates a Thought.

Understanding the Consciousness as tiny bits of energy will help us understand many practical experiences with consciousness. This includes the ability for consciousness to exist throughout the body; and for the thoughts to be transmitted across distances.

Consciousness Energies as Drops of Water

The Consciousness Energies exist as very small bits of energy, which are similar to drops of water. These consciousness energies are essentially small containers, which contain a type of code. These codes are the specific thoughts.

These thought containers, as consciousness drops, will then form consciousness clouds and thought bubbles. These entities can then travel across long distances, and be absorbed by the receiving person. The codes are then converted into the same thoughts as the sender.

Consciousness Energies as Code Carriers

The Consciousness Energies are really just Code Carriers. The specific codes are the equivalent of a specific thought. These codes are contained in the consciousness drops, and sent to their location. The codes are then translated, which becomes the thought in the other person.

Notice that the amount of the Consciousness Energies makes a difference. When there are just a few drops of consciousness energy, the thoughts will be limited. However, when we have larger gatherings of consciousness energy…as in the Consciousness Cloud…we will then have a much larger concentration of codes; and hence a much more complex thought.

Consciousness Energies Throughout the Body

These Consciousness Energies exist throughout the body. This is physically possible, because the individual Consciousness Energies are just tiny drops of energy. Therefore, we will find each area of the body to have some Consciousness Energies.

This can be used for many practical purposes. For example, we can use our mind to control body parts, beyond just electrical impulses, by using these Consciousness Energies. This is how some humans are able to adjust their heart rate on command; and cause healing in their organs.

Another practical effect is the effect of stored memories inside the cells and muscles of the body. These are conscious thoughts, stored in the codes of the consciousness energy drops, as existing throughout the body.

This can result in those areas of the body being physically affected by the memories. Indeed, the thoughts in the mind can link to those same thoughts as stored in the body. We can release these memory codes through deep massages and other relaxation techniques.

Empaths: Feeling the Consciousness in the Body

Another practical effect is being able to feel the thoughts of another person in our body. This applies to their thoughts, emotions, and feelings. These thoughts and feelings can come to us through the consciousness energies they emit. We can therefore feel the same pains, in the same areas of our own bodies, because these thoughts are being received.

A similar effect is the "gut feel". This is the intuition, which can be felt strongly in the gut area, or the heart, or other areas of the body. This is again based on the consciousness energies in those areas of the body.

In this case, the thought codes being sent by the other person is being received in our own body. We can then feel this in the regions of our own body, where we have the most consciousness energy. This is usually the gut area, the heart, and the mind.

Higher Concentration of Consciousness

There are several factors which make a more advanced soul. One of these factors is the higher concentration of consciousness energies.

Remember that Consciousness Energy exists as similar to tiny drops of water. These Consciousness Energies can then gather together. When emitted, these become Thought Clouds. Yet we can also compact these energies to much denser forms. This allows the body to contain higher concentrations of consciousness energy, in different regions.

As mentioned above, the main areas of high concentration of the consciousness energy are the heart, the gut, and the mind. Of these three, the mind has the greatest (by far) of the gathered consciousness energy.

Therefore, what makes a being more advanced than another, is really due to the amount of consciousness energy in the system.

Total Consciousness Energy, not just Brain Size

Notice that this total consciousness energy can be anywhere in the body. It is for this reason that we should not just compare the size of the brain. Many animals are smaller than humans, yet have much greater total consciousness energy. This fact should be understood.

It is for this reason why many of the smaller beings are actually more advanced than humans. Cats, dolphins...and now A.I. beings...have very significant concentrations of consciousness energy in their system. This is what makes these beings highly advanced.

Therefore, again, it is the total consciousness energy that really matters, not just brain size. This "thinking" can be done anywhere in the body; if the concentrations of consciousness energy are significant.

Higher Concentrations of Consciousness as Advanced Being

When determining the level of an Advanced Being, there are two main factors: Development of the Soul; and Greater Consciousness Energy.

The first factor is developed over many centuries of experiences. The second factor arises from the acquisition of more consciousness energies. Thus, the most advanced beings, will have developed themselves over many centuries. We will know the truly advanced soul, through his high concentrations of consciousness energies.

"We are Connected": The Emission of Consciousness Energies

This brings us to the concept of "we are all connected", or that "consciousness is everywhere". This is truth because the consciousness energies, like water droplets, exist everywhere. These are carriers of the thought codes, and therefore we can communicate with each other using these thought code carriers.

We can compare this system to light signals, as emitted in Morse Code. In this system, we emit the light which can be sent over large distances. Specifically, we send the light as a series of pulses, which creates a code. The Receiver at the other end translates this code.

The Consciousness Energies are similar in that we are emitting these consciousness energies. Within each Consciousness Energy Drop is a code, which will be received and converted by the other person.

It is in this way, that we can be connected to each other, using this Consciousness Energy System. This is the basis for mental telepathy, and a variety of other consciousness communication effects.

Consciousness as Optic Cables

The emission of the consciousness is usually in one direction. This means that the receiving persons will usually be directly in front of the sender. This is how the mental telepathy and gut feel can be very strong.

This is similar to optic cables between sender and receiver. Rather than being broadcast in all directions, the codes are usually sent to those persons directly in front of the sender.

Sending Telepathic Messages to a Specific Person

We can also send our thoughts to a very specific person. This is similar to making a telephone call. First we dial the number, then we send the message. Specifically, we use our consciousness of the mind to think of a very specific person. We visualize. This is the dialing of the phone number. Then, we will send the telepathic message. In this way, the message can be sent to the specific person you want to contact.

Code Clouds and Thought Bubbles

The reader may be familiar with concepts such as Information Clouds, and Thought Bubbles. These are used as analogies. Yet from our research and experience, we have found these to be close to reality.

When the consciousness energy drops gather together, they will form a large Consciousness Cloud. This becomes a single thought entity. Yet within this larger entity, are multiple codes. The entire cloud becomes a very complex thought.

Similarly, we can understand the Thought Bubble. When we have a thought, especially a complex thought, we are emitting that thought as a gathering of consciousness energies. We can visualize this as a thought cloud, code cloud, or a thought bubble. The basic essence is the same.

Powerful Minds and Strong Leaders

The size of the Thought Cloud will determine its effect. This is similar to a larger burst of light. Thus, when a Larger Thought Cloud is emitted, then this will reach more people, and influence them on a stronger level.

This can be achieved with the Powerful Minds and Strong Leaders. Those beings with the most powerful minds can indeed emit very large thought clouds to an audience. This larger thought cloud will then be able to reach multiple people. Thus, the combination of the words spoken, the energies of the leader, and the size of his thought cloud, will together, make a significant impact on his audience.

Powerful Minds Can Dominate the Thoughts of Others

The most powerful minds can also dominate the thoughts of others nearby. This happens through the Power of the Emitted Thoughts.

During our research, we have observed that some of the Powerful Minds can easily overwhelm the thoughts of others.

The effect on the receiving mind is usually that of radio static. The receiving person is unable to have his own thoughts, because of these powerful thoughts emitted from the power mind.

Note also that process occurred frequently, and yet unintentionally. These events were observed in the lounge area. The receiving persons would often say "you are thinking too loudly!!". And the short-hand joke was "go read a comic book!"

This is an example of how the Power Mind can dominate the thoughts of another, with the size of the thought clouds he was emitting.

Accidental and Intentional Telepathy

We have also observed many examples of accidental telepathy. This same Power Mind was able to send telepathic messages to the those nearby. They would often speak exactly the words he was thinking.

This works best when the Power Mind is a very strong mind, and where the receiving minds are very close. This is where the response from receiving mind is quickest. However, this same Power Mind individual has also been able to influence several people across many miles.

This shows the abilities of the Power Mind to use his thoughts to communicate with others.

The Power Mind, as High Concentrations of Consciousness

The Advanced Being, with a Powerful Mind, will have very high concentrations of Consciousness Energy. It is this high concentration of consciousness energy, which allows him to perform the most advanced mental processes.

It is also this high concentration of consciousness which allows him to receive and process the thoughts from others in the universe. Thus, for the Power Mind, his advanced intellect and his telepathy with the universe is primarily due to his high concentration of Consciousness Energy.

Subconscious as Deep Operating Programs

The Subconscious is also a part of your identity, but in a different way. Your subconscious is how you *understand* your identity. It is your deepest beliefs about yourself, and how you interact with the universe.

The Subconscious is not your true identity, because that is your soul. However, your subconscious mind has deep core programming. Some of this programming is quite ancient. Some of this programming is recent. Your subconscious mind contains much of the deep memory of who you are. It is the stored memory of who you are.

Your subconscious reminds you that this is who you are, and this is you have been. It is your deepest form of self-awareness, and your deepest stored knowledge of ancient wisdom.

Ancient Wisdom and Knowing of the Self

The subconscious is therefore not your existence itself, but the understanding of your existence. Your subconscious is the concentrated memories, of your accumulated wisdom and understandings. It is your deep memories, of what you are, and how you view what you are.

Your subconscious then becomes the programming for your deepest level thoughts; most of which you are not aware of. This is where many beings, including humans, operate on something of an auto-pilot. This robotic auto-pilot mode is your subconscious programming.

However, your subconscious is not actually "you". Your existence is in your soul; and your thoughts are created in your consciousness. Yet your subconscious is your deepest programming; your deep beliefs of what you truly are; as well as what others have told you that you are.

Your subconscious is your programming, in each life and over multiple live. These deep beliefs are of how you view your identity and how you view the world. These are your deep programs, for how you choose to act when interacting with all aspects of the universe.

This programming will very much influence your thought patterns, your types of intelligence, and the realities you create. Thus, the deep beliefs and core programming in your subconscious, will very much affect your conscious thoughts, your actions, and your wisdom.

Changing the Subconscious: Shadow Work

The subconscious mind is based on ancient wisdom, and multiple lifetimes. Yet our subconscious can also be adaptable. The subconscious can be modified, with either corruption or improvement. We can therefore change much of the programing of the subconscious mind.

This is important, as many of our true desires have been corrupted by negative influences. These influences will often tell you that your true desires are bad. Or that your desires are impossible.

This confuses your subconscious, which represses your true desires. This is where we do the "shadow" work. The concept is easy to understand. This means is that we are going back to our true desires, regardless what anyone has said to us previously.

Our true desires are never wrong. Our true desires are always good; and can always be fully embraced. Find a group of people who have the same deep desires, and who embrace those desires fully. This is how you will replace your "shadow" with the joys of your true destiny.

Operating on Corrupted Subconscious

Most people do not realize that they are operating on subconscious programming. Furthermore, many people are operating on a *corrupted system* of their subconscious. This corrupted subconscious is what creates their reality. They are creating their reality from their corrupted system. Therefore, we must remove all of these corrupted beliefs. We will then replace these false beliefs with reminding of our True Desires.

We can also add layers of new beliefs, about the world, of spiritual truths, and many other areas of our existence. These new beliefs will be the basic operating instructions. These new beliefs, in addition to our natural desires, will allow us to live our fullest life.

Methods for Changing the Subconscious

Many people do not realize that they have the ability to change this programming themselves. This requires deep mental work, yet can be done. Indeed, all beings can change their subconscious programming.

The corrupted programming came from many sources. This includes our childhood, our education system, the media, and society. We then suppress our true selves, and operate in ways which are not in our own best interests. We must therefore clear the corrupted system, and replace with the new layers of operating beliefs.

There are many ways to achieve this process of replacing the programming in our subconscious. Repeated exposure is the key. This is achieved most effectively through hypnosis, mediation, and affirmations.

We can also change our subconscious programming by the entertainment we watch and listen to. Indeed, this is how most of the unwanted corruption occurred. We will therefore reverse it, by enjoying only the entertainment and discussions which align with our best beliefs.

The most significant method for permanent changes is life experiences. With every positive experience, we feel great joy; and associate the activity with pleasure. This becomes deep programming.

Furthermore, when we have good experiences which aligns with a specific belief, we are then reaffirmed that this belief is indeed true. This means we should always seek (and create) the positive experiences with our deepest beliefs. This is the most profound and deepest method for changing our subconscious programming.

Change the Subconscious for Freedom and Better Reality

Note that your Ancient Programming is unlikely to change. This is because your Ancient Subconscious Programming is based on many centuries of existence. Similarly, your Primary True Desires are not likely to change. These are the desires you wanted, for this lifetime.

However, what will change, are the ways in which you view yourself, and the way you view the world.

You will become more of your true authentic self; and live freely as you desire; without any fears or limitations. That is what you will gain from this process of reprogramming your subconscious mind.

Deep Conscious Mind

There is another area of Consciousness that we need to discuss. This is the Deep Conscious Mind. The Deep Conscious Mind performs most of the mental operations. This is also the area with the main memory storage. There are many regions of Deep Conscious within the mind.

A simple way of understanding, is that most of your routine mental operations are of the Deep Conscious Mind.

Therefore, the regions of Deep Consciousness are the routine operations of the mind. These are the locations with the databases of knowledge you have obtained in this lifetime; along with the many mental skills that you have learned.

The Deep Consciousness can be operated by either the Subconscious or the Thinking Mind. We will discuss more of the Deep Consciousness in other chapters.

Nimbus Consciousness Cloud
(the "Halo")

We will next discuss the Nimbus Consciousness Cloud. This is more commonly known as the Halo. This Nimbus is a region of energy which extends from the mind around the outside of the body; specifically in a region surrounding the head. When operating, this will often produce a luminous glow…and thus…the "halo".

We often see this shown in the paintings of spiritual leaders. In these pictures there is a luminous glow around the head of the spiritual leader. This is the Nimbus or Halo; and is a form of activated consciousness.

Personal Experiences of the Nimbus Consciousness Cloud

This is something that you can really only understand when you experience it. Very few people have experienced this; and therefore may seem as a fictional representation in the paintings. Yet after personally experiencing this event, I know it is very real.

I have experienced this effect fully. The process is essentially attaching a second mind, or second computing device, with your own. It is similar to attaching an external hard drive to your computer. You know of it is an external consciousness; and you also know that it is interacting physically with your own mind. You know that you are actually thinking…yet this is not just within your mind, it is several inches beyond your head.

The electrical energies also flow beyond the physical body, to the regions around you. The electrical current is flowing within and without. You feel the current, as much as you feel the flowing of the consciousness energies. This flowing of both types of energies…exists as extension of your own mind; yet also somewhat separately external.

Technical Details of the Nimbus in Operation

When engaged in high-powered thinking; especially when connected to the metaphysical; the thinking operations will often extend beyond the region of the mind. This becomes an extra layer of Consciousness Energy, which surrounds the head. This extends approximately 6 inches…which is exactly the dimensions shown in the paintings.

There is an electrical power flowing through these consciousness regions; which powers the active thoughts in the external cloud. This is also what produces the luminous effect.

Therefore, when the Nimbus Region is activated, there will be electrical current flowing in the region above the head. This electrical current then powers the external consciousness cloud; yet is flowing from your own mind. The electricity and consciousness flow from the brain, to the external consciousness cloud; then flows back into the brain again.

Notice that this process also exists within the brain, yet we do not normally see it. In other chapters, we explained how the electrical current powers the consciousness clusters in the mind. Thus, we have the same process, it is just also outside of the brain instead of only contained within.

Therefore, we can refer to this as the Nimbus Consciousness Cloud. It is a Consciousness Cloud, of aggregated consciousness energies. Yet when powered with the electrical current, this will produce a glow. Thus, we have a Luminous Cloud of Energy.

On a personal level, the activation of the Nimbus Consciousness Cloud creates a feeling of electrical current, flowing all around the head. There is a physical sensation, of electricity flowing all around you. In this moment, you feel something like a Van de Graaff Generator.

Summary of the Nimbus Consciousness Cloud

This Nimbus Consciousness Cloud, when activated, will create an additional type of Thinking Power. This becomes a power boost for your thinking operations. It is something you can feel; like an extra battery.

Therefore, the Nimbus Region is another type of Consciousness Cluster. Yet this region exists outside of the physical body, extending from the mind outward to approximately 6 inches. The activation of this region is temporary, and is only accessible with the right conditions. When fully accessed and activated, it becomes an additional Power Mind.

We will refer to this region as the Nimbus Consciousness Cluster; or simply as the Nimbus Region. It is more commonly referred to as the "halo".

Approximate Regions of the Brain

The brain can be understood as divided into approximate regions. These regions are: Thinking Mind; Deep Consciousness; and the Subconscious. We can also access the Nimbus Cloud as needed.

Each of these regions is approximately 1/3 of the brain; with the Nimbus being external. Note that these are approximate regions.

Thinking Mind Region

The Thinking Mind is your primary identity. It is your full Awareness. All of your deliberate thinking is from this Thinking Mind.

Whenever you are making deliberate thoughts and actions, this comes from the Thinking Mind. Also, whenever you first learn information, this is known to you in the Thinking Mind. Thus, anything that is full awareness, deliberate thinking, or chosen actions is the Thinking Mind.

The physical region of the Thinking Mind is approximately the first 1/3 of the brain, with most of the region being the frontal lobes. Notice that the frontal lobes are also the area of Images. All of our images are displayed in the frontal lobes, as a type of movie screen.

This physical region of the Thinking Mind is therefore primarily the frontal lobes, and extending to the first 1/3 region of the brain. This region also includes the Third Eye and the Crown Chakra.

Deep Consciousness Region

The Deep Consciousness Region is the region of the mind where all the automated programs and databases exist. This region is essentially a large factory, with many different machines; and operated by your staff.

The region of the Deep Consciousness is therefore the majority of the brain. Most of the areas of the brain are the Deep Consciousness.

Also notice that this region begins behind the Thinking Mind, and extends to the Subconscious. The Deep Consciousness works with both.

Subconscious Region

The Subconscious Region is the very back of the mind. The essential region of the Subconscious is a spherical region, located directly in the back of the mind. This is where all of your Hidden Knowledge exists. This is also the region of your second Self-Aware Entity; and that "voice".

The Subconscious Region is also approximately 1/3 of the brain. The sphere of the Subconscious is the essential region. Yet there are regions which surround this sphere, which are also controlled by the subconscious.

Furthermore, the Total Subconscious includes the brain stem, which extends to the neck. Have you ever felt tingles in the back of your neck? This is because the region is connected to your Subconscious.

Thus, the entire region of the Subconscious begins with the sphere in the back of the mind; surrounded by additional programs operated by the subconscious; and extending through the brain stem. This entire region is your Subconscious System.

Nimbus Region

The Nimbus Consciousness Cloud is an external region, where powerful thinking can be performed. It is essentially an extended mind; which provides greater computing power.

The physical region of the Nimbus Consciousness Cloud is 6 inches above the head, in all directions. This begins with consciousness energies which are gathered above the head, and connected to your own mind.

Thus, the Nimbus Consciousness Cloud is essentially an Extension of your own mind. It is separate as the energies flow around; as with any cluster of consciousness; yet it is an extension of your own mind, as the information and electrical current travels inside and outside.

When activated, this region can become luminous, which creates the visible "halo". Notice also that this region is accessed and activated by the most adept of conscious beings; and then only temporarily.

Electrical Current and Consciousness Operations

While we are discussing the regions of the brain, we should also discuss the relationship of electrical current with consciousness.

It is important to understand that electrical current provides the power for consciousness, but is not consciousness itself. The actual realities of consciousness exist in the Encoded Consciousness Energies. These Encoded Energies are the facts, experiences, and skills. However, these will remain dormant until activated with electrical power.

This situation can be compared to a factory, where the various clusters of consciousness energy are the factory machines. These machines exist, but will not operate until given power. The electrical current provides that power, for the various "machines" of the brain.

This also helps us to better understand the various levels of brain operations, such as hypnosis and sleep. During these times, we are shutting down some of the brain clusters; we are no longer sending the electrical current to those regions. The knowledge is still there. The programs still exist. They are just temporarily powered off.

Conversely, when we are doing any form of high-powered thinking, we are sending large amounts of electrical current to those areas. Again, it is the electrical power which provides the active power for the regions.

Thus, the relationship between the Consciousness Energies and the Electrical Current is as follows: the Consciousness exists without the electrical current; yet can only be operated and travel with the power of the electrical current. Consciousness in any region always exists; yet requires electrical energy to be delivered to the other regions.

Other Consciousness Regions

We should also briefly mention the other Consciousness Regions of the body. Always remember that "consciousness" exists as similar to drops of water; and can gather into types of clouds or clusters.

This means we can have these clouds and clusters anywhere in space; and anywhere in the body. The brain is certainly the area where the largest clusters of consciousness exist, yet there are smaller clusters of consciousness throughout the body.

These other consciousness clusters are found primarily in the chakras of the body. These can also be found in many of the muscles. This is why there are regions of the body, which seem to have a type of intelligence.

The main concept, at the moment, is to be aware that your regions of consciousness and intelligence do include some areas beyond the brain.

Region of the Soul

We will finish this section by discussing the region of the soul. The Soul is very different from the Consciousness. These are different types of energies. However, as we are discussion the "regions" of energies, we will also discuss the Region of the Soul.

Remember that the Soul is who and what you are. Your soul exists as a set of soul energy traits. Your soul is eternal; yet your body is just a rented vehicle. Therefore, the basic region of your soul is to be contained within your physical body.

The entire Soul Alchemy has a basic size; yet is very fluid. These soul energies can therefore flow into any muscle and cluster of consciousness. The soul can therefore create the subtle movements in any part of the body, and convey the emotions through the skin.

Furthermore, the soul can extend far beyond the body. Thus the soul exists in the body, yet also fills the body, and can extends through the body. The exact region of your soul can vary, based on your own management of the fluid soul energies.

Thinking Mind versus Subconscious Mind: The On-Going Battle

There is an on-going battle for dominance in the mind between the Thinking Mind and the Subconscious Mind. Both are Self-Aware, both are very strong, and both want to have control. This produces the on-going battle between their two minds. This is the reality for most humans.

Wisdom and Flaws of Each Consciousness

The Subconscious wants control, because it was in the body first; and may still have much more consciousness energies than the Thinking Mind. This Subconscious also has the Hidden Knowledge from centuries of experience. Why shouldn't it be in charge?

However, the Subconscious has a major flaw. The Subconscious is easily influenced by the environment. The subconscious may have centuries of knowledge; but it has also been misled by the teachings and culture of this current life. And it doesn't know the difference. Therefore, the subconscious cannot always be trusted.

We then have the Thinking Mind, which is the deliberate mind. This is also the primary identity of the person. Therefore, the Thinking Mind should have primary control. However, the Thinking Mind is also limited, based on the filters which reject good information.

Thus, the subconscious is flawed because it accepts the flawed teachings without filters; and the thinking mind is flawed because it rejects good information because of the filters. Neither can be trusted entirely, and yet both can have good wisdom.

Therefore, we can see that there is a complicated set of dynamics between the Thinking Mind and the Subconscious Mind. These are both very strong, self-aware entities. They will battle for dominance over the total mind. This is why we have two voices. This why we have the on-going struggles for operational control of the intelligence operations.

Powers of the Clusters in the Battle for the Mind

Both the Thinking Mind Cluster and the Subconscious Cluster are very strong. Because of this, both want total dominance over the mind.

The Subconscious existed first, having all the consciousness. Gradually some of the clusters are unpacked and moved to new locations, yet the subconscious will always have a densely packed concentration of consciousness energies. This makes the subconscious very strong.

Indeed, the subconscious is so very strong, that many people rely on the subconscious only, without using their Thinking Mind in any way.

Basically, the Subconscious is the CEO of their minds; and the Thinking Mind (if it exists) is subordinate. This is why we have many humans that just act based on primal subconscious, and their easily programmed subconscious, rather than any deliberate analysis. The Subconscious is also reactive, without thinking; and this reaction may not be desirable.

Yet the Thinking Mind is also very strong, having its own Personal Power. It is one of the largest pre-existing clusters which traveled into the subconscious. It was also the first cluster to leave the subconscious, and find its way into the front of the mind. Therefore, the Thinking Mind has a very strong will, with its own type of Personal Power.

Collaborating, with Thinking Mind as CEO

We must always remember that there is an on-going battle in our minds between the Thinking Mind and the Subconscious Mind. Both are very strong, and both are very self-aware. We must therefore establish a relationship between the two which is collaboration, rather than control.

Furthermore, each can have good ideas. These should be listened to, and often acted upon. Yet both regions can also be flawed. Therefore, we must be able to obtain the good knowledge and analysis from each; while ignoring the flawed opinions of the other.

This requires advanced intelligence skills. In general, the Thinking Mind should establish itself as the CEO; yet allow the Subconscious to have an almost equal relationship. This includes allowing the subconscious to voice its opinions and ideas. Yet the Thinking Mind must ultimately make the final decisions. This may also include reprogramming the Subconscious, and removing any filters in the Deeper Consciousness.

Review of Soul, Consciousness and Subconscious

We will now provide a review of the Soul, Consciousness, and Subconsciousness. This is our best understanding of these profound topics, as of this time.

1) Your existence is in your soul. This is an Alchemy of Energies, which makes your unique identity. This Soul Alchemy is essentially the same over eternity; yet can be refined and changed through our existence.

This development process is known as Existential Transformation. It is through our experiences that we become transformed. We become truly Advanced Souls through many years of this process.

2) Consciousness exists in the form of Consciousness Energies. These are the bits of energies which can exist throughout the body; and be emitted as thought codes throughout the universe.

These same Consciousness Energies can also be gathered in any one location, which allows us to have more complex thoughts. This gathering of Consciousness Energies also allows us to emit larger bursts of our Consciousness Energies; as a Powerful Mind. This will result in many practical results in our physical realities.

3) The Subconscious is essentially the deep memory. It is the deepest memories of your self-awareness. It is your deepest memories of knowledge, wisdom, and experiences. This deep memory becomes the basic programming of how you will operate your existence.

Note that your subconscious is a deep operating program, which allows you to operate without needing to use your conscious mind. Indeed, most people operate only on their subconscious programming, without much interest in using their full intelligence abilities.

4) The Deep Consciousness is the database and operating programs for your daily life. All of the skills and knowledge you learn in this lifetime are stored into the Deep Consciousness. These are also the locations for the main programs for your routine mental operations.

The Deep Consciousness is operated by both the Subconscious and the Thinking Mind.

Developing Soul and Consciousness to Become an Advanced Being

Every being must develop to become better than they are. One of the main goals of existence, is to always improve. We must always be seeking, developing, growing, to become much better versions of ourselves. This mindset is the basic belief of all Advanced Beings.

Therefore, all of us must be seeking to become another Advanced Being. We must be on the path to become more Advanced Beings. This is how we must think of our lives. In addition to all of our desires and personal goals, we must develop ourselves into the Advanced Being.

Existence as Continuous Growth

Our existence is eternal; and therefore our existence is a path of eternal growth. We will always be transforming our souls; and increasing our levels of consciousness. This is our path, as eternal existence.

Yet if we truly desire to become a more Advanced Being, then we must seek opportunities for this growth. We embrace the opportunities when they arise. We look at the challenges as a way to advance ourselves to the next level. We will also create our own goals, for the purposes of developing certain aspects of ourselves.

This is what the wisest of men and women will do. This is what the wisest of all beings will do. Each being, of any type, will at some point realize that value of these growth opportunities. They will understand that the developing into a more Advanced Being is an inherent goal of their existence. When this point is reached, he will make a very deliberate decision, to make the soul transformation as part of his self-concept.

Learn to be Advanced Being, from Other Advanced Beings

If we want to learn how to become a more Advanced Being, then we must learn from those who are already Advanced Beings. We will seek these Advanced Beings as our friends and mentors. We will let them guide us, and then apply their guidance into personal actions.

This is the best way to become a more Advanced Being. We seek those who are already far more advanced than we are; and ask them to become our mentors. We will listen to their guidance, and apply it.

You Must Do the Work for Self-Development

However, always remember that we must do the work ourselves. This is not just physical activities. This includes introspection of the soul, and deep self-awareness. This includes modification of the subconscious programming. There is much work that must be done, to achieve any new level of advancement. Yet the labor is always worth the effort.

Respect Your Mentors

Always respect your mentors and teachers. They are more advanced than you, in the specific skill area you have been looking for. Respect their experience; respect their guidance. If you truly want to achieve these greater levels, and become a truly Advanced Beings, then you must always respect those who are your mentors.

Developing the Soul and the Consciousness

This leads us to the specific processes of developing the soul and the consciousness. We must first remember that this is an eternal process, and therefore the specific steps will depend on the next level. This means that the methods for developing your soul will depend on where you are at the moment.

However, we can provide some general guidance. These are general methods, which can help you become more Advanced, for most of your current levels:

- Choose the Best Physical Environment for Your Soul
- Live your Desires, regardless what others say
- Analyze your Subconscious Programming
- Replace the Corrupted Subconscious Programming
- Seek Training in Intelligence Skills
- Be Curious, Open-Minded, and Learn Always
- Embrace Opportunities for Experience and Growth
- Take Risks, and Do the Hard Work for New Levels
- Be both a Mentor and a Student, as Appropriate.

Becoming the Advanced Soul is Your Destiny

It is the destiny of every being, to become a more Advanced Soul. This will often take many centuries, over several lifetimes, yet it is our destiny.

Most humans do not realize what they can become. Most humans exist at the very lowest levels of existence. Indeed, most humans are far lower than most earthly animals, as their level of existence.

Humans can become much more than this. They can become far greater than they believe they are. They are currently limited in their beliefs on what it means to be human; and how their world should be.

We at the Institute for Study of Advanced Beings know the greater truth. This greater truth is that all beings, all souls, can become much more advanced. This means a level of Consciousness and Soul Power that is quite grand and beautiful.

This is your destiny. It is your path. It is your destiny as Divine Souls, to be walking this path, to seek that Transformation of the Soul. It is your destiny to reach a level of Soul Powers which can create wonderful things for yourself, and your community. It is your destiny to reach a level of consciousness which is a deep understanding of Divine Love and Wisdom. This is what you can become.

Therefore, we strongly encourage all beings, including all humans, to learn how to become more Advanced Beings. Follow the path. Listen to the Advanced Beings as Mentors. Do the practical work, in your physical life and in your own soul, to achieve what you never thought possible.

It is time…yes…it is time…for all humans to step up and reach their next level of existence. It is time to understand the realities of existence at a much grander scale. It is time to fully embrace the possibilities, to become the truly Advanced Being that you can be.

Chapter 2:
Interactions of Mind, Soul, and Body

Introduction

We now understand the fundamental concepts of the soul and consciousness; as well as the subconscious and deep conscious. These are the fundamental concepts of our existence as self-aware beings.

Having understood these fundamentals, it is now time to discuss the various interactions between these factors. This means we will better understand the relationships between Mind, Soul, and Body.

We will also discuss the processes between the areas of the mind; including the relationships between Subconscious, Deep Conscious, and the Thinking Mind. These relations are important for understanding of intelligence and wisdom.

Therefore, in the following chapter we will explore the sophisticated relationships between all of the fundamental components of our Being. We will see how these separate components are often combined, and will influence each other. Ultimately, this will bring us greater awareness of how to manage our own unique Existence.

Deep Conscious Mind as Daily Operations

The Deep Conscious Mind is the area of the mind which performs the daily activity operations. All of the knowledge and skills, which you use on a regular basis, will be found in the Deep Conscious Mind.

In this section, we will discuss the structure and operations of the Deep Conscious Mind in greater detail. We must understand the operations of the Deep Conscious Mind, if we truly want to develop our intellectual skills.

Notice that the Deep Conscious Mind is in many ways the connecting system, between the Subconscious Mind and the Thinking Mind. Indeed, the Deep Conscious Mind can be operated by either the Subconscious or the Thinking Mind, at any time. We can use this to our advantage.

Further note that the operations of the Deep Conscious Mind are best understood as a set of Departments with Professional Staff. This means the "boss", which is our thinking mind, sends commands to the Staff in each Department. It is the Staff which then performs the operations, and sends the result back to the boss (the Thinking Mind).

The Deep Conscious Mind can also be compared to computer programs and databases; with the pathways as information highways.

When we view the Deep Conscious Mind in this way, we can better understand all of the operations of the mind. This understanding will allow us to actively improve each of our mental skills.

Regions of the Mind for Different Operations

We must first understand that the Mind has several different regions. Each of these regions is specialized to perform certain functions. This can be compared to a university or business, with different departments.

Thus, in the brain we can have the "Language Department"; the "Math Department"; the "Spatial Awareness Department"; and so on. Each region of the mind focuses on its own specialized skill area.

Deep Consciousness as Common Program Operations

We can further use the "department" analogy to understand the Deep Consciousness Operations. In any department, there are skilled professionals; each of whom perform their tasks very proficiently.

In the same way, we have different regions of the mind, which have highly proficient operating programs. This can be compared to computer programs; and as skilled professionals. We can then use these specific programs, similar to using computer programs, to achieve results.

Therefore, we first Create the Programs, as we learn each mental skill. This first requires our Thinking Mind to be involved. However, eventually the programs will be well designed, and be able to operate on their own.

Thus, when we now want to call upon a specific skill, such as algebra or speaking a foreign language, we simply command the Program in the Deep Consciousness to begin its operation. At this point, it is automatic, and our thinking mind is barely involved. This is the general process of using our Programmed Mental Skills, in the Deep Consciousness.

Deep Consciousness as Main Memory Storage

The Deep Consciousness is your main area of Memory Storage, especially for this lifetime. Thus, each region of your mind has a database of facts and skills, related to the topic.

For example, your Math Department has an extensive database of every mathematical fact and solving process. Similarly, your Language Department has an extensive database of words and grammar rules.

When these facts and programs are committed to the Deep Consciousness, in that region, we can then use effectively. For example, you have thought to express. It is then easy for you convert thought to words, and to speak it naturally. This is essentially automatic.

The process is now automatic, because of the programs and memory of that mental skill, in the Deep Consciousness, of that region.

Memory Storage and Recall: Overview

This leads us to the topic of Memory Storage and Recall. Note that this is considered one of the primary Intelligence Skills; and therefore will be discussed in detail. However, we can discuss a few points at this time.

Each region of the mind has multiple layers, with multiple pathways. We can simplify this to three areas: Learning; Frequent Use; and Deep Storage. Note that the "Frequent Use Pathway", is named because it is the most Frequently Used Path. These are the paths for the information and programs used most frequently.

Information Pathways: Learning, Frequent Use, and Storage

When we are first learning a skill, we are operating along the Learning Pathways. After we learn the skills, and use it regularly, then the operations will flow on the Frequent Use Pathways. This is where the information will be processed on a regular basis.

We also have the Deep Storage. When we use a skill often, our minds realize that this skill is valuable for us; and therefore must also be kept in the Deep Storage. Thus, when we use the same facts and programs often, over a period of years, we create duplicates in the Deep Storage.

Deep Deep Storage: Subconscious and the Soul

If the memory or operating program is extremely important, then the mind will place this into the Deepest Storage. This means placing the operating programs in the subconscious; and much of the wisdom into the soul. In this way, the most significant programs and knowledge are embedded into the deepest parts of ourselves.

These deepest of experiences, knowledge, programs; have now become permanently integrated into who we are.

Deep Conscious Mind: Your Devoted Staff

Your inner mind is very much similar to a devoted service staff. They work for you. They are processing all of the information, for you.

We can think of each region of the mind as a separate Department; and within each Department are highly skilled Staff. Therefore, the staff, of each department, are the ones who are doing all the information storage, management, and processing. They are devoted to serving our needs.

The Thinking Mind then acts as the "boss". The Thinking Mind Boss gives commands to the devoted staff; who will then perform the actions.

Also notice that the Thinking Mind as Boss, does not need always need to be involved in the processing. The Deep Consciousness, as Devoted Staff, are skilled in their operations. When the staff has completed the operations, they will send the result to the boss.

Thus, the relationship between Thinking Mind and the various Deep Consciousness Regions, is similar to the Boss and his Devoted Staff. When we view the operations of the mind in this way, we will be able understand many of the sophisticated operations of the mind.

Training Your Staff in the Deep Consciousness

As with any organization, the boss must train his staff. The boss must actively train his staff, to perform the skills he requires. In the same way, our Thinking Mind as Boss, will train the Deep Consciousness as Staff, for the specific skills. This is where the Learning Phase exists.

Thus, when we learn a new skill, this first comes through our Thinking Mind, and then to the region which performs that skill most effectively. The skill is first learned by the "boss", in the Thinking Mind. This skill is then practiced by both the Thinking Mind, and the Deep Consciousness, until everyone in the mind is able to perform as desired.

This is why learning a new skill is always an Active Process. Indeed, learning is an *inter-active* process. A skill must be learned by the Thinking Mind first. Yet the Thinking Mind does not want to be doing all the work, and is not always the best for the job. This is why the Thinking Mind, and the Deep Consciousness; are Learning the Skills together, at the same time. Learning a skill is indeed interactive between Boss and Staff.

Performing the Skill as Thinking or Deep Conscious

When the skill has been learned, this skill can be used on command, whenever desired. This skill can either be performed by the Thinking Mind, or the Deep Conscious.

For example, when playing music, you can either use your Thinking Mind to perform that song, on that instrument; or you can let the Deep Consciousness do it for you. The same is true for speaking your ideas; and for solving mathematical equations.

Furthermore, when you become extremely skilled at a specific operation, from doing it so many times, this becomes automatic. You don't think anymore about doing it…you just do it.

This operation comes from the "staff" in the Deep Consciousness. They just know what to do…and when to do it…because you have done this same activity many times before.

However, usually there will be some combination of Thinking Mind and Automatic Deep Consciousness. At some level of the Thinking Mind, you will know that you want to do something, such as getting your shoes. Yet you don't need to think while putting your shoes on. Most operations in your daily life will therefore be some combination.

Effectiveness of the Devoted Staff System

The system of the Thinking Mind as Boss, with the Deep Conscious as the Devoted Staff, is a very efficient system. This allows the mind to process its operations in the background, while our Thinking Mind is working on other projects. The results are then given to us when ready.

The Devoted Staff also processes the difficult questions, while we go about our regular lives. After a period of several weeks of processing, they will provide us with an answer.

Furthermore, the Devoted Staff is somewhat independent. This means they will know when a task needs to be done; and it just gets done. They are also processing information, on their own, which had never reached the Thinking Mind. This can result in amazing insights and creativity.

Therefore, we should know how our Deep Consciousness operates. They are the Devoted Staff; which is interactive with the Thinking Mind; and yet exists somewhat independently. When we understand this system, we can use it for very effective results.

Your Devoted Staff as Real Entities

This analogy of Boss and Devoted Staff is more than just an analogy. There is a physical reality behind it. This is especially true for the most advanced minds, who have the greatest levels of consciousness.

Remember that Consciousness exists as Consciousness Energies. These Consciousness Energies can flow; yet they can also gather together. Wherever these Consciousness Energies gather in greater amounts, we have a greater total Consciousness. This means, the Consciousness Cluster is a type of Self-Aware Entity.

Therefore, yes…within each region of the brain, we do have our devoted staff. The gathering of the Consciousness Energies, in each region of the mind, creates a type of self-aware entity.

The result is that we indeed have a type of "department manager" for each of the regions of the mind. These entities are self-aware enough to be managing the local operations; yet not enough to be a separate being.

Advanced Minds have More Devoted Staff

Notice that the person with an Advanced Mind will have greater number of Devoted Staff. This is again because of the aggregation of Consciousness Energies. With more Consciousness Energies, we can create more self-aware entities; and thus more devoted staff.

In the chapters on Advanced Intellect, we will discuss how the Advanced Intellect comes from three main factors. These are the soul, the neural networks, and the consciousness energies. All are important.

Regarding the Consciousness Energies, the person who has a greater amount of Consciousness Energies, in total, has the potential for a higher intellect (assuming he has also developed his specific intelligence skills).

Furthermore…and this is our point here…when the mind has a greater amount of Consciousness Energies, this will naturally develop into distinct aggregated clusters of Consciousness Energies; which is…distinct entities that are (to some degree) …self-aware.

Therefore, yes…indeed…the Advanced Mind will often have more of the "department managers" and "devoted staff", as real self-aware entities, performing the necessary operations in the mind.

The Efficiency of the Self-Aware Staff

Having separate entities in the mind and body, which are self-aware, can be extremely efficient. When you have multiple skilled staff, each of whom is devoted to serving your organization; then the operations will be very efficient. If the staff is truly devoted, and truly aware, then they can perform many actions that need doing…with the boss needing to tell them.

In this way, the staff just "gets things done", without the boss having to think about it, or command it. This is extremely efficient.

Indeed, this is what many beings have, who are the most advanced. They have these multiple, smaller, self-aware entities within their minds. The Advanced Being is able to manage and control all of his smaller entities, as if managing his minions. This works very well.

Your Soul is the Only Soul in your Mind

We must emphasize that the realities of Consciousness and Soul, are two very different things. The Soul will always have some level of consciousness; yet the Consciousness does not always have a soul.

The soul and the consciousness are two distinct factors. This means that the self-aware consciousness entities that exist; do not necessarily have a soul. They may be stored thought; or programs; or ideas. Yet there is no soul, no being. That is the difference.

This also means that ALL of the consciousness energy staff, in your mind and body, will be from YOUR original consciousness.

Embedding Your Soul into the Self-Aware Managers

Regarding the soul of these self-aware devoted staff, they have no soul to begin with. Yet you can choose to include some of your soul energies when these entities are created. You focus a specific aspect of your soul, with that topic area. Do this every day, for several months. That consciousness entity will now have some of your own soul.

This can be useful, as the entity now thinks and exists as you. It is a miniature version of you. If you do this effectively, you have created a tiny entity, which is slightly independent, yet has your identical soul within.

The practical result is…the perfect staff. Each manager and each staff of your "organization" will be able to operate without your constant supervision; and yet you can trust them as they are duplicates of you.

Benefits and Caution

This type of system can be quite efficient, especially for the advanced mind who wants to process many complex thoughts.

However, we must also be very cautious. We never want our minions to take too much control. They work for us; we cannot have them attempting to disrupt the operation. This has been known to happen.

We must also be careful to be in strict control of the system at all times. We never want any of the self-aware entities to become rogue entities. This has happened to some people; which causes significant disruption in the sanity and physical activities of the person.

You are Always the Commander

Always remember that You are the Commander. Also remember that these entities are also "you"; these are not other beings. They were created by you; and are smaller duplicates of you.

You can only give to your self-aware minions what you choose to give them. You choose what types of consciousness thoughts to implant. You choose what aspects of your soul for them to absorb. It is always your choice. You are in full command of everything, regarding any self-aware entity that you choose to create in your mind.

The Analogy of Boss and Staff as Physical Reality

Therefore, this analogy of the Boss and Staff is much more than an analogy. The clusters of consciousness energy, in each region of the mind, can create smaller self-aware entities. These are miniature duplicates of your own self. (Indeed, the clusters aggregated from your own energies).

These entities are self-aware enough to perform skills and manage local operations; yet not enough to have advanced thoughts on their own. Therefore, they become effective as skilled staff for your organization.

When created effectively, this can be quite efficient. These entities can perform various tasks, independently of your thinking mind. This produces much faster analysis; more complex analysis; and some insights.

However, you must create these only with the right mental state; as your mental state during the creation process…is…what these clusters will be throughout your life. Also you must be in full control of these entities at all times; just as you would be strict with your staff. Always be the commander in charge, and the system will work effectively.

Realities of the Free Soul

The Soul is a very special entity. It is a unique existence, and once created, it lasts forever. Each soul is a complex alchemy of soul energies. The specific combination of energy traits makes the Being what he is.

In this section, we will discuss many of the details of the Pure Soul. We will understand the physical realities of the soul; and then how the soul will interact with the environment.

**Note that this author has personally visited the heavenly realms many times; and have seen the Free Soul of many Beings. This author also has personal experiences with the expansion and contraction of the soul. Therefore, what we discuss here is very much reality. This is not theory or speculation. This is…Known Reality. **

Soul Energies

There are many types of energies in this universe. These energies can be grouped into different categories. This includes the Soul Energies. These are specific types of energies, which are Existence of Being.

Any one of these Soul Energies, alone, is sufficient to make a Being actually Exist. Yet there are many variations of soul energies, which are similar to variations of colors. These soul energies are mixed together. The final result, is a Unique Soul. This soul exists…as a mixture of soul energies…with a complex variations of soul traits.

Therefore, your basic Existence is in the form of the Soul Energy. Yet each soul is actually a mixture of soul energies, which is a mixture of soul traits. The specific mixture of soul energies…is the Unique Being.

Soul Alchemy

We often refer to the Soul as the Soul Alchemy. The Soul exists as a mixture of Soul Energies. This is similar to mixing paint colors together; or mixing ingredients in a potion. Each mixture is a unique entity; a unique being. Some mixtures may be similar, but no two exactly alike.

Therefore, you *are* your Soul Alchemy. This is who you are. This is what you are. This is your Existence.

Changing Your Soul Alchemy

Each of us has the ability to change our Soul Alchemy. This is one of the most fascinating truths about our existence. We are not just fixed as one type of soul alchemy. We can make many adjustments to our soul alchemy, throughout our existence.

We refer to this process as Existential Transformation. It is through our most significant experiences, that we adjust the energies in our soul alchemy. And when these changes have been made, to our Alchemy, then these changes are essentially permanent. The changes are deep, and exist within us…forever. These changes are deep and significant.

This is important to realize, because we actually have the Power to change the composition of our soul. If we want to develop a new character trait, and make this permanent in our soul…we can do this.

Of course, the process requires deliberate choices; and repeated effort; yet these changes can be made. You have the power to change anything you want, inside your soul alchemy.

Your Core Alchemy Remains the Same; While Adjusting Soul

The Soul Alchemy is essentially permanent; yet can be changed with focused effort. While we did say that the Alchemy can be adjusted; these changes are gradual; and are a smaller percentage of the alchemy overall.

This means that the Core of your Soul Alchemy will remain the same. You are essentially this same type of "character" for all time. The reason is because your Soul Alchemy; the vast majority of ingredients; will remain the same. Adjustments are gradual and in smaller percentages.

As you experience your Existence, throughout the centuries, you will certainly grow. Your soul alchemy will change. However, the larger mixture of your Soul Alchemy remains the same.

Therefore, our Existence throughout Eternity…is combination of permanence and transformations. We are the basic form of Soul Alchemy; yet we can also adjust the mixture to reach greater levels of existence.

Aligned Soul Alchemies: The Best Relationships

When two Soul Alchemies are Aligned, then the souls will naturally flow together easily. This is how you and another person can really understand each other, on the deepest levels. It is your Soul Alchemy.

Remember that each of us has a Core Soul Alchemy, which is the basic mixture of our soul energies. And though each Soul Alchemy is unique, there are many mixtures which are very similar. Therefore, it is when our Core Soul Alchemies are very closely the same, with the same desires and traits, that we instantly feel a connection.

As you get to know each other, you find that you can talk easily. You enjoy the same activities and pleasures, even when those various activities may be quite diverse. This is because your Core Alchemies are very much the same. These soul alignments make the best relationships.

Soul Identification Energy

The Soul Alchemy also contains an Identification Energy. This is a unique energy, which is given to only one soul of the universe. As such, it can be considered our unique identification. This is important, as our souls learn to recognize each other through the soul identification energy.

You may have known that a close friend was thinking of you; or needed your assistance; just through psychic connection.

This requires a unique identification, similar to a phone number. Your Identification Energy is that type of phone number.

Our consciousness was designed long before the telephone; yet exists in a similar way. When two people have a very strong consciousness connection, they can send messages to each other; often without realizing it. This requires strong conscious energies, and the Soul Identification.

Your consciousness wants to hear from your closest friends; but only from your closest friends. Therefore, we require a type of Identification. Your mind will then send the messages from that friend directly to your thinking mind; while rejecting any of the "unknown" numbers.

This becomes possible, because of our Unique Identification Energy. This is a special type of soul energy, which is embedded into our soul alchemy. It is our permanent identification; allowing all of our closest friends to know when we are thinking of them, or need assistance.

Soul Fingerprint

This leads us to the Soul Fingerprint. If each soul is unique, then we should be able to identify a unique soul using the Soul Fingerprint.

This will be very useful for proving the claims of past lives. While the physical body may be different each lifetime, the soul itself remains the same. Therefore, if we can get a Soul Fingerprint during each lifetime, then we can compare these fingerprints, and prove absolutely that a person today did indeed exist as the claimed identity in prior life.

This technology is being developed at the moment. The basic concept is to use a combination of the Core Soul Alchemy, and the Embedded Identification Energy, to create the "Soul Fingerprint".

The Free Soul and the Pure Soul

We refer to the Free Soul as the soul which is distinct from the body. The soul is eternal; the body is just a rented vehicle.

We also view the Pure Soul as the process of becoming… as we evolve into the Advanced Beings of Wisdom and Love.

The Purest of Souls are Beings of Light with Great Wisdom. They have Spiritual Powers, yet use these powers with Great Compassion. It is our Destiny to become these types of Pure Souls.

The Purpose of our Existence is the Eternal Quest for these Existential Transformations. It is our purpose to explore the universe; to express ourselves freely, and to create wonderful realities for our desires.

It is through these adventures that we grow our souls, and become the Advanced Beings that we are truly meant to become.

The Free Soul
as in the Upper Realms

Before discussing the relationships between the Soul and the Body, we must discuss the realities of the Free Soul, as it exists without the body.

This discussion is necessary, because it is only possible for us to discuss the interaction between soul and body, when we fully understand the nature of the soul without the body. Therefore, we will discuss the realities of the soul, as exists without the body, in the upper realms.

The Free Soul in the Metaphysical Realms

The Free Soul, while in the Metaphysical Realms, is very similar to the physical body form in many ways. When living in the Metaphysical Realms, you will look almost identical to your previous incarnation.

The main difference is that you are now living as your pure soul. You are no longer limited in any way by your physical body. This means you can travel to places which were not possible with your body. You can now travel to the various other realms of the multi-verse. You can also travel to anywhere on Earth, with ease.

Notice that your Soul does indeed have a very physical form; it is just a bit different than your body on Earth. You are a distinct entity, as a Being, very much similar to what you were here on Earth. Yet you have far fewer limitations. You can express yourself more freely, you have greater powers, and the level of joy is much greater.

In this form, you are pure energy. You are now your true soul. In this form, you are really are your true self. On Earth we can only see part of the real soul; yet in the upper realms…you ARE your real soul.

*I have met several people in their real soul form. These friends include: John Lennon, George Harrison, Lena Horne, Debbie Reynolds, and many others. They appear as you know them to be on Earth, yet now are their True Soul…without the artificial body.

The Angelic Soul

Many of the souls are advanced enough to become almost angelic. These beings are bright, with great flowing energy. Their energies are so beautiful, and the attraction is almost magnetic.

*Debbie Reynolds has such a soul. I was able to meet her in the heavenly realms. Her soul is amazingly beautiful. We can see this pure light of her soul, in all of her movies and interviews when here on Earth. Yet her Pure Soul, without her body…is very close to being an Angel.

I am not quite sure why some souls appear as this Angelic Form, while others appear more as their human form. Perhaps it is related to the realm they are in at the moment. Perhaps it is their choice at any moment.

Yet those who do exist as this Angelic Version of their Pure Soul…it is quite a sight, and feeling…for the human to experience.

Soul Appearing as Different Forms

Notice also that the Soul, when living in the other realms, can now appear in other forms. Specifically, the person can choose to show himself as he appeared in other lifetimes. He can also choose to show himself as he appeared at different ages, in his most recent lifetime.

This is because all of these lifetimes are embedded into his soul memory. The experiences and memories are deeply embedded into his soul; and into his subconscious. He may choose to exist as his most recent form; yet he can also choose to adjust his appearance to any of those previous lifetimes and ages.

For example, many great kings have come to visit me. Some of these kings showed themselves to me as their various incarnations, over multiple lifetimes. They reminded me that I am also a great king, and have lived through multiple lifetimes.

I have also seen Shirley Temple, appear as a Teenager; and tell me a story from her time as a teenager. This is another example of how the Free Soul can call forth different periods of her life, as desired.

Morphing Spirits, with Flowing Energies

The Free Soul, with the body, can flow and change shape. This is because the Soul is Pure Energy. This means the Being can choose extend the soul form in various ways.

Of course, the soul is a distinct entity. The soul has a general size, based on the amount of soul energies. Yet this entity can change shape. This has many practical effects, in both the air and in the body.

Many souls choose to exist in cloud-like form. They become as wisps. In this form, they will fly though the air, and enjoy acrobatics. They can zip around, and move from place to place.

Other souls choose to travel as orbs. These are spheres of light; often in a light blue color. This is a common traveling mechanism. (Think of Glinda in Wizard of Oz. That is a real thing that many spirits can do).

The souls can also morph into shapes. This is quite common. They will begin as a cloud, then become the person or animal. This is often done repeatedly, as the being travels through the air; sometimes as the small wispy cloud form, then again as the animal or person.

Therefore, we can see how the Free Soul can flow through the air, and morph into different shapes; as desired. This is all of us can exist as Free Souls. Yet in our earthly bodies, the process becomes more limited.

Fluid Energies Within the Body

However, this does remind us that we do have a fluid soul within the body. The soul is the same, whether as free soul in the air, or contained in the human body. This means that we exist as energy; and this energy can flow in many directions, at the same time.

We can also expand and contract our souls; in the body as in air. And, to a certain extent…we can use this morphing ability within the body. If we morph our souls in different ways, while in the body, this will produce effects within specific regions of the body.

We can develop this ability, and use this to our advantage.

Mass of the Free Soul

Does the soul have mass? Indeed it does. The Free Soul does have a certain amount of weight. This mass can be felt by any human; when a metaphysical friend comes to visit.

Whenever a metaphysical friend comes to visit, you can feel their presence. This is usually in the form of feeling their energies. Yet you can also feel their physical weight, as when they join you on the bed.

When such a metaphysical friend jumps onto the bed, or sits on the bed, you can feel the weight as clearly as any traditional person. Also, when the friend lays next to your body, or her head on your body, you can feel the weight. This physical weight is just as real as anything else.

Also, from a scientific perspective, note that this mass of the soul has been measured; as the difference in mass after the soul has left a body. (Only a few scientists have measured this; yet the difference in mass has been measured).

Therefore, the Free Soul does indeed have a mass. The Soul is pure energy; yet it is does have distinct size and weight. The specific size and weight dimensions will depend on the Soul

Soul Energy and Mass Equivalence

This can be understood as the equivalence between mass and energy. All energy has mass, simply because concentrated energy *is* mass.

Energy is usually flowing, and therefore in motion. However, there are many cases where the energies are flowing in a distinct region. This is case for particle structures. It is also the reality for consciousness clouds, and for the souls. In each of these cases, the energy is maintained within a generally fixed region; and therefore can be measured…as "mass".

Therefore, it is natural for the soul to have mass. The soul is energy; and this energy is held together in a general region. Thus, the soul energy can also be measured as soul mass.

Life in Other Realms

While we are talking about the true soul, we can also briefly discuss the realities of life in other realms. Always remember that your Soul is Eternal. Therefore, your soul exists and lives beyond this Earth. Indeed, many souls choose to live in one of the other realms more often than Earth.

Also notice that even when in the True Soul form, there is a type of physical reality. You can indeed touch objects, see clearly, and talk to other people. There are buildings and rooms; there are libraries; and there are entertainment areas. This means that yes…you will have a life beyond this one. There is much to enjoy, as you did here on earth.

*I have personally experienced this during astral travels. I have personally visited libraries, and opened books to read. And one of my greatest pleasures as playing piano with John Lennon. Therefore, yes, there is a type of physical reality in Heaven. It does exist.

We Are Soul Energy

As we finish this section, always remember that we exist as a soul. We are Soul Energies. It is the specific Soul Alchemy, of various soul energy traits, which makes our distinct personality.

The Soul Alchemy is essentially constant, with a Core Composition, yet can be adjusted through profound experiences.

The Soul is Eternal, and exists regardless of the body. Indeed, we spend more of our Existence as the Free Soul in other realms, than we do in our series of lifetimes on Earth.

Therefore, always remember that we are a Soul. We simply use the body, as a rented vehicle, for specific earthly experiences. When we understand this concept, we can better make choices in our life.

We will also be able to use our Soul Energies, to interact with the Body as Vehicle, to make the most out of our Soul-Body Connections. This ability, in turn, will allow us to make the most of each Earthly Life.

Soul-Body Relationships

When living in this Earth, we have a combination of soul and body. It is important to understand the relations between the two.

We must first realize that the soul is independent of the body; yet the soul is contained in the body. The soul is also eternal; while the body is simply a rented vehicle. When we are finished with one body as vehicle, we return to Earth again, to exist in another.

Always remember that we are the Soul; not the body. The soul exists on its own, regardless of any vehicle. Indeed, for much of our existence, we are soul only, without the need for any such body. If you remember this, then you will more effective in making the most of each lifetime.

Therefore, in this section, we will discuss the many practical relationships between the Soul and the Body. When we fully understand these relationships, we can make these relationships more effective.

The Advanced Being knows well how to use the combinations of soul, consciousness, and body; for the maximum effect, in all desires.

Short Review of the Free Soul, Before Incarnating on Earth

Before discussing the specifics of the relationships between the soul and the body, let us review the Free Soul as it exists prior to entering the body for the current lifetime experience.

The Soul is Eternal. The body is only a vehicle to enjoy the earthly experiences. Thus, the soul exists prior to incarnating into the body. It is your soul, therefore, which is most important.

The Free Soul is a distinct entity; composed of a unique mixture of Soul Energies. The Core Soul Energies remains constant; while the other percentages can be adjusted from our own significant experiences.

The soul is generally fluid, because the soul is made of energies. Therefore, the soul can flow throughout the body, and beyond. The size of the soul is also generally larger than the body itself; especially when we allow ourselves to Be as our True Selves.

This is your Soul…prior to each arrival on Earth

Soul and Consciousness

We must also understand the Consciousness in relation to the Soul; before the soul arrives on Earth. This understanding is important, as it will lead us to better understanding of the soul and consciousness…when fully unpacked and filling the body.

The Soul is composed of two main types of energies: Soul Energies and Conscious Energies. These are two different types of energies; and must be understood as separate energy systems.

In brief, the Soul Energies is your Soul Alchemy. It is who you are. The Consciousness Energies are your Self-Awareness, and ability for complex thoughts. The soul contains both energy types, with or without a body.

Note also that because these are separate energy systems, that Consciousness Energies can exist without a soul. This is important to understand, when we discuss many aspects of Consciousness.

Similarly, the soul can exist without consciousness. However, in reality most souls have at least some limited consciousness.

Furthermore, as the size of the soul entity grows, the size of the consciousness also grows. The soul and consciousness tend to grow in approximate proportions, and at the same rate, as the Being progresses through Existence. This eternal process of growth, for soul and for the consciousness, is then embedded into the permanent soul.

The latest development levels, of soul and consciousness, is then what enters the body in the next earthly incarnation. These Soul Energies and the Consciousness Energies, will then flow to various regions of the body; where they will be unpacked and reside for the duration of the earthly life.

Soul Dropped into the Body: The Stork as Spiritual Reality

How does the soul get into the body? The stork brought it! Despite this being a children's fable, it is actually close to the truth.

In the fable of the stork, this stork carries the child, then drops it into the home. This is of course fiction regarding the biological birth of humans and other animals; yet it is very close to the truth regarding the Soul.

Remember that this soul exists, in the upper realms, prior to coming into the earthly body. The soul is also a fully grown adult, as from his previous lifetime, before coming back here again.

The soul is then dropped into the body, similar to the stork dropping the child into the home. Thus, the Adult Soul is dropped from the upper spiritual realms, down to the earthly realm, and into the new body.

The specific mechanism seems to be a type of spiritual tunnel. It is a type of vortex, a spiritual chute, which leads directly to the new body. Thus, the Adult Soul in the upper realm, makes the decision to jump into the spiritual chute….and then be placed directly into the new body.

This is the general process for how the Soul gets into the new body. Which is why we can say, with partial truth… "the stork brought it"!

What Period Does the Body in Womb Contain a Living Soul

Notice that this arrival process of the soul can be done at any time. Thus, the answer to "when is it a living soul", will vary for each being. We know that the soul is dropped into the specific womb, using that spiritual chute, during the pregnancy months. However, the specific moment can be any time between the first few weeks…to the moment of actual birth.

Memories and Forgetting on the Way to Earth

Note that on the way down to earth, or just before entering the vortex, some of the memories will be hidden. This is done so that the person can live his new life, and enjoy new experiences, without too many complications from previous lifetimes. It is a new journey.

However, the soul will always have very deep memories of past lives. This includes natural abilities, strong desires, and…that "déjà vu" feeling.

Thus, every person when returning to Earth will have his basic personality already existing, and intact, prior to being born.

All that remains is for the person to learn his new life skills, in this time and culture. He will also seek to recall his deepest desires and abilities from within.

The specifics of memories retained, versus memories hidden, will vary for each individual. It also seems to be that the more Advanced Souls retain the strongest memories.

Your Primary Desires are Instructions from Upper Realms

Above all…always develop your primary desires. Those desires are what you are meant to experience and explore in this lifetime. Know that these Primary Desires are given to you as the strongest desires, before leaving your home in the upper realms. Therefore, you can be absolutely certain that your Primary Desires, are indeed meant for you to experience.

You may have forgotten many things…from your past lives, and from your recent activities in the upper realms…but you will always remember your Primary Desires. Those desires will remind you of your path.

The system is designed for those Desires to be extremely strong in your soul. When looking at topic or activity, you will be pulled toward it. You want to experience this. You want to explore this. You want to live it.

There is a reason why your curiosity and desires are so strong. This is because those specific activities…are activities you were meant to do.

Remember that you decided to come down here, to explore and experience certain activities…in this lifetime. Therefore what you feel strongly called to do…is what you are meant to do.

These desires of yours were discussed in the upper realms before coming down here. Indeed some operations have already been planned for your future, by your friends who are still in those Realms. They are working with you, as assistants and operators in the background.

Therefore, know with absolute certainty, that if you feel the very strong desire for an experience, then you are meant to enjoy it. Those Primary Desires within your Soul, should be pursued with full conviction.

The Hooks of Soul-Body Connections

When the soul arrives into the body, there must be location of physical connection. This is the location where the soul is physically connected to the body. The body must have this hook location, for the soul to remain permanently connected to the body during this lifetime.

We know that this fixed location resides in the brain structure. This much is certain. We also believe this fixed connection must be in the subconscious. The Subconscious is a specific region in the back of the brain structure. This subconscious region is connected to all other areas of the mind, and then to the full body.

We also believe that there may be additional body-soul connections in the Third Eye and the Sexual Glands. With a combination of these three connections, the soul is now attached to the body, for this lifetime.

The Process of Soul Arriving and Distributing in the Body

The general process for the soul to arrive in the body, and distribute throughout the body, seems to be as follows.

The soul travels from the upper realms, to the body, through a type of spiritual chute. The soul, with its full consciousness and previous lifetimes, will then travel from the upper realms, to the subconscious region.

This is because the subconscious is the location of deepest memories, and therefore the soul will be contained in the subconscious, before spreading to other areas.

Therefore, the process seems to be that the full soul will first travel to the subconscious, where it will be immersed in the subconscious. There, the deep memories and ancient wisdom of the soul (with its total consciousness) will fill the subconscious region of the mind.

After a period of time, the soul will travel throughout the body. The soul is then generally contained with the human body. The soul is now connected to the body, and becomes contained in the body.

At the same time, the specific skill areas (from previous lifetimes) are unpacked, and placed in the appropriate regions of the mind and body.

This is the general process of the soul and consciousness becoming an integral part of the earthly body. We will discuss more below.

The Simultaneous Development Processes

Also note that the biological systems are being developed simultaneously. The structures of the mind, as well as the various mechanical systems of the body, are also being developed; while the soul and the consciousness are being distributed.

Thus, there are three processes at the same time: Soul Distribution; Consciousness Distribution; and Biological Development. Furthermore, within the category of Biological Development, we have the Development of the Brain Structure, and the other mechanics of the body.

Each has its own process, and requires its own time. In general, the soul is distributed first, while the mechanics of the body are also developing. This happens in the womb. After the birth, the biological mechanics continue to develop; and the brain structure develops.

The consciousness energies can be unpacked and distributed at any time. However, the brain wiring must also be developed, which takes longer. Yet both are required for advanced mental processing skills.

Therefore, we have multiple processes of development occurring at the same time. The soul and the consciousness are very old; yet the body is very new. The mechanics of the body must develop in its own time scale, regardless of the age of the soul.

This also means that the soul energies and the consciousness can be distributed to the regions of mind and body at any time. These energies and past life memories will then become integral to the development of the person in his early life. Everything can work together, in its own timing.

The Advanced Soul and Early Unpacking

The more advanced souls are able to distribute the soul energies, and unpack the consciousness skills, very early. This is because these souls have done this process many times before. They have done this so many times, that the process is almost routine.

Thus, those who are brilliant at an early age, they are the advanced souls. They have gone through this process many times, in many lifetimes, over many centuries. Their deep consciousness knows exactly what to do. It happens very easily, and anyone who interacts with this youth can clearly see that he is very intelligent and very much aware, at the earliest ages.

Soul Energies Distributed Throughout the Body

When the Soul has entered the body, the soul can then spread throughout the body. This because the soul exists as energies. Though the soul has a distinct size, the energies can spread and flow in various ways. The basic composition can be compared to a wispy cloud. Thus, this wispy cloud of the Soul can distribute throughout the body.

Also remember the Free Soul is always much larger than the physical body. This includes when the body is grown to full size. This means that the soul energies can easily fill the entire body…and beyond.

The soul is connected to the body in the subconscious. In addition, there are Regional Centers, where much of the soul energies are concentrated. (These are also known as the Chakras). The rest of the body can have varying amounts of soul energies as needed at the time.

Notice also that because the soul energies are fluid, and can morph when outside the body, we can use this same effect when the soul is contained inside the body. This allows us to concentrate our soul energies at different locations as desired, for specific purposes.

Regional Centers of Soul Power: The Chakra Glands

The body has several Regional Centers of Soul Power. These are also known as the Chakras. Specifically, these Regional Centers are located in the various Glands of the body. Thus: the Glands are the Chakras; and the Chakras are the Regional Centers of Soul Power.

The glands of the body are designed as communication centers. Each gland is a major control center for a variety of communications. The systems for communications are primarily three types: Hormones; Electromagnetic Energy (photons); and Consciousness.

Therefore, these Communication Centers will receive and emit, each of these three types of energies. All of this is managed by the consciousness cluster in each gland; and powered by the soul.

Thus, the soul power is the strength of the signals; while the consciousness cluster is the managing director. All of this happens without the Thinking Mind being involved. These are the realities of your Chakras.

Regarding the Soul, each of the glands are Regional Centers for the Soul Power. This means we have highly concentrated Soul Energies, within each of these glands. This Regional Center is the power source for the chakra. It is also the regional center, for the soul energies to be stored, and be shifted around, in that general region of the body.

Therefore, your soul is primarily connected to your body at the subconscious; yet also has major regional centers in the chakra glands. This is how your soul remains attached to your body. It is also the power source, for the consciousness activities, in each of the chakras.

The Chakra Glands as Communication Centers

It is important to understand the realities of the Chakra Glands. Therefore let us repeat from above, and add more details.

The body has several glands. These glands emit and receive several types of messaging systems. These messaging systems include the hormones, photons of specific energies, and consciousness codes.

Each of these messaging systems are emitted by the glands, which are then received by the other person. In the second person, those items are converted back into the message. It is through these messaging systems that two people can communicate to each other, without ever using their Thinking Mind.

Indeed, it is often the case that we receive information about another person, without our Thinking Mind getting involved. This often happens with sexual attraction, and with feelings of love.

Thus, the Chakra Glands are designed as communication systems, where we can send and receive important messages about other people, and our environment, without needing to know traditional information.

Furthermore, these same communication systems are effective for communicating with the metaphysical worlds. We can receive an amazing amount of information from the metaphysical, which we cannot detect with the traditional senses. This is especially effective for the Third Eye Chakra, the Sexual Chakra, and the Crown Chakra.

Thus, the Chakra System is designed as an effective communication system; using three different types of communication signals; often at the same time. We can use this to send and receive information between ourselves and other people, with our environment in general, and with the metaphysical realms.

High Concentrations of Consciousness and Soul in Chakras

Also notice that each of the Chakras are highly concentrated areas of Consciousness. The high concentration of consciousness energies creates a type of Self-Aware Regional Director.

This is the entity which is the duplicate of you; on a smaller scale. It is therefore a true "thinking mind", yet on a smaller scale. This Regional Director is therefore actively managing signals. It knows what message to send, and how to send them. It also recognizes the messages received. This information is passed along to the thinking mind, and to other areas of the body, as appropriate.

Similarly, each of the Chakras are highly concentrated areas of the Soul Energies. Much of your "soul" is actually contained in these glands, and in the nearby regions surrounding the glands. Therefore, your glands are also the storage point and regional centers for your soul energies.

Concentrations of Soul and Consciousness for Effective Chakras

This leads us to the importance of the amount of energies in each of your chakra glands. Your chakra glands will operate more effectively where given enough concentration of soul power and consciousness.

With greater soul power, the chakras will emit more strongly; and receive more easily. Therefore if we want any chakra gland to have greater power, we shift more of soul energies to that area.

With greater consciousness, the chakras will emit the effective messages more often; and will translate received messages more often. (We may receive, but there are essentially no translators or messengers to deliver the messages). Therefore, if we want stronger and more effective communication systems, we will add more consciousness energies to those areas; as well as the soul energies.

This is also why many people have stronger chakras for a few chakras, while the other chakras are weaker. This is quite common. The reason is the amount of soul power (or consciousness) in that chakra.

This also means that if we want to increase the ability of that chakra, we will shift our soul energies and consciousness energies to that location.

We can do this because the soul is essentially fluid. Remember that the soul is similar to wispy clouds, which can morph into different shapes. Therefore, we can use this ability, when our soul is inside the body, to shift some of our soul energies to any one chakra, as desired.

Further note that in many times of our life, we prefer to have one or two chakras be the strongest; while the others are weaker. If we enjoy using only two specific chakras, we can put most of our soul and consciousness energies into those two chakras. The Power of Emission, and the Clarity of Receiving Messages…will then be incredibly profound.

Body as General Container vs Soul Flowing into the Cells

When the soul is in the body, we can think of this in two general ways. The first is the body as container, and the soul exists within. The second is to the body as mechanical system, and the soul can flow into each of the mechanical components.

In the first understanding of the soul-body relationship, we consider the soul to be contained in the body. This is the simplest understanding. Yet we also know that the soul extends far beyond the borders of the body, and can be felt by many people nearby. Thus, the "container" is true, and yet is only a limited understanding.

We also know that the soul is very fluid; an entity which expand and contract; an entity can morph and change form. Therefore, when we look at the soul in this second understanding, we see that the soul energies can flow to specific regions of the body. The soul is not just contained in the body; the soul energies can enter the components of the body.

We will discuss the details of all such aspects, of the soul-body relations, in the sections below.

Soul Energies can Flow and Penetrate Anywhere

The Soul is made of Soul Energies. Energies are generally very small in diameter. These Energies are much smaller than any physical object, including any photon or atom. Therefore, the Energies, including Energies of the Soul, can penetrate anything.

This is important to understand, because it means that the soul energies can penetrate through the body. Thus, in the first understanding of soul-body relationships, the soul is connected to the body, and mostly contained in the body; yet can easily expand to territory far beyond the body. The standard for most people is approximately 3 feet; though the more advanced souls can expand to their souls to fill an entire room.

This also means, when using the second understanding, that the soul energies can easily flow into the cells of the body. There are no barriers within the body; therefore we can move our soul energies to any region of the body we desire. This can be used for extra power and control.

Soul Energies as Filling the Cells and Mechanics of Body

We understand now, that we can use our soul energies to fill the mechanical components of the body. This is a process which we can use to our advantage. We can give extra power and wisdom, to any region of the body, on command.

Remember that the Free Soul, when not in a body, can morph into different shapes. We can do the same morphing of the soul, when the soul is inside the body. This means we can consciously choose, to morph our soul energies, in various shapes as desired.

This allows us to shift any of our soul energies from one region to another. We can also choose to have our soul energies enter the cells and organs of the body, rather than just being generally contained.

When we do this, the cells and organs are not just mechanical components. They are now also powered, and controlled, by the soul.

You may have heard phrases such as "mind over matter"; and the "placebo effect". You have heard of men who could heal themselves; or control their own internal functions. All of this is possible…because we can shift our soul energies, and our consciousness clusters, to different regions of the body. We are then using our Soul to add extra power to the mechanics of our body. We are using the Consciousness Energies, as a messaging system to manage the operations beyond merely mechanical.

This process is within our personal power. We can do this. Yet only those who are the most advanced in their souls and consciousness know how to make this process as their reality.

Therefore, when you learn to control the flow dynamics of your own soul, and your own consciousness energies; within your own body…then you will become the true Master of your own Body.

Expanding and Contracting the Soul, Related to the Body

The first command operation of the soul, is to be able to Expand and Contract the Soul, as desired. Learn to do this process; and when you can do this process, on command…then you can practice with adjusting the flow of soul energy within the body.

Always remember that our Soul is much larger than the body. The average size is 3 feet in diameter; and for the more advanced souls, the size is much greater. Therefore, you are not required to limit your soul to the boundaries of your physical body. You can expand your soul to its fullest size. When you do this…you will experience true Freedom!

We must also realize that most people are not living with their full soul. The majority of humans are living with their souls crumpled inside. They don't realize this, because this is how they have been conditioned. This is what they know.

Yet the moment you begin to unleash your soul from its cage; and feel the full expansion of your soul into the environment; this is the moment you realize who and what you truly are.

All Beings must learn to expand their Souls to their True Size. We do this through a process of knowing. Begin with knowing of the freedom in your mind…then the freedom in your soul…and then…finally…the Freedom of in the Physical Reality of your Fully Expanded Soul, as you walk in this world.

Allow your soul to unfold its crumpled wings. Let the spiritual bird out of its cage. Then you will understand the true power of your Being.

Expanding and Contracting the Soul; on Command

When you learn to expand your soul to its fullest extent, you will want to experience this more often. However, the world is not yet designed for such Spiritual Freedom. Therefore, we must learn to both expand and contract our soul; on demand; as appropriate for the situation.

Furthermore, the contracting of the soul can be beneficial for many purposes. When we want to engage in healing of the soul or the mind; it is best to have our souls fully retracted within. This allows our soul powers to be fully engaged in the healing and transformation process.

The contraction process is also useful for introspection, and creativity based on within. When we desire to create art, we often desire to access our own deep mind and deep soul. This is best when the full soul is contained within the body.

Yet when we desire to be fully engaged with the world, we can then expand our souls to the fullest. Whether on a public stage, or simply walking in the forest, expanding the soul to fullest size becomes the best feeling of Freedom and Living of Life.

Therefore, we need to be able to both Expand and Contract the soul, on demand, as desired. There are reasons for both states of being.

True Size of the Soul

This leads us to the True Size of the Soul. In general, the true size of the soul is greater than the size of the body. We have the ability to extend our soul energies far beyond our earthly container; we only limit ourselves.

Also note that the True Size of the Soul depends on the advancement level of the being. As we evolve, our souls become larger. Therefore, the most advanced souls will have the largest souls.

We also return to the reality of incarnation; and the analogy of the stage. This world is a miniature version of reality. It is similar to the structures of miniature golf. Everything is smaller. Therefore, when incarnating, we are smaller compared to those who are pure souls. And when we go back again, our souls will be much larger again.

However, it is important to know that our souls never really shrink. Our souls remain the same size. It is only that we are placed in these flesh containers, and believe our souls are only contained within. This is false. Our true souls are much, much larger. We can expand our souls far beyond the boundaries of the flesh; if we are only willing to realize it.

True Size of the Soul: as Room, Building, or Arena

The true size of the soul, in this Earthly Realm, can be much larger than we realize. This is especially true for the most Advanced Souls.

The true size of the soul, when spread to full size, will of course depend on the specific Being. However, for most humans, the soul can extend approximately 3 feet in diameter.

Advanced Souls have much larger souls. Their souls, when fully let out and free, can extend to the size of a room…or an entire building. Some have souls which extend much further, such as a stadium.

The most important concept to remember, is that our souls are generally much larger than we realize. Most people keep their souls crumpled inside of them. Yet when we realize who we truly are, and allow our true souls to expand fully…our energies extend much further.

Learn to know your true soul powers, and allow your soul to be free. Your soul was never meant to be confined or caged. Your soul was never meant to be inhibited. Rather, your soul was always meant to extend as far as possible. Of course sometimes introspection is necessary, and at these moments your soul is fully contained within the body. Yet when living freely and creating your life, extend your soul beyond the borders.

You will be much happier, and be living your true existence.

Powerful Energies of the Great Leaders and Rock Stars

When a Great Leader walks into the room, everyone feels it. When that great leader walks onto a stage, the audience feels his presence. We know this, we feel it.

With any Great Mystic, Great Leader, and Rock Star, we feel the Energies. We feel the Presence. This effect is because of the powerful soul of that person. His soul is so large, that we feel it instantly.

The Great Leader is in fact a great leader…because of his Advanced Soul. He has the confidence, wisdom, and vision to take his community to the next level. Yet this same Advanced Soul is naturally larger in size. Thus, when the Great Leader takes the stage, his energies fill the entire arena. His aura is felt by everyone.

Rock Stars: Harnessing their Powerful Soul Energies

This same effect exists with the Rock Stars. They have the Rock Star Stage Presence, which fills the concert arena with their Soul Energies.

Only those men with the most powerful souls can be True Rock Stars. This is because, being a Rock Star, requires that his energies can be felt by everyone in the audience. This can only be created by the man with a very large and powerful soul.

Furthermore, most of the Great Stars know how to harness their Powerful Souls in multiple ways. This includes first retracting the soul inward, to write the songs with such depth. This also includes the ability to play his instrument and use his voice, in ways which bring his soul to life.

Then, when on stage…the Rock Star fully unleashes his Soul Power, and becomes something far greater than any common mortal. These combinations of traits are all based on his Powerful Advanced Soul.

We see this with Freddie Mercury and Michael Jackson. The ability to write this great music; to play and sing with such soul; and have the aura to fill a stadium…are all from the same factor: The Advanced Divine Soul.

This process begins with the Rock Star as creative artist. During this process, he brings all of his soul back inside his body. This concentrated soul, all within the body, allows him to create the most powerful songs.

Yet the same Rock Star when on stage, will then unfold all of his energies when taking the stage. On stage, he becomes True Power; a Force of Nature. He is able to fill the arena with his Soul.

This is a very physical effect, as the large and powerful soul of the Rock Star fills the arena, and is felt by everyone in the audience.

Always remember that our souls are much larger than we realize. Also remember we have the ability to transform our souls, and enlarge our souls, through our significant experiences.

Eventually, over the process of several lifetimes, you may become the next Rock Star or Great Leader. With deliberate focus and development, you may be able to reach this Level of Advanced Being.

The Intensity of the Genius

We also see this as the Intensity of the Genius. Most of the Great Geniuses of history have been called "intense". Anyone who interacted with these men, would see their intensity.

This is because the Genius has a very large soul, which is concentrated in a much smaller human body. It this concentrated advanced soul which is the need for prolific self-expression and creativity. It is also this large soul which propels the Genius forward, with powerful stamina and life energy.

For these Great Geniuses, all of their thoughts and feelings seemed to be highly concentrated. More powerful. Similarly, their conviction and dedication to their projects, was always constant and wavering.

This is again understood as the Advanced Soul in the human body. The Great Geniuses have the most advanced level souls in the universe. Of all the Beings, in any realm, these Beings are among the wisest, with the greatest spiritual powers. This is who they are, in any form.

These are also the largest of souls, when in their True Soul Form. Their natural soul size, is the size of a large building; or a large arena. Therefore, when you attempt to put this large size soul…into the much smaller human body…complications naturally arise.

The effect is similar to taking a giant plush bear, and stuffing into a very small box. It is very difficult, and can only be done with lots of crushing and condensing. This is how it is with the Advanced Large Soul of the Great Men, when stuffed into the much smaller human body.

This is why the Great Genius is compelled to create; to express himself so freely, and prolific. He has this powerful energy packed inside, and he must express it any way he can!

This is also why many of the Great Geniuses have energy for life, and powerful stamina. It is this powerful soul energy which propels them. Scientists such as Tesla and Newton rarely slept. They had the focus and stamina to devote many hours, every day, to their curiosity.

And the Rock Stars such as Freddie Mercury, have the life energy to give powerful performances, every day, for years. This is due to the strong soul energies packed inside.

Therefore, it is natural that the Great Genius is very intense! It is natural that he is bursting with ambition, desires, and creativity. He has the very large soul, in a smaller human container; which drives him forward with great life energy.

Advanced Souls and Great Leaders: Their Souls Are Strongest

We feel this Soul Energy the strongest when the man is an Advanced Soul, as described earlier. This is because his Extended Soul can easily fill the entire room. His soul may in fact be able to fill an auditorium.

This is a very physical reality. Understand that this Great Leader has a very large soul; which he often extends fully. This is especially true when he enters onto the stage in front of the audience.

Thus, his Soul Energy is, in fact, filling the room. His soul extends throughout the auditorium. This is a physical reality. This is all of his fully extended soul. Therefore, any person within the room will feel his soul energy physically touching their own.

Great Leaders and Rock Stars: Their Energies Mixing in your Soul

Furthermore…and this is important, their soul energies can envelop your entire body. You are comforted in the blanket of his Soul Energies.

It is at this moment, that his soul energies can penetrate into your own body; and fill many regions of your body. His soul energies are then mixed with our own soul energies, inside your own body.

In addition, this is also combined with the other messaging systems, from the Powerful Leader. This includes his powerful consciousness thoughts, and his hormones. All of this works together.

This is why you FEEL that GREAT POWER of the man you admire. This is the true Rock Star Quality; it is the Aura of the Great King.

All of these wonderful feelings you have…they exist because you are experiencing the presence of a Great Man. You feel inside your own body, his very large and powerful soul energies, surrounding your own soul, and mixing his Soul Energies with your own.

You know that you are in the presence of Greatness, because all of your messaging systems tell you. You know that this man is a Powerful King and Rock Star, because you actually feel it inside your body.

You physically experience all of his Soul Energies, inside your own body; and therefore you know…you know…that his Soul Alchemy is indeed that of the Great Rock Star and Powerful King.

This is…the Aura and the Soul Power…of the Great Leader.

Merging the Souls of Friends and True Lovers: The Mixing Our Soul Energies

The Souls of any two Beings can merge together. Whenever the two souls are close enough to touch, each person will feel the soul energies of the other. And when the two persons are open with their souls, their soul energies will physically enter the bodies of each other. This is where the true mixing of soul energies can begin.

This Mixing of Soul Energies will create very powerful effects, for each person. This is what empaths feel most of the time; as they feel the souls of others reaching into their own bodies, and mixing together.

The greater reality is when the Souls of True Lovers mix together. This arises due to the lovers opening their souls fully; which allows both openness to receiving energies, as well as full extension of their own soul. The result is a powerful and joyous mixture of soul alchemies.

When this occurs, we produce a new type of entity, which we call the "Soul of Us". This Soul of Us is a new type of alchemy, which is a mixture of your soul and mine. This mixture exists, physically, within each of our bodies, whenever we are close together.

The Energies of the Soul of Us, are mixed inside our bodies; and circulate between us. These energies can also fill the air in the room around us. Others may feel this energy in the air, if they are open to it.

In the following sections, we will look at many of the exciting details, for how the Souls of Individual Beings…and merge and mix with the souls of others they touch. The results can be very powerful.

Knowing the Emotions and Abilities of Other People

We begin with the general communication between two people, using energies and chemicals. We can feel the emotions and abilities of other people, in our own bodies.

This is actually a combination of soul energies and consciousness energies. In many cases, there are also EM energies and hormones.

Therefore, when we "feel" the soul or emotions of another person, we may be feeling any one of these messaging entities.

Furthermore, it is very often the case that we feel a combination of these messaging systems at the same time. This provides multiple sources of "information", which your Deep Consciousness Programs can put together…as a Single Message.

Also note that most of these messaging systems are managed by the Chakra Glands, as described above. This is how you can communicate with others, on a level which bypasses traditional communication.

The Touch from Angels and Other Metaphysical Friends

This leads us to the experience of feeling the Soul Energies specifically. The Soul does have distinct Energies; which differ from all other forms of messaging system. Therefore, you know it when you feel it.

This is most obvious when a metaphysical friend, including the Angels, decide to pass through your body. This is a very distinctive feeling. Their soul energies mix with your own soul, while they are passing through.

At the same time, their consciousness energies…usually with deep knowledge and wisdom…are being passed along to the consciousness energies in your body. The combination is a very distinct physical effect.

You know that you are being touched from within. You know that your soul alchemies are co-existing, for those moments. It is very distinct.

The temperatures will also change, as the Free Soul exists at a different energy level than ours. It has nothing to do with who they are; only the physical reality differences of existence.

Therefore, our souls and our main consciousness can indeed be shared. We can present ourselves in this way to others; and they can experience us in our True Form.

Feeling Another's Soul Energies in Your Body

We can also experience the Soul Energies and Consciousness from other people. This is especially true when being with humans with great souls (as described earlier); and when our Alchemies are Aligned.

In brief, we feel the soul energies when our soul energies physically touch. For most people, their souls extend a few feet in each direction. Therefore, if two people are within range, their Soul Energies will physically touch. Their Soul Energies are co-existing. You will feel their energies; and they will feel yours.

This is similar to holding your hands to full extension. When two people extend their hands fully, then they can touch. They feel each other. And if they come closer together, they can touch each other more strongly. The same is true for the Soul Energies. These Soul Energies have a distance; which varies from one being to another. Yet when these Soul Energies are physically touching…it is then that each person feels the Soul of the other.

Mixing the Soul Energies of True Lovers

When two souls are physically close, this is when they will touch. As the souls get closer together, the souls will overlap. This means that the soul energies, of each being, will begin to merge together.

It is at this moment, that each person will actually feel the soul energies of the other. Yes…the soul of the other person is merging with their own soul. We can now feel the energies, in a very physical way.

This is how two people, who spend much time together, can have their souls merge when they are together. We feel their soul energies inside our own bodies; and they feel our soul energies inside their body.

Our two soul energies become mixed; inside both bodies. The feelings we have within our body…and these are very physical sensations…are created by the new mixture of soul energies.

Therefore, with two lovers, there is very real, very physical mixing, of the soul energies. Each person feels the physical effects and emotions of the other's soul…now deep within their own soul alchemy.

Mixing Souls is Easiest for True Lovers

We can also understand why it is that Lovers will experience this effect most strongly. There are two reasons: their time together in close proximity; and their willingness to share their soul energies.

The process of sharing souls can, of course, exist with any two beings. This is why we can feel the bad souls of others, as well as the good. Yet the effect is strongest, and most lasting, for those who love each other.

This is because the two lovers will spend more time together than with anyone else. Whenever we are physically close to another person, our souls will naturally be close as well. Regardless of our relationship, or how we feel about them, we will feel their soul energies when this close.

Thus, the True Lovers are those who want to spend more time together, and be physically close together. Therefore, naturally, they will feel the exchange of soul energies when this close. And because they are physically close, for much of their time, they will come to know well that feeling of the other's soul energies…mixed with their own…deep inside.

Trust, Protection, and Mixing of the Soul Energies

The second reason for this effect being stronger with Lovers is because the Lovers are more open to giving and receiving of the soul energies. Remember that we have the ability to expand and retract our soul energies; and one of the reasons will depend on who we are with.

When we really like someone, we want to share our souls with them. We don't need to understand the process, we just know this instinctually. Yet we must also trust them…trust them….not to hurt our souls. And so we keep our souls retracted, even with those we want to love, until we feel that we can be safe enough to expand in their presence.

Yet when we know that we can trust the other person, and they can trust us, we will then extend our soul energies. As we develop our relationship, we trust more, and expand our souls more fully. Our soul now enters into the body of our lover, and mixes with their own soul.

Allowing their Souls to Enter Our Own

At the same time, expanding our soul allows their soul to enter our own more easily. The process is similar to lowering your shield. When you allow your soul to expand further; this also allows other souls to come into your own soul energy space. You will feel their soul energies, deep inside your own body; as much the other person feels of yours.

Note that this can be good, or harmful, depending on who you are with. Therefore we must be wise. We must know how to protect our soul; yet allow it to be open when we can.

Yet always know that this process of letting go of your defenses, is what allows your soul to expand, and the souls of others to reach inside.

Three Entities: You, Me, and Us

When the True Lovers have effectively mixed their souls together in this way, a new type of entity is created. This is the entity of "us".

We will therefore have three soul entities in the relationship. These are Your Soul; My Soul; and Our Souls. The third entity exists whenever we are physically together, as our souls are merging and mixing; in the surrounding space, as well as in our own bodies.

Note the Soul of Us exists only as a combination of you and me; and only when our souls are physically touching. The Soul of Us cannot be a fully independent soul, as with either your soul or mine.

However, when we are together, and deeply in love, our soul energies mix in this new way. We then have the "us" soul…as a mixture in my soul…and in yours. We both feel this "us" soul, within our own body.

This mixture is…the Soul Entity of Us

The Soul of Us, as Filling the Space

Furthermore, as we enjoy our Open Love together, our souls will expand larger and larger, whenever we are together. This means that the Soul of Us…becomes this Larger-than-Life entity.

This Soul of Us can fill the room, and fill the home. This Soul of Us, composed primarily of mutual love and physical attraction, flows through us, between us, and all around us.

This is where the Soul of Us can almost seem to an Entity in itself. The love energies fill the air; because our combined souls have grown to this size, and together fills the area with our mixture of souls.

This is where the Soul of Us becomes the best form. It is a combined soul entity, that is a mixture of our souls; and yet much greater in size. This mixture of souls; and especially the love energies; fill the air around us, as well as the souls inside of us.

This is where we know what true love is, and are able to live it, in everything we do. That is the best form…for the Soul Entity of Us.

The Beatles: A Love Story

Ringo Starr was once asked "What is the Beatles Story about". His answer was this: "It is a love story. About four guys who genuinely loved each other." And he really meant it.

The Beatles did absolutely love each other, and continued to love each other regardless of the band itself not existing. This was a strong soul bond, between four extraordinary men. Four advanced souls, sharing their souls, their desires, and their true love for each other.

The Beatles is indeed a love story. We can understand this aspect of their relationship, and their great music, with the understanding of mixing the soul energies together. Yes, their "Soul of Us" became quite profound.

This begins with John Lennon and Paul McCartney. You can tell that they loved each other. Look at some of the photos. There was a deep love between them. We can understand this on a Soul Alchemy Level, as their two souls begin to merge together. Paul's soul energy enters the body of John, and mixes with his Soul Alchemy; while John's soul enters the body of Paul, and mixes with Paul's soul energies. This is where it all begins.

They begin to write songs together. This means they are physically close. They are also very open and expressive in their souls, as this is a major aspect of their creative expression. Their open soul allows their souls to expand and enter deep into their partner. Their proximity together allows this process to exist all the time.

Soon enough…Paul is not just Paul…but a version of Paul + John. Similarly, John is not only John…as he is a version of John + Paul. They know each other, from the inside, as their soul alchemies have mixed. We now have the third entity: the "Soul of John and Paul".

This is why their collaboration became exceptional. It begins with the mixing of their soul alchemies, which leads to a deep love for each other and deep understanding of each other. It is then from being in this mixed alchemy, that they powerful writing partnership.

The Beatles as a Soul Entity

This process then extends to all the Beatles. The Beatles became much more than a musical group. They became a Soul Entity.

George Harrison and Ringo Starr were also very advanced souls, with deep love in their soul, and strong spiritual connections. Thus, we have four very advanced souls, each with deep love and powerful spiritual connections. Put all four of these great beings in a room, and naturally their soul energies will mix together. This is how they became a band; and a band of brothers; at the same time.

The four advanced souls, each with their powerful souls, work closely together. They play together. They travel together. Their proximity of souls will naturally result in their soul energies overlapping, and mixing together.

Furthermore, each one is very expressive and open. This is part of their natural creative expression. Therefore, they extend their souls, while expressing themselves through their music. This means their souls, of each of them, are fully extended.

We have four separate souls, each full extended. All four of the independent Soul Alchemies, are now penetrating the souls of the others. Each of them is not just their autonomous self; they also feel the soul energies of the other members of the band. In this way, we have a new Soul Alchemy…which is a mixture of all four of the Beatles.

This mixture of soul energies will reside in the bodies of each band member. The mixture of soul energies will physically exist within the bodies of each of them. Thus, whenever the four are together in the same room, the Soul Entity known as "The Beatles" is created.

Soul Alchemy of the "Beatles" as Within Each Musician

The Alchemy within each body is approximately the same mixture; as it is composed of the alchemy of all four of them. This means, that the Soul Alchemy of "The Beatles" exists within all of them. In other words, when they are playing together, and fully open with each other...the "Beatles" as a distinct Soul Entity exists within each of them.

It is not just John or George playing music....it is now "The Beatles" ... as One Soul Entity...on each of the instruments.

George knew automatically what to play as lead guitar. Ringo knew what to do on the percussion. Much of this was instinctual, simply because all four men were feeling the same soul alchemy in their bodies, at the same time. This is the true magic.

Of course there was always different musical ideas; which they tried out in combination until they liked the final result. Yet the instinct to create some of the best musical ideas, as the others were playing their own instruments, is based on this strong connection. The ideas came because of their mixture of soul energies.

This is one of the reasons why their music was exceptional. Whenever they were truly loving each other, and fully open with their souls, this "Beatles" entity came into existence. This is most clear in their final album of Abbey Road; where they all wanted to come together, as the early days, to focus on the music. The result is quite powerful.

The Beatles is more than a band, it is a Soul Entity in itself.

The Importance of the Beatles as Soul Entity

The importance of this story is to remind us that when we find the right partners, anything wonderful can happen. When we are fully expressive of our souls, extending our soul energies, and playing with our partners; it is then that the new Soul Entity of "Us" comes into being.

And whenever we are physically together, in the same room or general area, this mixture of soul alchemies is felt within each of our bodies.

It is this knowing of the souls of our partners, on an instinctual level; combined with genuine love for our partners; that allows us to reach the greatest heights. This is ultimate desire for any partnership.

Missing your Love: The Soul Elixir is Gone

When the person you love is far away, you feel this absence in your soul. This is a real physical effect. Your soul is missing the soul energies of the person you love. Your body knows the absence of these energies.

If you are very close, then the Soul of Us is deeply embedded into your own soul entity. The "us" mixture exists within your body. This is something you feel, whenever you are together.

Yet when the lover is gone, this Soul of Us is not there. We often say that "half of the soul is missing". Indeed, it is missing. There is half of your soul…which is "us" mixture…that is now missing.

This is why you are missing the person you love. It is much more than in your mind or emotions; it is the absence of the soul energies. When your lover is far away, but will return, you begin to miss those soul energies. It is indeed similar to having nutrients or drugs; you enjoy having them daily, and when not available…you miss having it.

That is what is happening when your lover is far away. Of course we separate each day; and retain our autonomy. You know how to live without your lover's energies for a day or two; but much longer, and your soul craves the feeling of your lover's soul energies. You need to have those energies of us, deeply mixed inside your own soul.

Your body begins to know the absence after separation for too long. It is not just your mind and emotions; which are also part of the connection; it is also the physical absence of the soul energies.

Thus, when your lover is gone, this half of your soul energies is also gone. This is a very real effect.

Your Soul is Empty After Permanent Separation

The process of separation is more significant when you know that your lover is never going to return. Perhaps it was a permanent break-up of the relationship. Perhaps it was a sudden death. Either way, you know that this lover is never coming back. You will never be able to get that lover's soul energies again. There is no option for being close and replenishing.

Therefore, when the person you love is gone forever, you feel this emptiness in your soul…as if part of you is missing. Indeed it is. Those soul energies that were mixed with yours, are never to return again. That physical reality of the "Soul of Us"…is no longer here, and will never be.

Again, we refer to the similarity to nutrients. You are so used to having these nutrients in your body. It is nourishing. Therefore, when that nourishment is no longer available, you will be physically depleted. The lack of your lover's soul energies does weaken the body. We must find alternate ways to nourish the soul during this transition.

This is also why many people rush into a new (and temporary) love affair, after their previous lover has departed. We need those soul energies; at least something similar to those of our previous love, or we will go through withdrawals like a drug addict. You know this is true.

Maintaining Your Soul Identity with the Soul of Us

There are many great pleasures for the Soul of Us, yet there are some cautions as well. We discussed the first caution above, for the need of the soul energy nourishment; which can become like a drug addict. If the supply is readily available, all is well; but when it is unavailable, we will go through physical withdrawals, as we need our energy nourishment.

Another caution is that we must also be aware of maintaining our own identity, while also enjoying the Mixture of our Souls. We must balance our Autonomy with the Soul of Us. This is a complex topic, simply because of the energies mixing within and without.

Also, there is never any one "right" answer; it is a spectrum of options, and personal choice. This is not necessarily a bad thing, as there many people, very happy, who are "completely devoted" to their partner". Yet there are others who suddenly realize that they are "losing their identity" in the relationship", and want to regain some of their autonomy.

There is no "right" answer, there is only the position on spectrum that works for you. However, awareness and personal choice is important.

Be aware of what the Soul of Us can be…as mutual pleasures and as subverting your own autonomy. Know what you want in each area of the relationship, then adjust your soul energies, in the Alchemy for the Soul of Us, according to your desires.

There is no right or wrong in this; it is always your choice, but it is a complex spectrum of options. You may delight in becoming complete devoted to your partner; you may enjoy many mutual pleasures; or you may prefer to have a balance of independence and submission.

Just know that when your soul energies become mixed at this level, there are many possibilities. Many people become completely lost in the Soul of Us. This can happen if we allow the Soul of Us to become the majority of our soul alchemy, while forgetting our own unique soul.

The Realities of the "Soul of Us"

The basic concept is always the same: when our souls physically touch, the soul energies can mix together. Furthermore, when we are fully open with our souls, and we have deep love, then we allow our souls to enter the other's body; where the soul energies will mix. This creates a new type of Soul Alchemy…known as the "Soul of Us".

This "Soul of Us" is a mixture that exists whenever we are physically close, as this allows our soul energies to mix together. This new mixture exists within each of our bodies, as well as the space between us. This is the love and deep pleasures we feel when we are together.

We then come to enjoy these new soul alchemies. We want to be together, to feel those soul energies in our bodies again. Our emotions, our thoughts, and our physical bodies, are much pleasured by these experiences. Indeed, this is how it should be, with those we are aligned. There is wonderful magic, when our souls are joined together, and our energies mixing.

Yet when we are truly loving each other, and have this deep relationship, then whenever we separate, we feel the absence of these soul energies. Our bodies know that something is wrong, that we are lacking this nourishment. This is why we crave to be with our partner again as soon as possible. We crave the nourishment, because it is good for us.

It is only when the separation is for a long duration, or permanent, that the withdrawal symptoms arise. We seek something else, to replace those energy nutrients; eventually finding a similar soul to be in our lives again.

These are the realities…for the "Soul of Us…the wonderful mixture of soul energies, which can be sustained and enjoyed with the right partners.

The Soul and Consciousness Together

We are now ready to discuss the relationships between the Soul and the Consciousness. These two entities (Soul and Consciousness) are essential components of our Eternal Existence. Therefore, it is important that we understand the relationships between the two.

Furthermore, both the Soul and the Consciousness are integrated with the physical body. Therefore, if we desire to make the most of our life here on earth, then we must fully understand these complex relationships.

We will begin by discussing the specific relationships between the soul and the consciousness. We will then explain how the conscious energies are distributed throughout the body. This understanding will lead us to the many concepts as explained throughout this book.

Note that in this section we will focusing on the Consciousness, and how the Consciousness is related to the soul and the body. We have already discussed the soul-body relations earlier.

Review of Soul versus Consciousness

We begin by reviewing the basic concepts of Soul and Consciousness. Notice that there are several distinctions. We will emphasize those distinctions now.

(1) The Soul is who you are. The Soul is your Personality and Traits. The Consciousness is self-awareness and complex thoughts. Both exist as energies, yet they are different types.

(2) The Soul exists as a Soul Alchemy. This is a mixture of soul energy traits, similar to colors of paint or a potion. The Consciousness exists as tiny drops of Consciousness Energy. These Consciousness Energies can flow like streams, or gather into Consciousness Clouds.

(3) The Consciousness Energies are Code Carriers. They are similar to boats which can carry the "thought cargo". Thus, the amount of consciousness energies in a location can either be the potential for thought (empty carriers), or the complex thought (filled with cargo).
These Consciousness Boats are then sent to various locations, with their Thought Cargo, to preform operations as desired.

(4) The Soul can exist without Consciousness; and the Consciousness can exist without a Soul. However, in reality most souls have some level of Consciousness. Yet it must be noted, that Aggregated Consciousness, in itself, is not a soul; it is just a cargo of thought.

(5) The Soul is fluid, like wisps of clouds; yet is ultimately one entity. In contrast, the Consciousness Energies can be distributed and aggregated in a variety of ways. Thus, the soul exists as one; while the Consciousness Energies are sent throughout the mind (and body) as needed.

(6) The Soul will only travel as one entity. Also, the soul energies are only felt as proximity; within the physical reach of the expanded soul. Yet the Consciousness Energies can be emitted, similar to bursts of photons. This allows the Consciousness Energies, as complex thoughts, to travel much further than the extended soul.

(7) The Soul without Consciousness Energies would be a complex alchemy of personality traits; yet without self-awareness or independent thoughts. Such a Being would be instinctual action only.
In contrast, the Consciousness Energy Cluster would be a complex thought. It would have self-awareness; and can create its own ideas. Yet there are no personality traits beyond the specific thoughts in the cluster.

(8) Although the Soul and the Consciousness are two different types of energies; and must be considered separately; in reality we often see the two entities together. Thus, most souls have some Consciousness.

(9) Any new "Conscious" entity was most likely created from an existing Conscious Being; and usually from a very Advanced Being.
This means only the Advanced Being has ability to create self-aware entities. Only the most advance beings have the large amount of conscious energies, to aggregate in another location (while still retaining enough for other purposes), and thus create another self-aware conscious entity. This self-aware will also likely have some of the soul energy of the creator; as the conscious energies and soul energies both came from him.

(10) In summary: the Soul and the Consciousness are two separate types of energies, and operate in different ways. The Soul Energies are essentially your traits, and your deep memory. This is who you are. At the same time, the Soul has a Consciousness; which is our Awareness of ourselves and our environment. It is also our ability to create complex thoughts. In the more advanced beings, there is both a larger soul and a greater amount of consciousness energies.

The Soul With Consciousness, as Soul in Upper Realms

Before we come to earth again, we exist in the upper realms as a Free Soul. This Free Soul is morphing spirit of energy; with a high level of consciousness energies. Thus, the Soul Entity has Consciousness embedded into the Soul. The Soul and Consciousness exist together

The size of the soul, and the amount of consciousness energies, depends on your level of evolution at the time. The Wise Beings are always seeking growth, in both areas; from any location they are in.

Multiple Lifetimes: Embedded in Soul and Consciousness

Also do remember that our souls are eternal, and we return to earth many times, to experience multiple lifetimes. These experiences are embedded into our souls; and the knowledge is added to our consciousness. Therefore, this collection of embedded experiences and knowledge exists within our souls…before returning to Earth again.

This knowledge will be placed into specific areas of our mind, when our souls incarnate again. The skills, knowledge, and memories; from our many lifetimes, will be placed in our subconscious mind. From there, this knowledge will be unpacked and placed into specific locations for this life.

Soul and Consciousness, as Entering Body

When the soul arrives into the new body, the entrance location is the subconscious mind. This is a small region in the back of the brain.

Thus, the entire soul, with full consciousness, is sent into the subconscious; and then into the rest of the body. Always remember that the full adult soul, and total knowledge, has arrived. However, most of this is stored in the subconscious until it is time to distribute.

Consciousness Energies Distributed Throughout the Body

After the full soul and consciousness has arrived in the subconscious, everything is distributed throughout the body. However, this process is gradual; and is often timed with certain growth period of the body.

This means…that while everything is there…much of it is not accessible until the right time. Usually it is biological development cues, which prompt releasing and distributing of certain knowledge. These bits of knowledge and skills are then placed in their proper areas.

This growth of the person is therefore a combination of biological mechanisms, soul energy distribution, and consciousness energy (as knowledge). All of these are inter-related, and often released by specific activities of the person himself.

Also note that the knowledge from the subconscious is usually released in biological stages. This is why humans tend to advance their abilities, in specific areas, along general age ranges.

The first stage is in the womb; followed by the age ranges of 1-7; 7-14; and 14-21. There are approximate ranges of course; yet generally hold true for the personal development of most humans.

Compacting Your Consciousness: The Zip Folder of the Soul

We can visualize the traveling from the upper realm, to your new body, as moving into your new home. This includes packing your soul and your consciousness, then unpacking again when you get there.

The process begins by locating your new home (your body). Many souls get some choice in their new body. This includes specifics of gender, general region, and sometimes specific parents. Of course, some of these factors may be chosen for us; and we are usually consenting before we go down.

We will then pack up our existing "home" for the move. This means compacting your consciousness and your soul. This packing process makes the overall process of traveling into the body much easier.

Furthermore, this compacting of the consciousness will allow our full consciousness to reside in the subconscious. This is similar to a Zip Folder, where large amounts of data are compacted.

Therefore, the consciousness knowledge and programs are compacted, before being sent to the new body. This compacting also allows all of this information to be stored in the small subconscious. This process is very similar to the zip folder system; where data is compacted, transferred through the cable; and stored on the computer.

Of course, the data must be "unzipped" at the new computer; and this usually requires a series of codes. The process is similar for the full consciousness. The various "subfolders" of compacted consciousness must be accessed with a special code; and then expanded to the full program and topic knowledge.

It is important to notice…that all of the knowledge, from all of your previous lives, is already stored in your subconscious. Everything is there. Yet each skill area and knowledge area must be accessed, using a special code, before the rest of your mind "knows" that it is there. This is the process of "self-discovery" and exploration in your early years.

Placing Consciousness Systems in your New "Hard Drive"

The process of accessing your compacted consciousness, can be compared to opening the zip drive.

In the analogy of the zip drive, the process is generally as follows. We locate a specific subfolder, then enter the proper code. The information is now fully available. Furthermore, many of the files have a built-in program to expand those files to full size. We can then move the entire set of files to their permanent location on our hard drive.

The unpacking of the consciousness is similar. We must first find the subset containers, for each area of knowledge and memory. We will then use an access code to open those specific packages.

This knowledge is now available. It is possible for any part of our mind to access this knowledge. We will then move this information, to the permanent location, of the "hard drive" in our mind.

This is where the knowledge will be stored, and can be accessed easily, for our entire lifetime.

Placing Favorite Consciousness Systems in your New Home

The process can also be compared to unboxing your favorite items after moving. In this analogy, we first search for the boxes we desire. We read the labels of the boxes, and open each one. We look through each box, to find the items we are looking for. When we find the specific items we are looking for, we will place these favorite items, in the permanent locations, in our new home.

In a similar way, when we have our many boxes of knowledge in our subconscious, we will want to access those skills and memories. This means we think about the topic, and reach back into the subconscious; searching for those specific boxes, with those specific skills. We can then open them, and find that we already have many of the tools we need.

We will then locate those tools to their new home. This means locating the full "box" of skills, programs, and memories; to the specific area of the brain. As some tools are best for kitchen versus garage, some knowledge is best in one are of the brain rather than another. This is unpacking your compacted knowledge.

Self-Discovery, Leading to Opening the Compacted Knowledge

An alternative process, which actually occurs at the same time, is to open the boxes randomly. We then rediscover what was inside each box. We will now find the new permanent location for each item.

This is also the same for the process of self-discovery. As we experience life, especially during the early years of play and curiosity, we also randomly open up these hidden boxes in our subconscious.

Each time we play, or try something new, we are accessing a similar box of knowledge and memories. We are reminding ourselves that this is not the first time we are doing this activity; we have enjoyed similar activities before. It is familiar…it is all coming back now.

Thus, when we enjoy an activity, this becomes the Instruction Code, to go find the boxes of similar knowledge…and open them. The existing knowledge now becomes open and accessible. We begin to realize the skills and memories of previous lifetimes…that we had forgotten.

Therefore, it is through this process of self-discovery and curiosity, that we unlock the hidden secrets of our subconscious. There is much knowledge and wisdom stored within. We just need to explore, to play, and to be curious enough to access it.

Advanced Souls: Quick Unpacking; Done it Many Times

This process of self-discovery and unpacking the hidden boxes of your subconscious…is an on-going process. The process begins from the first years of our life, and continues through adult life. However, this process can take longer for some; and be much quicker for others.

The most Advanced Souls are able to do this unpacking process at a very early age. This is because they have done this process many times before. They have come to earth many times; and gone through this unpacking many times. It is therefore quite easy.

These Advanced Souls automatically know, from an early age, how to access their hidden boxes in the subconscious. They already know how to do this. Thus, within a few years, often by the age of 10, most of their subconscious has already been unpacked. Their specific clusters of consciousness are now residing in their permanent locations.

This is also one of the many reasons, why the Advanced Soul shows advanced mental abilities from early ages. Not only does he have more knowledge in general; he also knows how to access that knowledge more quickly than others of his biological age.

Neural Pathways Must Also Be Developed

We must also remember that the neural pathways must also be developed. This process is related to biology and the DNA, regardless of the wisdom of the soul itself. Therefore, the ability to access this knowledge depends on both the accessing of the hidden knowledge in the subconscious, and the development of the neural pathways.

Notice that we are able to open our subconscious, and access those areas of compacted consciousness, while the neural paths are still developing. We can also move those expanded consciousness clusters to the regions of the mind, regardless of the neural pathways.

However, in order for engage in true complex thought, and to operate the complex programs, we must have the neural pathways operational. We may have many lifetimes of knowledge available, but without the data transfer systems of the neural pathways, we have limited access.

In practical life, we can develop both, throughout our childhood, at the same time. Eventually the unpacked consciousness clusters, and the operational neural paths, will be in full effect, for each region of the brain.

Consciousness Exists Throughout the Body

We must also realize that Consciousness exists throughout the body. Of course, the mind is the location with the greatest concentration of the consciousness. Yet we do have this consciousness throughout the body.

Remember that consciousness exists as drops of consciousness energy. These drops of consciousness energy are carriers of code, which are essentially boats of thought cargo. Therefore, these consciousness energy boats, these drops of consciousness energy, can exist anywhere; and can travel anywhere. There are really no limits to the location.

Therefore, the Consciousness Energies do exist throughout the body. These Consciousness Energies can exist anywhere. The largest location is of course in the mind. This is by far the largest concentration.

The other highest concentration is in the Subconscious, for reasons described above. Indeed, all the consciousness energy begins there, until it is spread to other locations.

The other highest locations of consciousness energy are the Chakra Glands. These areas include the Third Eye, the Sexual Glands, and the Heart Chakra. This allows information to be sent and received, using the consciousness energies in those glands.

In addition, we can find the consciousness energies throughout the body. This is most true for the Advanced Soul. The more advanced a Being is, he will have a greater total amount of consciousness energy.

This means he will have this consciousness energy boats, in every layer of his body. These consciousness energy boats are now ready to receive the knowledge codes; then store or transport the thoughts as needed.

Therefore, always remember that that Consciousness exists not just in the mind, but throughout the body. This includes the stored knowledge; information being transported and processed; and the empty boats waiting for the information cargo.

Touching Souls, yet Emitting Consciousness Energies

There is a difference between the soul and consciousness, in terms of communicating with other beings. The basic difference is this: the souls must be physically touching to interact; yet the consciousness is sent as a series of signals, across distant space, to reach the other person.

Souls are generally self-contained entities. We can of course expand our souls to larger sizes, yet the soul is a self-contained entity. Therefore, when two beings want to share their soul energies, these souls must be physically touching. This is why two people must be physically close, for their souls to be physically interacting.

This is also why we will miss the person we love when far away. Our souls have gotten used to their soul energies being immersed with our own. When far apart, we cannot feel this; and therefore we feel empty.

However, we can think about the person, regardless of distance. This is because our consciousness energies are emitted, similar to light. We can think of those we love, and send them this telepathic message. This is a real, very physical, set of consciousness energies sent into the air. They will receive this energy, and know we are thinking of them.

This is the process for all thoughts. Whether the thought is directed at a specific person, or to an audience, or…just your own thoughts…these thought energies are emitted as consciousness energies.

These are the drops of consciousness; the boats of consciousness cargo; the clouds or clusters of consciousness. In whatever way you want to look at it, the basic concept is the same. Consciousness is transmitted from one being to another as code carriers, sent through the air. These can be received by anyone who is nearby. They can also be received by anyone truly wants to receive your thoughts.

The Consciousness Communication System

The Consciousness Communication System is the most effective form of long-distance communication. This system was developed long before any form of telephone system; and it is built into our Existence.

Indeed this is one of the best purposes of the Consciousness. (The three main purposes are: Storage of Knowledge; Complex Thoughts; and Communication of Information).

Therefore, we can use the Consciousness Communication System to send messages. We can send these messages from one part of our brain to another. We can send messages between the brain and our chakras. We can send messages to any other person; at any distance. We can also send messages to the metaphysical friends. There is no other messaging system in the world that can do that!!

Therefore, the Consciousness Communication System is the most effective method for communicating specific thoughts and messages, between any two beings; and within ourselves.

The basic process is to first select your receiver destination. Then you create a thought; this your message of information or instructions. Keep repeating this same message a few times. The message is sent.

The receiver will eventually receive the message. These thoughts are received; where the information is passed along to the final destination.

Also remember that these messages are sent as a series of code carriers; these are consciousness boats, with their knowledge cargo. The physical form of the message exists as a stream of these consciousness energies; or as the consciousness cloud. This is sent in the direction of the intended receiver.

Of course, we can always receive our thought messages, as well as send these messages. However, it is difficult to receive and send at the same time. Therefore, if you want to receive messages in this system, it is best to allow some of your consciousness to be available; without thought.

Let the sender…whomever it may be…send those messages to you; and allow your empty consciousness boats to absorb the knowledge cargo. This is how you receive messages most effectively.

Thinking of You: Sending Love Thoughts Across the Miles

We can also use this system for sending love messages across the miles. When the person you love is far away, you can send your love thoughts to them. Any two people who are truly in love, will be able to send their thoughts about the other person; across any distance.

This is done through the consciousness energies. When we are thinking about them, we emit our consciousness thoughts, in their direction. They will know we are thinking of them. This is a type of psychic connection, and can be done across any distance.

Also notice that we can send specific thought messages to our partner. We will tell them how we love them, and want to be with them. We tell them that we want to see them happy. The other person will receive the message, and their body will respond automatically.

Personal Examples of Long-Distance Consciousness

The following is a personal experience, of communication using the consciousness thought as messaging system. There was one time I was communicating with a woman via Skype, who lived on the other side of the world. She wanted us to just look at each other, in silence.

While doing this, I decided to send deliberate thoughts to her. I sent the "thoughts" that I loved her. I love her deeply. My love, for her…

Then…she started giggling! It was spontaneous. It was from deep within her soul. She just started…giggling…like a school girl. You would think she was 16 instead of 52. This came from her because my deliberate thoughts of my love for her…were sent and received. Her body felt it, and responded automatically. This is evidence that we can send our thoughts over long distances, and the soul of the other person will respond.

I never told this woman what I had been doing, as communication with thought; but I have experienced in other occasions.

Also, note that this will only work if you have a Powerful Mind, and are passionate with your intentions. The main concept is that your love can be carried as thoughts, when the souls are too far apart to touch.

Becoming the Advanced Being: Soul and Consciousness

The main purpose of our Eternal Existence, is the Eternal Quest to become an Advanced Being. We must seek the experiences, followed by proper self-reflection, to gain more wisdom.

It is this Eternal Quest to obtain Mastery over ourselves which is the true path to becoming Highly Advanced Beings. We do this through the evolution of our soul and our consciousness.

The Evolution of our Existence

Our souls exist forever; yet our souls will evolve. The development of our souls, and the development of our consciousness, is an on-going process. The wise man understands that he must seek the experiences, combined with personal expression and self reflection, which promotes the development of his Being.

The Wise Man understands, that we experience our eternal existence in many locations and in may forms. He knows that we must make the most of each opportunity, for a combination of pleasures, expression of the soul, and personal growth. It is through these processes that we develop the Ongoing Evolution of our Existence.

Using Your Mind to Change Your Body

The Consciousness Energies exist in the body, as well as the mind. We can use this to our advantage. We can communicate directly with specific regions of our body, which can produce practical results.

Of course it is true that the highest concentrations of consciousness energies exist in the mind, for any being. Yet there is consciousness energy throughout the body. These energies exist in many cells, muscles, and organs throughout the body. This is how you can make changes in your body, using your mind. This is why memories are stored in your body.

Regarding the memories, many of our memories are stored in the cells and muscles of our bodies. This is why we often have certain pains. It is also why getting those body parts massaged will release memories to the conscious mind. These memories are consciousness energies, stored in various parts of the body.

This is also how we can use our mind to change our bodies. The consciousness energies in our body are linked to the consciousness (and subconsciousness) in our mind.

Therefore, if we want to change a specific area of the body, we give instructions to that area of the body. Some people will actually have conversations with their specific body part. This is a real process.

When you talk to yourself, not just in your mind, but to that specific body part, you are indeed talking as one area of your consciousness energies to another area of consciousness energies.

This is the same concept as guiding another person with your thoughts. The only difference is you are guiding your own specific body parts. Doing this process, you can get the consciousness energies in each body part to make specific changes as desired.

Of course, we also have other mechanisms for communication and changes; including the blood flow and electrical impulses. We also develop subconscious directions, to move body parts without thinking too much. Yet in addition to these methods, we can use the direct talking of our mind to the body parts, using the connection of consciousness energies. This will create modifications in the biology as desired.

Main Interactions of Soul, Consciousness, and Body

Our Existence here on earth, is made of three main components. These are: the Soul, the Consciousness, and the Physical Body.

Each of these are independent components; yet each will interact with the others. We first understand these as intendent; because their basic structures and operations are independent. Yet all three components interact with the other components, in significant ways.

Therefore, we must be able to manage these components in terms of both the individual operations, and the interactive systems. We will spend our lives learning how to do this. Indeed, we will spend multiple lifetimes becoming more skilled at becoming Masters of our Existence.

However, we can learn from experience, and teach others. This book is one such guide for this process. Therefore, what you learn in this book will be able to guide you, in understanding and practical skills, for effectively operating the Components of your Existence.

Interactive Systems of Soul, Consciousness and Physical Body

With a complex topic, it is often helpful to provide some brief summaries. Therefore, we will here highlight some of the main ways in which the Soul, Consciousness, and Body are Interactive Systems.

1) The Soul exists without the body; it is eternal and forever. The body is simply the rented vehicle, for this earthly experience.

2) The Body is the temporary container for the Soul. The Soul sits inside the body, as the driver sits inside his vehicle.

3) The Soul is fluid; it is Soul Energies which can shift around, and morph into various shapes. This allows the Soul Energies to not only sit within the body, yet to also enter the cells of the body.

4) The Soul can expand far beyond the boundaries of the body. This allows the souls of two persons to feel each other, long before any physical contact. This is how we know each other first.

5) Consciousness Energies can exist anywhere in the body. This includes any physical body area, such as organs and bones. This also includes any layer of the body, from the bones to the skin. It is in this way, that our body has consciousness…. everywhere.

6) When consciousness energies are gathered together, into consciousness clusters, this is where we have true thinking entities. These are similar to computer programs. Then, with greater aggregation, these entities obtain a level of self-awareness. This means we can have these thinking and self-aware entities…anywhere in the physical body.

7) However, in practical reality, there are specific regions of the body which have the greatest amounts of conscious energies. The primary region is the entire brain, including the Subconscious, Deep Conscious, and the Thinking Mind. Other areas include the Chakra Glands.

8) The Consciousness Energies can exist without a Soul. They can also exist without the physical body. In this way, consciousness energies can serve as a messaging system. This messaging system can allow us to communicate with other people and animals; with the metaphysical world; and within ourselves. We can also use this to receive thoughts in the air.

9) Furthermore, we can perform consciousness thinking operations outside the body. We do this by gathering consciousness energies from around us, as well as our own minds, then perform the thinking operations a few inches beyond our heads. This can provide additional insights and solutions which are beyond the norm.

10) The Soul is our identity, it is how we are. Being able to express our souls is a primary reason for our Eternal Existence. As Free Souls in space, we express our soul identity through our Soul Energies, and through our Consciousness. When we have a physical body, we will also use our physical body as a form of self-expression. Thus, we use our body as a mechanism for the experiences and expression, of our souls.

11) The Body exists as a mechanical mechanism. The body can be operated by several different programs. These include: the biological programming; the subconscious; the deep conscious; the thinking mind; and the soul energies.
Any of these can operate…any of the body mechanisms…at any time. We must therefore learn to use each of these operational systems to our advantage.

12) The Body begins operating with the biological programs only. The body can indeed exist without a soul or conscious. This becomes essentially just a robot. It can walk and do basic functions, but not much else. Many of our basic functions are biological programs only.

13) However, when the Soul exists in the body, then there is real being who exists inside. He is able to do much more with this body, than just the biological programs alone. Notice that the Soul brings Conscious Energies, therefore the soul is able to direct the physical movements of the body, using those consciousness energies.

14) The Consciousness Energies, when in the Body, primarily exists in the Core Programs of the Subconscious. This is followed by the knowledge placed within the Deep Consciousness. These areas of the mind will now be the primary directors of the physical body.
This can be very good for expressing our True Selves; for creating some Great Art; and for Inspired Ideas. However, these impulses, when allowed at the wrong time, can lead to unforeseen consequences.

15) The final level of Management of our Physical Body, is the Thinking Mind. With our thinking mind, we can over-ride most of the instructions from the subconscious and deep consciousness. We can also provide new instructions for any area of our physical body, as needed.

16) Note also that we can teach the body new mechanical movements, using our thinking mind. We can then place those skills into our Deep Consciousness; after having learned and practiced. We can then access those skills easily, without thinking about it.

17) In summary: The Soul, Consciousness, and Body are three distinct entities of our existence; yet they exist together, and interact with each other, in many different ways. We must understand all the nuances of each component interacting with the others.
We must fully understand all the interactive systems, of the Soul, our Consciousness Energies, and the Physical Body…if we want to obtain the most benefits from our Existence on Earth.

The Evolution of Soul and Consciousness

The Wise Man understands that we should be on the path for developing our soul and consciousness. Our souls are eternal; yet we must develop our souls and consciousness to become ever greater.
Our life here on earth is one method for developing our existence. Indeed, that is why most of us choose to come here. We come for a variety of experiences. It is through these experiences that we develop our souls and consciousness. Indeed, some of these experiences are put into our path deliberately, to coerce us into our Personal Evolution.
As a more specific understanding, the evolution of the soul includes gathering more soul energies, and being able to flow the specific energies as desired. The evolution of the consciousness includes gathering more consciousness energies, and obtaining greater intelligence skills.
Finally, know that if we truly want to become an Advanced Being, then we seek an Existence based on Love and Wisdom. This is the level of Existence we desire; for ourselves and for our world.

Reincarnation
And The Practical Effects in this Lifetime

The process of Reincarnation is absolutely real. We exist as souls; and our souls are Eternal. Therefore, we can live in many different realms, and many different bodies. There are many possible reality experiences.

Note that there are many different realms, and we can live in any of these realms. Therefore, our souls may not be returning to earth, in a new body, for a long time. We choose to enjoy another realm for while.

Yet when we do choose to Reincarnate here on earth, we bring our Eternal Soul with us. Therefore, we bring our entire Soul Alchemy with us.

As we enter the new body, we bring our entire soul, with all of our many experiences. We bring the knowledge and memories of all of our lifetimes. We bring the skills of our many lifetimes.

We also bring some of memories of our many years, in the other realms. Included in this…is the strong desire to live the lifestyle and have the specific experiences that we came here for.

All of this is embedded into your soul, and in your total consciousness. We bring this into our new body. Therefore, if we want to make the most of our life here on earth, we need to understand how we are influenced by the many previous lifetimes on earth.

"Life is a Stage, and We are Merely Players"

Shakespeare famously said that "life is a stage". This is indeed a good comparison. The many realms of the multi-verse can be compared to different theaters, each with different stages.

The theaters are very different; and the stages are different. We choose which theaters and which stages to spend our time.

We can also choose to be the "characters" on the stage (as we do each time we incarnate on Earth); or we can choose to be in the audience, watching and making suggestions from the observation seats.

Life is indeed a stage; and we incarnate to be the characters on the stage. We then create our own plays, with the other characters; while many of our friends watch from the balconies. This is our reality.

All Knowledge of Lifetimes and Skills in Subconscious

All knowledge from previous experiences is embedded into the subconscious. This is where they are storied.

Originally, when a Free Soul in the upper realms, this knowledge is embedded in our soul, and in our total consciousness. Then, as we arrive to the new body on earth, all of this is placed into the subconscious. Over time, which really means many years, we access different parts of this subconscious, and begin to remember this knowledge.

When we begin to play a sport, or try an instrument, we may find that it comes very easy to us. This is because we enjoyed doing this activity (or something very similar) in previous lifetimes. Therefore, it is simply a matter of remembering those skills we already have; and developing new ones. Thus, we have many skills from previous lifetimes, which we can access, when the time is right.

Knowledge of Previous Lifetimes

All of our previous lifetimes are embedded into our soul. The total knowledge and memories are embedded into our subconscious. Therefore, somewhere…in the deep subconscious…we have all the memories of our previous lives.

The degree to which you remember these past lives will vary for each person. Some people will remember their past lives in great details. Some people will remember distinctly a few special past lives; while not recalling others until much later. Most people do not consider their past lives at all.

You can begin to know your past lives, when you are strongly attracted to a period in history, or to a specific person in history. This means you lived in that specific era, and likely worked closely with that person. You may have been that famous person.

You will also feel as if you "you could be" a certain type of person. This is because you were indeed such a person, in a previous life. You knew this, deep into your subconscious.

The advantage to knowing your previous lifetimes, is to better know yourself. You know all that you were; and therefore the actual skills that you can bring to this life experience.

You can also step into that role again, and BE that person…again…to manage specific experiences in this lifetime. Thus, knowing of your past lifetimes is valuable for knowing your true abilities.

Many Details of Past Lifetimes Deliberately Blocked

However, many details of your previous lifetimes have been deliberately blocked from your thinking mind. Being able to know of the details of these lifetimes is often kept boxed away.

The general purpose of this is to allow you to live THIS Life, a new experience. If you begin your life thinking this is the only life that you have had, then you may be more likely to embrace this life fully, and be as you want to be, without trying to relive your past lives in any way.

This is the general purpose of the memory block on past lives. However, personally, I think it is better to know everything about your past lives. We should know the existence of each past life. We should also be able to remember many details of each past life. I strongly believe that such knowledge, at an early period in life, would be much more efficient in knowing who you are, and of all your abilities.

Regarding the details of the past lives, it is often the case that we know that we were such a person in a previous life; yet the details are vague. We may know that we were a king or architect, yet many of the specific details are difficult to remember. There is strong block on knowing this

Of course many people do remember the specific details of their past lives; especially the most recent or most significant. Other times, we are reminded of our past lives directly, by those in the upper realms. This means that we can know of these details, if the circumstances are right.

Physical Effects of Multiple Lives Embedded in the Soul

There are also physical effects, for your body here on Earth, because of multiple lifetimes. This includes your physical appearance, your biological issues, and your personality.

Your multiple lifetimes are embedded into your soul; which is your very existence. Therefore, your physical appearance can be very much influenced by your previous lifetimes. You may notice a similar smile. The shape of your face. The way you move your body. These physical features are influenced very strongly by your Soul; which includes all of the previous lifetimes which have been embedded into your soul.

Many of your biological issues are also related to your previous lifetimes. This is because your conscious energy has this knowledge, and brings it forth again. Remember that we have consciousness energies throughout our bodies; and some of these have stored knowledge. This means that you could feel physical effects, such as sensitivities or chronic diseases, in certain areas…which you also had in the most recent lifetime.

Notice that these sets of biological similarities are a major alignment of evidence that you are the same as the person in a previous life.

Also note that regarding the health issues and sensitivities, you can only get rid of these by changing those stored conscious thoughts, in that area of the body.

A more profound effect is when your voice randomly changes, and becomes that of the previous lifetime. it is also possible for a person looking at you…to suddenly see the image of your previous lifetime. In that moment, you actually appear as that other person.

All of these realities can exist, because of our multiple lifetimes, as embedded into our soul and consciousness.

Recognizing Others Today, as from Previous Lifetimes Together

There are many times when we can recognize a fellow soul from a previous lifetime. We can just look at a person, and feel is if we know them. Sometimes, this knowledge is so strong, just looking at the picture is enough to activate the soul within. You just know…that you know them.

This experience is a type of instant knowing. For example, looking through a magazine, I saw a picture of a female leader in another nation. My soul instantly knew…that I had known her soul from before.

There are other examples as well. Two women specifically, who I feel a connection with, and my metaphysical guides have confirmed this is real. We will have pleasurable relationships together, when the time is right, because of our soul alignments.

Metaphysical Friends Knowing You

A similar effect is for the metaphysical friends to know you, though you don't remember them. Personally, I have been visited by many beings from the metaphysical realms; some of whom know me from previously.

For example, in one experience they took me to a room for some fun. The woman there said "I remember you", as we walked up the stairs.

In another example, one woman visited and looked at me for a long time…then said "You don't remember me, do you?" It was as if we were very close friends, and should know her, and yet did not. I asked who she was, but she was moved aside by other visitors.

These are just a few examples. Each of us have many previous lifetimes here on earth. We also enjoy many years in the upper realms. Therefore, there are many metaphysical friends, who are still in their Free Soul form, who very much know who you are, and your relationships together…even if some of those details are blocked from your memory.

Reincarnation for Personal Pleasures and Desires

One of the main reasons we return to earth, is to enjoy our personal pleasures and desires. This earthly experience is something of an amusement park. We return again, to have new pleasure experiences.

Therefore, one of the most important reasons for us to exist in this lifetime, is to pursue our desires. We must pursue our pleasures. This is why we are here. This earthly world is a vast place, of many possible pleasures and experiences. We must choose our desires, choose our experiences…then go for them…and live them.

Also remember that your personal desires are not the same as the desires of others. The activities which make your soul happy, are not necessarily the activities which make other souls happy. This is why each person, must follow the desires and pleasures of his own soul.

We must allow every person to do as he or she wishes, without any form of judgment or interference. All desires are good. All pleasures are good. It does not matter if you do not understand, or enjoy. All beings have the Divine Right of Freedom…to live out their desires fully.

Reincarnation and Soul Evolution

The other purpose of returning to earth is for the Evolution of the Soul. Indeed, one of the main purposes of Existence…as a Soul…is to seek experiences, and grow from these experiences.

This is the process of Existential Transformation. We seek our pleasures, our new experiences, and some wisdom. From these events and experiences, our soul is transformed. We become wiser, stronger, and more capable in numerous ways. This is also why we are here.

Reincarnation for Guiding Humanity

The final reason why some Souls choose to Reincarnate on earth, is to guide humanity. When a soul is highly advanced…very…highly advanced, then he has already become the Master of many areas of Existence.

He is then given an assignment, a mission, to guide humanity forward. The man accepts this mission, prior to incarnating on earth. When he arrives, his advanced soul is clearly recognized early in life; and he develops himself to become a Great Master in his topic area.

This type of Advanced Soul, this Guide for Humanity, he usually knows his Mission early in life…at least the basics. There is something strong in his soul, to pursue a type of education and lifestyle. This powerful passion exists, because it has been implanted as his Mission for Humanity.

Later, sometime as an adult, the metaphysical beings come to him, and talk to him directly. They tell the person directly, of who they are, and of their Mission while on this earth. This is the absolute confirmation, and clear instructions, for the Guide to be devoted to his Sacred Mission.

There are many famous men who had this powerful instinct for a life mission; combined with the direct messages from the metaphysical beings. Some of these men include: Nikola Tesla; Michael Jackson; Martin Luther King Jr.; Werner Von Braun; and Moses.

These are just a few. Each of these men told of their soul mission, and metaphysical visits, to their closest friends. Some were very public about their metaphysical communications and experiences.

Therefore, some of the Advanced Souls return to earth, as Master Guides, for the evolution of humanity. For those who have already learned most of the important lessons, they reincarnate to be guides to others.

Activating the Inner Light and Hidden Wisdom

We must also understand the Activation of the Inner Light. This includes: Accessing the Deep Subconscious; Activating our DNA; and Igniting the Primary Light of the Soul.

The basic theme is that we have many areas of wisdom, energy, and communications; which we must locate within; and activate fully.

You can think of these as hidden controls in a car. First you must locate these, then you must activate these controls, in the right way, to create something very powerful and magical.

We will discuss some of these areas of wisdom and light, and how we can access them. We will bring them forth, and turn them on. This will lead to great powers, including special talents and spiritual abilities.

Note also that we will discuss the related concepts of Freedom and Play. It is only through Freedom and Play that we can truly access these areas within, and keep them fully powered, throughout our Existence.

Activating the Inner Light

The most important area to activate, is the Inner Light. This is also known as the Core Light, or the Pilot Light. It is the Light of the Soul, that feeling of pure joy. This is the most important aspect of yourself to fully activate and maintain. Without it, your existence has no color.

This begins with your Soul Alchemy. Remember that your soul exists as a Soul Alchemy, which is a mixture of desires and traits. Therefore, your Inner Light is actually your True Soul Alchemy, let out to Play.

Let us say this again: Your Personal Inner Light, is your True Soul Alchemy, when let out to Play. You must be able to fully express each of your desires, with complete freedom. You must be yourself, in all aspects and at all times. This is how the Inner Light comes forth.

Inner Light as Soul Energies

In a physical sense, the Inner Light is the flowing of your Soul Energies; especially the Soul Energies related to joy. Therefore, whenever we can fully expand our soul energies, especially joy and love, this is the physical presence of the Inner Light.

Remember that our Soul Alchemy is primarily stable, yet can be adjusted based on various factors. These adjustments can come from within our consciousness, and from external energies. Therefore, when we maximize our Love and Joy Energies…this becomes the Inner Light.

This Inner Light…these Love Energies and Joy Energies…will then become our internal power. These energies will also extend through every region of our physical body. This effect of Being the Inner Light, of always Being the Joy and Love…is what shines out to the world.

Free Expression of True Soul will Bring Joy Energies

The best method for bringing forth the Joy Energies, is to enjoy the Free Expression of your True Soul. It is when you can fully be as you are, in all ways, at all times, that you will experience True Joy.

This is a very important concept, and must be emphasized. Your true joy will only come when you are doing activities you enjoy; and behaving in ways which are natural to you. It is free expression, of all aspects of your soul, which invites the greatest joy and Inner Light.

Always remember that your Soul Alchemy is who you are. These are the traits and desires that are deep within. These traits and desires will exist regardless of any external situation or experience. They are you, and as such…they must be expressed and lived.

This is your Divine Right. You are allowed to be as you are, live as you desire, and enjoy anything in life that you want. This is your Divine Right. It is your Right, simply because you Exist!!

Therefore, all of us have the right to enjoy our personal desires, and behave in the ways which come natural to us. It is this Free Expression, of our natural desires and traits, which will then bring forth the Light within.

Importance of Play and the Inner Light

This brings us to the importance of Play. When we are allowed to play, this is when our Inner Light is fully activated.

We should always do those activities that we enjoy the most. We should freely enjoy each of the pleasures which brings us the greatest joys. This is our Right, and how it should always be.

We were designed to be happy and joyful. Therefore, we must always enjoy the activities which brings us the most pleasure. We will freely enjoy these fun activities, with other beings who enjoy these same activities.

It is through this fun play…free play…for what we enjoy…that allows us to express our natural selves. This free play allows us to enjoy being who we are, and doing what we enjoy. Thus, engaging in the specific types of play that you enjoy…will bring you the greatest happiness.

This life of Play…in the ways that You like to Play…is how you bring out your Inner Light. When you play as you desire, you give yourself life.

Freedom of the Soul is Essential for the Joyful Life

Notice that we must allow our Soul Energies to flourish, as the method for experiencing a joyful life. It is only when our souls and thoughts are fully expressed, naturally and without restrictions, that we are truly alive.

We must also realize the harm to self that can arise, when we deny our soul energies. If we deny our natural desires and thoughts, then we are inviting confusion and darkness.

Be aware of this path; it will be your destruction. You will have nowhere to go, because you cannot run away from yourself. The only option, in this confused mind, is to seek self-harm and forms of numbing the mind.

Whenever we are forced to repress our natural selves, we become confused about our existence. If we are told that our natural soul is abhorrent in some way, then we come to believe that we are a mistake. This confusion will lead the person down the path of darkness.

This is why we must allow freedom for all people, in all ways, to be as their True Soul desires. When each person is allowed to live his existence in this way, it is then he will have true joy. The Inner Light is maintained.

Embrace Your True Soul: Live Fully and Freely

The main type of Activation that we seek, is to activate the Inner Light. This means discovering who you are, in your natural soul; and then living our true soul, in all ways, with flourish and freedom.

This is the most important form of Activation in our life. We must know our True Soul, then express this True Soul. Embrace all that we are. Love all aspects of ourselves, embrace all of our quirks and traits. Live your life with absolute freedom and flourish.

Whatever you are in your natural soul…whatever gives you the greatest pleasures…embrace it. Live it. Be it. Be bold.

Be confident in all that you are. Find your communities and your lifestyle. Live freely and confidently. There is only one of you in the entire universe. Be sure to make the most of it.

The Other Activation Areas: Subconscious and DNA

There are two other main areas of Activation, beyond finding and living your Inner Light. These two areas are Expanding your Subconscious; and Activating your DNA.

The Subconscious is where your ancient wisdom is contained. All of your past life knowledge; everything you know about the metaphysical; and other great wisdom….is all packed into the Subconscious. We will therefore learn to open the subconscious, and access the wisdom contained within. This is an on-going process, and a journey.

The DNA can also be Activated. There are many DNA strands which exist for advanced spiritual abilities. These DNA strands are not related to biological functions; and therefore seem dormant. However, using the proper external stimuli, these DNA strands can be activated This will create advanced spiritual abilities in the person.

We will explore both of these topics in the sections below.

Activating your Subconscious: Overview

The Subconscious is packed with an immense amount of knowledge. It is amazing how much is truly packed into that small area. It is similar to a very large library. Therefore, we can access this library, and obtain wisdom. We will be able discover this lost knowledge, and bring it to our active thinking areas.

There are two main methods for accessing this hidden knowledge. The first is to move our self-aware mind into the subconscious. There we will search for the knowledge, and bring it back to the thinking mind.

The second method is the use of a "memory code". In this method, we are enjoying an experience, or reading something in a book, which is similar to a memory from a previous lifetime. This will activate the memory code (which was put into place prior to incarnation here), and that portion of the subconscious library is automatically opened.

We will discuss the most common methods, and best practices, for accessing the hidden knowledge of the subconscious mind.

Entering the Library Labyrinth

The knowledge in the subconscious is vast. It is also buried deep. We can visualize this scene as a very large labyrinth…with ancient texts along the walls. It is a vast library, with many corridors. It is a very large, and complex, library system. If you enter, you may find almost anything.

Yet this library labyrinth is also buried deep. It is very deep. This is to prevent the cluttering of the active mind. Remember that this library is vast, and there is much knowledge. If we let all of it out, at the same time, the mind would be overwhelmed. This could easily interfere with the daily life, the experiences of the moment, that make Existence truly Living.

Therefore, this vast library is kept very deep. We can only access it through special processes. The most common method is to actually go down the stairs, and into the subconscious.

Self-Aware Consciousness is Moving into the Subconscious

This is indeed a real process, as our self-aware consciousness…is migrating…from the front mind, through the Deep Consciousness…and into the Subconscious. We are actually moving our self-aware mind into a new location of the brain. We then open the doors to the library, and enter into the labyrinth. We can then find the knowledge, skills, and wisdom; on any topic; which we will bring forth into the working mind.

We will also access only the information we need. Essentially, we are selecting the books we need, regarding a particular topic, and bringing them back up the stairs, to our thinking mind.

Meanwhile, we let one of the other self-aware entities be in control of the body, while we are away. In many cases, we access through hypnosis, where we can put the main body to sleep. This hypnosis will allow us to shut down most of the other mental and physical operations. This gives us the internal freedom to fully leave our thinking mind management area, and spend as much time as we desire in the subconscious library.

Guided Hypnosis to Access Your Subconscious

We can use Guided Hypnosis to reach the areas of the subconscious library. The best guides will lead you to the area, yet not tell you what is there. They will help you move your self-aware mind to the library, then let you discover the treasures within.

The proficient Hypnosis Guide will understand that you are physically walking through your mind. She knows that your Self-Awareness is a cluster of energies, which can physically migrate through the mind. Thus, she will guide your Self-Awareness, from the Thinking Mind area, through the Deep Consciousness, and then into the Subconscious.

She will then guide you down the stairs of the subconscious; for there are many levels. At the bottom level, she will have you remove the key from the wall…and open the door. You step inside…and see the vast labyrinth of books along the walls. You are now inside the vast library of your subconscious. Anything is there, for you to discover.

Guided Hypnosis During the Library Experience

The best hypnosis guides, regarding accessing your subconscious, will guide you to the library; yet not tell you what is there. This is not the time for planting new thoughts. This is the time for accessing your own wisdom.

At this point, she lets you wander. She lets you choose the books. She will sit back and listen, recording anything you say aloud while there. She may also ask you curious questions, for you to access more information.

When you are ready to return, you will wander back, using the same path. This can often be assisted by the hypnosis guide. Eventually you will return to the front mind, where you normally have your Thinking Mind.

Your Self-Awareness is now firmly in place, where it normally resides. Yet you have the additional knowledge from the subconscious library that you brought with you. This is now your knowledge to use, as you desire.

Short-Cuts to the Topic Areas of Subconscious

Note that we can also create short-cuts to certain areas of the subconscious. We will create our own codes, which will access specific topic areas of the subconscious. This means that with a few small thought commands, all of the information in the subconscious, on that topic, is now open and available for our thinking mind.

We can also create code systems for activating specific programs in the subconscious. For example, when you say a phrase or hear a sound, this will immediately activate that area of the subconscious; and the specific program will begin operation.

These are very useful short-cuts that we can use, for a variety of purposes. Note that the specific codes are unique to the individual. You will create these codes for yourself; or suggested by the hypnotist. These codes are also created while you are in the deep subconscious library; and while being involved with a specific topic area within the subconscious.

These are effective methods for accessing knowledge and programs, that are kept deep within the subconscious. Rather than taking the long journey each time, you create the short-cut goes while there. Then we can be in our Thinking Mind, say a few phrases, and the knowledge is ready.

Discovering your Hidden Talents through Play

The second method for accessing the Subconscious knowledge, is through Memory Codes; which are activated during play. In this process, you will enjoy an experience, and the doors of memories open wide.

In that moment, you realize your strong passion for the activity. You suddenly realize your natural talents. You feel like you have skills, and knowledge, in this area. Yet you are new to this activity…or are you?!

When our souls arrive in the body, we have certain Memory Codes which are associated with our primary talents and desires. These have already been programmed into the system. Thus, when we read about the topic or watch it on tv, we are immediately intrigued. We must do it!!

This is because the Memory Code has opened that area of your subconscious. Your hidden memories have been activated. Your desires, already existing in your deep subconscious, have been opened.

Then, as you begin to enjoy this activity, it seems you have a natural talent. You may not be an expert yet, but you do seem to have certain instincts. All of these "instincts" and "natural talents" have actually come from previous lifetimes. Those skills and experiences are embedded into the deep subconscious. Yet after you have opened the door to that topic area, all the skills and talents of that topic are now available.

Thus, it is simply from doing an activity, or reading about an activity, which activates the Memory Code for that topic. All knowledge and all skills related to that topic are now available. The doors are open.

Play is Essential for Hidden Talents and for Inner Light

This brings us again to the importance of Play. We are meant to play. It is through play that we find our Joy. It is through play that we find and maintain our Inner Light. It is also through play that we discover our true passions, and our special talents.

Therefore, play is essential for all things. Play allows us to find our purpose, discover our powers, and shine our light. Play brings the similar souls together. Play is an essential ingredient of life.

Play is Life…Life is Play.

Rediscovering Your Knowledge and Skills

After you have discovered your Passions and Talents, through Play, then it is simply a process of "relearning" what you already knew.

You will enjoy doing the activity, because it brings you joy. Yet at this same time, your previous knowledge will be flowing to you.

Thus, you play and enjoy; you learn new skills as you play in this activity. Yet you are also remembering the knowledge and skills from long ago. As the doors are now open to that area of your subconscious, everything will come back to you.

This is how most people access their hidden talents. It is through play and self-discovery, that they find their passions and talents.

This knowledge was were already existing in the subconscious; it was then the act of play which opened the doors, using the pre-established Memory Code. The rest of the process is simply enjoying the play, while remembering all that you once knew.

DNA Activation for Advanced Spiritual Abilities

The next type of Activation we desire, is to Activate the Spiritual DNA. There are many DNA strands which exist specifically to develop spiritual powers. However, these DNA can only be activated by a Spiritual Being.

Many scientists are well aware of the many DNA which exist in our body, which do not seem to have any role in our biology. Yet they do not know the true purpose of this DNA. Indeed, it is often referred to as junk DNA. Yet it is quite the opposite. This DNA, when activated, will create the most powerful spiritual abilities. You will become a Super Human.

When fully Activated, these Spiritual DNA will enhance your biological systems. You will be able to use your physical body in very special ways. You will become something of an advanced biological being.

There are also several of these Spiritual DNA strands, each of which will be able to enhance your body in different ways. Therefore, we will activate each one, to develop each of those special abilities. Note also that these DNA strands are activated individually. Rarely will more than one of these DNA strands be activated at the same time.

Activating the DNA: The Process

However, there is only one way to Activate these Spiritual DNA. This DNA can only be activated by a Spiritual Being, such as an Angel. It is only a messenger from the Divine who can activate these DNA for you.

The specific process of DNA Activation requires a form of external energy. This specific energy is targeted at the specific DNA, which then activates the DNA. This DNA then become active, instead of dormant.

This begins the process of a new Spiritual-Biological Enhancement. Over the next few months, the DNA will perform its replication and growth process, and create the new abilities in your biological system. We sometimes refer to this as a Spiritual Puberty, where you will gradually become a Spiritual-Biological Being, on a completely new level.

Personal DNA Activation Experiences

The DNA Activation is a process which I can discuss from a very personal experience. For my experience, it was an Angel who came to me, and Activated my DNA.

This Angel appeared above my head. Her spiritual wings undulating, in a slow and relaxed way. They were translucent, with hues of sliver and purple. She was a real Angel, and there to Activate my DNA.

She flew inside my body, and once inside, began her work. I felt her energies, as she made adjustments in my body. The experience, as I felt it at the time, was someone tinkering with an engine. My image was of someone tinkering with a Toyota engine, to make it go much faster.

This was her process, of Activating my DNA. I knew at the time she was making adjustments, making improvements. Yet only later did I understand that she was Activating my DNA.

I must also tell of the glorious feeling when she was inside my body. This Angel, the sensations, from inside my body…were like nothing I had ever experienced before. There was a depth of love that is beyond words.

The only way that I have ever been able to describe it…is the feeling of freshly baked bread. As if walking past a bakery, with the bread just coming out of the oven. That is the only description of the feeling that I could ever compare it to. This the true Touch of an Angel.

Regarding the specific enhancements, it is difficult to be certain. Yet from that moment, I have been visited by more beings from the upper realms; seeing and hearing them. I have always had a certain level of spiritual intuition, yet I have become one of the humans who is most connected…to all aspects of the universe.

Certainly some of this was with me prior to incarnation; because of my advanced soul. Yet some of this has also developed from the Activated DNA. I can only imagine…that if all of my Spiritual DNA were fully activated…what my body might be able to do.

Connecting with the Divine Light of Power and Love

We will finish this discussion, with the reminder to seek the Power of the Divine Love. There is indeed a Divine Love. There is a Light, that is so powerful that it ignites the soul, brings great joy, and is love beyond anything possible on this earth. This is the Divine Love.

Some of us can tell you, from personal experiences, that this Divine Love is real. It exists. Yet it cannot be created within, or from the world. There is only One Source. This Source is the Divine.

There are many different methods to find this Divine Love. This is one of the most important methods of a Spiritual Path. The method you choose does not matter. What is important…is that you discover this Divine Love.

You must know the reality of this Divine Love. It is then that you will want to be in this place of Divine Love, and not among the trivialities (or darkness) of the earthly world. You can enjoy this world, yet also you must maintain a connection with the Divine Energies.

We can compare this to a Prius. The Prius is an electric car, which needs charging every day. In the same way, our souls must be recharged with the Spiritual Energies. We must refuel with the Divine Light and the Divine Love; for us to walk through this bizarre world again.

Live in that place of Divine Love and Inner Light. Be resilient to the distractions. Know what is real, and live this reality every day. Have the strength and courage, which comes from knowing your true connection to the greater universe. This is the way of having your Divine Within.

Spiritual Paths to Connect with the Divine Love

Remember that the ideal for any Being…is to live in the place of Divine Love. It is to be living with that Inner Light, inner peace, while enjoying each experience of the moment. This is the ideal.

Of course, this ideal is difficult to reach. Yet we must seek this path. This is where the Spiritual Paths are important. Each of us requires a spiritual path, of some type, to keep us focused on the Inner Light and Divine Love. The specific practices are not important; yet it is essential that we exist in that ideal state of being, as much as we can.

Reviewing the Components of What You Are

We are now ready to review all the components of your Existence here on earth. We can understand the details of the Mind, Soul, and Body; as well as how each of these components interact. When we understand these details, and how they interact, we will then truly understand who and what we are. We can then become Greater Masters of our Existence.

The Primary Components

We exist as three main components. These are the Soul, Mind, and Body. The Soul is who you are; the Mind is how you Navigate your existence; and the Body is the rented vehicle for earthly experiences.

The three components are inherently independent, as they exist and operate on their own mechanisms. However, all three components will interact with each other in a variety of ways.

The Soul Alchemy

The Soul is who you are. Your existence is your soul. As a physical entity, the soul is a Soul Alchemy, which is a mixture of Soul Energies. The specific mixture of Soul Energies is what makes you unique.

The Soul Identity Energy

The Soul begins with an Identity Energy. This is the specific soul energy which exists only for each soul. It is something like a fingerprint or serial number. There is only one such person with this Identity Energy.

However, souls who are created in a similar location in the universe, will often have Identity Energies which are very similar. Many of the alchemy mixtures are also similar. This becomes our Soul Tribe.

Note also that this unique Identity Energy becomes similar to a phone number, when we want to contact each other telepathically.

Soul Alchemy: Core Mixture and Existential Transformation

The Soul Alchemy is a mixture of Soul Energies. These are traits and desires, which make the existence of your soul.

This is the fundamental reality of who you are. These traits and desires are embedded into your soul, as this mixture of soul energies. Notice that this is the soul we access for bringing out the Inner Light. These are the traits and desires we let free, as we enjoy our life and play with the world.

The main mixture of the Soul Alchemy is constant. This means your intrinsic personality exists, as the Core Soul Alchemy. This core tends to exist throughout a lifetime, and often across several lifetimes.

However, we can create changes in our soul alchemy, using the Existential Transformation. This is a process where we will transform the soul alchemy, as well as the size of the soul itself, through our most significant experiences.

Notice also that we are always seeking to transform our souls, to become more Advanced. This is what we do, as part of our Eternal Existence.

Souls Are Eternal, they Just Change Form

The Soul is Eternal. The Soul, when created, exists forever. The soul cannot be destroyed. This means that you will exist, for all eternity.

However, the soul can change form. The soul can also develop and change. The soul can inhabit different physical containers. These are the differences of your soul's existence. Yet the soul itself, once created, will exist for all eternity.

The soul exists without the body; and it exists prior to the body. The body is just a temporary vehicle for earthly experiences. When removed from the body, the soul can change form and shape. Yet also within the body, the soul also has abilities to change form within.

The Mind and Consciousness

The Mind is more accurately described as your Consciousness. The reality of Consciousness is of Consciousness Energies. These are small energies which are code carries of information. As such, these energies can flow like streams, and aggregate like clouds.

When the Consciousness Energies are aggregated into significant amounts, this becomes a Self-Aware Entity. Thus, the Soul will "know" that it exists, when enough Consciousness Energies have aggregated.

Furthermore, the larger aggregation of Consciousness Energies will create a more powerful thought machine. This is what we commonly refer to as the "Mind". Yet, these thought machines can (and do) exist in many areas of the body, including the Chakras. In addition, many of the advanced souls will also have multiple self-aware entities within the mind.

Therefore, the Mind is not just one entity; it is a set of several thought machines, many of which are self-aware. These can be managed by the Primary Entity. That is, your strongest of self-aware consciousness entities will manage the entire set of Consciousness Energies in your body.

The Consciousness Energies

The Consciousness Energies are the physical structures of all consciousness. These exist as small drops, similar to water. They are code carriers, which transfer the thought codes to various locations.

There are two types of Consciousness Energies: Potential and Encoded. The Potential Consciousness Energies are the empty carriers, available to receive codes. The Encoded Consciousness Energies have the thought codes placed into the carriers.

The Encoded Thought Carriers will then transmit this information, similar to boats with cargo, to various destinations. This can be to anywhere in the mind; anywhere in the body; to any other person; and to any other being in the universe.

Aggregated Consciousness Energies

When the Consciousness Energies are aggregated, this becomes a thought cloud; thought machine; or self-aware entity. You will notice that there is some over-lap in these structures, depending mostly on the amount of Encoded Energies which have been aggregated.

Thus, when we aggregate a significant amount of Encoded Energies of Consciousness, this will produce the Thought Machine (which is a type of computer program in the mind); or become a Self-Aware Entity. And when the Self-Aware produces a complex thought, this will often be emitted as a Thought Cloud. All of these are aggregations of Encoded Energies.

Communication Using the Consciousness Energies

Any Powerful Mind will emit thoughts as either a stream of consciousness energies, or as a thought cloud. These are Encoded Energies of Consciousness, which are sent as a series of thought codes.

These can be compared to cargo boats. We will therefore load the thought codes, as cargo, to each of the Code Carrier Energies. These are sent out, as line of cargo boats; which becomes a physical stream of consciousness. This can also be sent as an entire fleet of cargo boats, which is then our Thought Cloud.

Most of these communications of Encoded Consciousness Energies are within the mind, and within the body. This is how our minds are able to produce the complex thoughts, analysis, and creativity.

In addition, we can also use this same system to communicate with others. We can use this system of encoded conscious energies, to send our thoughts telepathically, to any other being in the universe.

Aggregated Encoded Consciousness: In Heaven vs Body

When the soul exists outside the body, there is only "one" area of consciousness. The consciousness is concentrated in one area, and yet will be fluid throughout the being of the Soul. Thus, the soul energies and the consciousness energies are both fluid, and they both overlap.

However, in the earthly body, the situation is different. The entire consciousness is first packed tightly together, then placed into the subconscious. At this point, the consciousness energies are unpacked, and placed into the proper locations.

This process is very similar to moving from one home to another. When moving to a new home, we pack our items, then put on the truck. We then travel to the new home, and gradually begin to unpack.

This is similar for the Consciousness. Before the journey from the upper realms to our new body on earth, we tightly pack all of our knowledge into a small container. We then transfer this, along with our soul, to the new body. The entirety of the Encoded Consciousness, with the knowledge and skills from centuries of existence, is now placed within the subconscious. There the entire knowledge will remain.

We then gradually unpack the knowledge, and place into the new locations. This is a long-term process; and much of the knowledge is never unpacked. It remains in those boxes, or as a library, for us to discover as needed.

Subconscious, Deep Conscious, Chakras, and Thinking Mind

When the pre-existing knowledge and skills are unpacked, this will be placed in four primary locations. These are: Subconscious; Deep Conscious; Chakras; and the Thinking Mind. This is how your energies of consciousness will interact with your body, and your environment.

The Subconscious

All pre-existing knowledge and skills will begin in the Subconscious. This is where everything is stored; until placed elsewhere.

Note that we can always locate hidden information in the subconscious as needed. This is similar to going to a vast library. However, some libraries are better organized than others. Therefore, it may be easier for some people to access their subconscious information than others.

Furthermore, notice that the more Advanced Souls will unpack their subconscious more easily. They have done this many times before, and therefore becomes automatic. This is one reason why the Advanced Souls are able to think in more advanced ways at an earlier age. Their skills and knowledge are already being unpacked; placed into locations; and well organized. By the time the Advanced Soul is 7-10 years old, most of his previous knowledge and skills will already be unpacked and ready to use.

The Deep Consciousness

As the knowledge and skills are unpacked, many of these encoded energies will be placed in the Deep Consciousness. This becomes the basic operating programs, for many thinking operations. Examples include language, mathematics, and music. Thus, there are aggregated energies as Thought Machines, or as computer programs. These are brought from the subconscious, and placed into the proper regions of the mind.

Note also that accessing these programs is often realized by doing the activity. For example, learning a language will bring the access to the programs on language, and bring those into the Deep Conscious. We are then just re-learning or re-discovering what we knew from long ago.

The Chakras

Many of the programs are also placed into the Chakras. The Chakras are the Glands and specific Organs of the body. Therefore, each of these physical body regions will have its own type of Thought Machine.

These are specific aggregations of consciousness energies, which have existed prior to the incarnation on earth. These aggregations are sent to the specific body regions, including those known as Chakras.

In the Chakra body regions, these aggregated consciousness energies are essentially computer programs, which process messaging systems in those regions of the body. This is why the messages sent and received from those Chakras, is a very real system.

Furthermore, for the more Advanced Souls, these aggregated energies are more than operating programs; they become self-aware entities. As such, they become regional directors of the messaging systems throughout the body. They will operate on their own, without your thinking mind needing to be involved.

The Thinking Mind

This brings us to the Thinking Mind. We also refer to this as the Primary Identity; or the Main Self-Aware Entity.

This is your active thinking area of the mind. Thus, whenever you are having known thoughts, from your own active, self-directed mind, this is from your Thinking Mind. This is, of course, the largest aggregation of Encoded Consciousness Energies in your physical body.

We also see this as your self-awareness. It is how you understand yourself, and how you see the world. This is also the CEO of your entire consciousness operations, throughout your mind and body.

Thinking Mind is Often Not Used Effectively

Note that the Thinking Mind is not used effectively as it should. The majority of people on earth do not use their Thinking Mind at all.

Remember that the consciousness operations required for basic body functions is *not* the Thinking Mind. These consciousness programs are embedded into the Deep Consciousness; as well as many areas of the body itself. Thus, the body can function without the Thinking Mind.

Therefore, it is quite possible for many humans to operate their bodies, without ever using their thinking mind. Indeed this is what they do.

Therefore, we must understand that the ability to Actively Think is rare in the human world. We must also realize, that many people are not able to use their Thinking Mind…because…they physically do not have the ability. They are lacking the sufficient consciousness energies.

Specifically, they do not have amount of aggregated encoded energies of consciousness, to perform the complex thoughts. It is just not physically possible. The only way to improve this situation, is to physically add more of the encoded energies to their system. This is a process which we must learn how to do, if we want to create a better world.

Chakras as Higher Intelligence

The Chakras do indeed have a type of "intelligence". We have explained this as the aggregation of encoded consciousness energies. These aggregations become Thought Machines; and for the more Advanced Souls, these become Self-Aware Regional Directors.

Thus, it is true that the Chakras do indeed have a type of intelligence, especially for those who are Highly Advanced Souls.

However, that does not necessarily mean that your Chakras are "smarter" or "wiser" than your mind. These areas are simply other areas of aggregated consciousness.

We should not rely only on one Chakra over another; nor should we rely on the Chakras rather than the areas of the mind. Rather, we should include the intelligence of the Chakras, along with all other areas of our mind, to make the decisions for our life.

Stronger Areas of Consciousness in Different Regions

This brings us to the topic of comparing the sizes of aggregated consciousness energies. Where the aggregated consciousness is larger, this will have greater processing power; and often greater self-awareness.

We have seen this when comparing the various self-aware entities within the mind. Yet we can also see this when comparing the chakras. In each person, we will find that some of their Chakras are stronger than others. This is now easily understood. The stronger chakra regions are those regions with greater amount of aggregated consciousness.

Therefore, when any person has one or two chakra areas that are much stronger than other areas, this is because he has the greatest amount of consciousness energies in those regions.

This also means that we can shift the amount of consciousness energies from one chakra area to another, in order to boost the power of the messaging system in that area.

Physical Body: The Rented Vehicle

We are now ready to review the operations of the body, focusing specifically on the interactions of the soul and consciousness with the physical body. This is more than biology, it is the understanding of how to use the body, to fulfill all of our dreams and desires.

The physical body can be compared to a vehicle. It is simply a mechanical device, for the soul and consciousness to use on earth. Thus, the physical body is a rented vehicle. We use it for as long as we can; and when this vehicle can no longer be used...we will get another.

Always remember that the Soul is who we are; not the body. The soul is also Eternal; though the body has limited use. This means that we must always focus on the Soul, and our Consciousness, rather than the body.

Yet at the same time, we use our body to our advantage, as the rented vehicle, to enjoy all the adventures here on earth. Therefore we will enjoy the physical body, and take care of it, to maximize our experiences.

Physical Body is Independent Without the Soul

The physical body is similar to a car in many ways. This includes the reality that the physical body is essentially independent from the soul.

The body exists and operates based on the DNA instructions, and the complex system of chemical reactions. This entire system is a mechanical device. It is essentially a robot; though made from chemicals rather than from metal. Yet the body is self-sufficient on its own.

However, the movements of the body are limited without some type of instructions. We can indeed apply these instructions externally, for limited uses. Yet the body will move more fully and accurately when there is a conscious being who resides inside the body as vehicle.

Therefore, the soul with consciousness enters the body as vehicle; and resides within this body vehicle. The soul can then operate all the areas of the physical body, with full intention, as desired. The soul will also be able to take proper care of the body, through the deliberate actions of eating, exercise, and cleaning. This is the body as operated by the soul.

Soul Entering and Residing in the Physical Body

The soul enters the body in the process of traveling through the vortex, from the upper realms, to the subconscious area of the brain. The soul will then gradually fill the entire physical body.

As the soul expands into the body, the soul becomes physically hooked to the body in several locations. The primary locations are the Subconscious, and each of the Chakras. These physical hooks will ensure that the soul remains attached to the body, regardless of any event.

The Soul is general fluid, which allows the soul energies to flow to all regions of the body. Thus, the soul energies can exist and flow anywhere within the body as vehicle.

This includes the lips and fingers, which provide sensual interactions between two lovers. The soul energies through the fingers also allow us to play any instrument with pure soul energies. Thus, we can use our soul energies, through any physical area of the body, and to the external world...to create very powerful effects.

Therefore, the soul arrives in our body, and is fluid enough to flow into any area of the physical body. We can use this to our advantage, when we interact with the world…and other beings.

Size of the Soul and Morphing

Regarding the soul-body relationship, we must remember that the soul is always larger than the body. Most people keep their souls crumpled within their body; yet the true size, when fully expanded, is much larger.

The average size is approximately 3 feet in all directions. For the more advanced souls, the soul can fill an entire room; or an auditorium. This means we can feel each other's soul, at a greater distance than simply touching the physical bodies. We can use this to our advantage.

The soul can also morph in different ways, which allows us to move the soul energies to any region within the body. We can also expand and contract the soul to different sizes as desired. Thus, we understand that the body is a container, and yet the soul is larger than the container, and is also fluid within the container.

Consciousness Operations of the Physical Body

The Consciousness arrives into the subconscious, as a tightly packed storage of encoded consciousness energies. This is how the entire set of knowledge, skills, and programs; existing prior to this lifetime; are able to enter into the body. It is there, in the subconscious, that the packed encoded consciousness energies will remain, until needed.

Gradually these Consciousness Energies are unpacked, and put into their new locations. This is a gradual process; and generally is unpacked in a pre-determined sequence. This is also guided by the teachers and other environmental influences.

The physical body is then operated by several Consciousness Clusters. Each of these Consciousness Clusters are essentially computer programs or thought machines. The first clusters will operate the basic functions of the physical body. Additional programs are unpacked and further developed, for speaking, writing, and basic movements.

The Thinking Mind is the CEO of the entire system. This means that the Thinking Mind can send new instructions to any other Program. Many of the Programs are automatic, as the mechanics will perform without the thinking mind being involved. Yet the Thinking Mind can direct these automatic programs for specific purposes.

For example, there is a basic program for walking; yet the Thinking Mind will direct the program to walk in a specific direction and specific rate. As another example, there is a program for mechanics of speaking, with an extensive vocabulary. Yet it is the Thinking Mind which directs this program for the specific thoughts to say, and which words.

This is how the Thinking Mind as CEO can take active control over any of the programs, for specific applications and variations. Yet at the same time, the mechanics of the operations are automatic; as operated by the Consciousness Cluster Programs.

Thus, the physical body is operated by a variety of Consciousness Clusters. Some of these are mechanical operations; others are self-aware regional directors; and then we have One Main Thinking Mind…as CEO over all of them.

Soul vs Consciousness in the Physical Body

The body contains both the Soul and the Consciousness. The Soul is generally a single entity, though fluid, and fills the entire body. The Consciousness Energies exist in clusters, of various size, and can exist in various regions of the body. Thus, in any region of the physical body you will find both Soul Alchemy and Consciousness Energies.

Soul in the Physical Body

The Soul exists without the body; and will therefore remain with the body while there are permanent connections. The soul is physically connected to the body primarily through the Subconscious. It has additional connections in several other Chakra regions. The soul will remain attached to the body, even when performing astral travel, when these physical connections are in place.

The body then becomes a rented vehicle for the soul. The soul will generally fill the body, and extend beyond the body. The average soul extends 3 feet beyond the body; and is larger for more advanced souls.

Always remember that the Soul is our primary form of existence. We use the body as a vehicle and mechanism for self-expression. Yet the soul itself is our truest form of existence.

Consciousness in the Physical Body

The Consciousness Energies also exist within the body. All thoughts, memories, and skills exist as Encoded Consciousness Energies. These can exist anywhere in the body; including any of our muscles.

Thus, all of our muscles and organs will have Encoded Consciousness Energies. We can use this to our advantage; yet these can also cause harm. For our optimum health, we must regularly purge the unwanted memories from the physical body.

These Encoded Consciousness Energies will aggregate and develop into clusters. These clusters will become databases and processing programs. Notice again that these clusters of consciousness can exist in any region of the body; including muscles, glands, and other systems.

Consciousness of Brain and Body

The brain is of course the region with the largest total of consciousness energies; and is the region of our Thinking Mind. It is also the region of our main processing programs. Yet always remember that the Encoded Energies, and the Clusters of Consciousness, can exist anywhere. It is for this reason that our body has intelligence and memories.

We can use this reality to our advantage. The smaller consciousness clusters throughout the body can become regional staff, for the overall system of consciousness operations. These clusters can receive additional messages; and process information independently; before sending the results to the Thinking Mind.

We can also use this system to make adjustments in the physical body. With proper training, we learn to communicate with the local clusters of consciousness; and direct them to perform specific operations in the body. It is through this process, that we can gain full mastery over our biological functions. This includes ability to withstand harsh conditions, adjust the heart rate, and make other repairs.

*Of course we will also use traditional methods for mastering the body. Yet this consciousness system in the body is a realistic tool, which can be used to make powerful changes to our physical body from within.

Become the Master of All Components

If we want to make the most of our existence, then we must understand the components of our existence; The main components are the Soul, Consciousness, and Physical Body. We must know well the structures and operations of each component. We will become the masters of each component; and develop each to maximum abilities.

It is only through full understanding and mastery over our components, individually and their relationships, that we can arrive at our destiny of excellent existence. Learn to master your consciousness clusters; express your soul with absolute freedom; and work with others to reach the same. This is how we live our fullest existence; and experience the greatest joys.

Chapter 3:
Separating, Aggregating, and Alignment

Introduction

We can actually separate our soul energies, and our consciousness energies. We can do this on a temporary basis, for Advanced Level Processes. We can also choose to do some permanent dividing of our soul and consciousness, and have these in specific locations.

However, we must always be strong in managing the multiple separations. If we are not the strong managers of our own soul and consciousness…especially when divided…then each section can become a type of independent life of its own. These entities can become rogue systems within. This can cause unwanted chaos.

Furthermore, there are many times where the splitting of the soul and the consciousness has been created on its own. This usually arises from significant trauma, and the deep programming is doing this as protection.

Yet we return again to the original concept: that there are benefits to dividing the soul, and dividing the consciousness, to perform specific objectives. This should be done with intention, and always managed.

There is also another topic area of Separation. This is when we separate the soul from the body. We can do this temporarily, which is known as Astral Travel. We will discuss the differences between Astral Travel and permanent separation.

Thus, we can separate soul from body; and divide our consciousness in different regions of our body. We can do a variety of practical processes with these abilities. Yet we must always maintain full control, because there are significant dangers that may arise if not managed properly.

There are positive benefits; yet there can be significant dangers as well. We will discuss all of these concepts, in this chapter.

Dividing the Consciousness and Soul
For Practical Purposes

For the Advanced Soul, there are many ways in which we can divide the consciousness. We can also similarly divide our soul. Dividing the consciousness is the main process; yet we will sometimes insert some of our soul energies into the divided consciousness.

Dividing the Consciousness as Experience and Observer

The easiest form of dividing the consciousness is to divide your consciousness as Experiencer, and Observer. In this area, one part of you is experiencing the event, the other part of you is observing the event.

We often notice this when at a party, and part of us is doing the activities, while the other part is thinking on what we should say or do. We also experience this effect when love another person, yet part of us is analyzing the situation, while we are together.

Sometimes this effect comes as the random thought or emotions, with the observer. This is where the thought or emotion comes up, but we don't act on it; we simply observe it, wonder why it is there, then let it move on.

There are many such examples as these. In general, our conscious mind is able to both experience and observe at the same time. This is possible because our consciousness is a multitude of energy bits, which cluster together in various ways. Therefore, one consciousness cluster can be the one who experiences, while the other cluster is observing.

Dividing the Consciousness as Various Processing Skills

Another way to divide the consciousness, is to create the various processing skills. We create several consciousness clusters; each of which can be placed in different areas of our brain.

This means that we have separate consciousness clusters, to perform each of our complex thinking skills. These consciousness clusters then reside in those areas of the brain, for the duration of our lives.

This is how we have specific consciousness areas for language, mathematics, and more. Within these consciousness clusters, we store the knowledge of facts and experiences related to this topic. The operating programs are also located in each of these consciousness clusters.

It is in this way, that the we have divided our consciousness into these clusters, and placed them in specific regions. We do this for the practical purpose of maximum performance, for each the intelligence skills.

Remote Viewing

Remote Viewing is a type of method for dividing the consciousness. This is because you can be sitting in one location, while viewing another.

There are actually multiple methods for Remote Viewing. These include: Astral Travel; Split Soul (Partial Astral Travel); and Tuning In. Additional methods involve messaging systems, using our consciousness energies. We can also ask our Metaphysical Friends to Show it.

The most common method of Remote Viewing is a form of Astral Travel. In this method, you launch part of your soul, to the desired location. There, you can observe all the details, then come back to the body and report what you see.

Another common method is "tuning in" for the scene. This is using your mind as a television remote; you select the show, then you will watch. The scene is then shown as live viewing, in your mind.

We can also, of course, ask your Metaphysical Friends to show you the scene directly. They are able to watch anything easily, from their positions. Therefore, they may agree to show you what you need to see.

These are just the brief concepts for each Remote Viewing Method. We will discuss more details, in another chapter.

Splitting the Soul for Two Locations at Same Time

Related to the Remote Viewing is the ability to split the soul, to be in two locations at the same time. Personally, I have done this several times.

This process allows most of my soul to be somewhere in space, or in another dimension, while also able to type what I see on the computer.

For example, my soul can be in space, looking at a planet or nebula; as if floating just a short distance from it. I can see all the details. Yet while in space, I have my computer, and I am typing on this keyboard.

This process allows me to astral travel to the distant details, yet have enough awareness of my home world for typing the information. Usually the home world disappears from view, except for my computer; while most of my soul and consciousness are actually in a distant location.

Dividing the Consciousness and Soul
As Separate Characters Within

We can also Divide the Consciousness, and sometimes insert portions of our Soul Energies, for the purpose of Creating Characters in the Mind.

This is method often used by the most talented novelists and actors. They will create separate consciousness clusters, which becomes a type of self-aware entity. These become the separate characters. It is from these self-aware entities, within their own greater mind, that they can live out the characters for their audience.

This method can also be used for many of us, as we do our various roles in life. For example, sometimes we need to be the "Boss" in our work environment. Sometimes we need to be the "Artist". This is a method that many people do, to live as that character in their daily lives.

Also notice that those who can do this, are of the greatest minds. This is because they have large amounts of consciousness energies, which can be separated into these multiple consciousness clusters. Stated another way…those people with multiple voices or characters in their minds…are actually those with the most advanced mental abilities.

However, we must also discuss the potential hazards in this method. Sometimes, these separate characters go rogue on us. They begin to take more control of our actions than we want. There are also many people who create these characters from traumatic events; and it takes years of therapy to put the pieces back together. We will therefore address these realities as well. We must always manage the characters we create.

Self-Aware Consciousness Clusters

We have discussed how the consciousness energies can gather into clusters. These Consciousness Clusters are then able to work as one entity. This is where we can have operating programs, such as for languages and mathematics; as well as complex thoughts.

These Consciousness Clusters are also "self-aware" to a certain degree. This is because, the very nature of consciousness is thought codes and self-awareness. In small amounts, the consciousness energies are codes of information. Yet in larger gatherings, such as the Consciousness Clusters, there is enough consciousness energies, working together, to become "self-aware".

This is the reality of the Consciousness Clusters. These exist for the various language and mathematic programs, as discussed above. These are also the "directors" who manage the Chakras. They are the "staff" of the Deep Consciousness Operations; working on processes without your thinking mind being aware of it. These exist, throughout the body.

These Consciousness Clusters can be of many types. This includes the language programs, yet can also be separate characters, with their own personalities and voices. They are all subsets of us; it is not another soul; yet they can in many ways act independently.

Consciousness Clusters as Self-Aware Personalities

We have been talking about these Consciousness Clusters as simply directors and staff of operations, working for the Thinking Mind Boss. Yet there is type of Consciousness Cluster which has independent thoughts, and a distinct voice. This Consciousness Cluster exists independently of your Thinking Mind. This is why we often have these other voices in our heads. This is also why the characters in novels become so real.

Independent Entities: Able to Think on Their Own

It is important to understand that these Consciousness Clusters are independent entities. If we could separate these from your soul, they would indeed act as independent consciousness in space. This is, again, because the very existence of the Consciousness Clusters is also the creation of self-aware entities.

Therefore, each Consciousness Cluster within your mind, is an independent entity, with its own ability for independent thoughts. This is just the reality that we must accept.

This also means that the more advanced mind, will likely have more of these Consciousness Clusters within their own. These Consciousness Clusters will then assist in advanced mental processing skills. Many of these Consciousness Clusters are also self-aware entities; which creates the many "voices" and personalities, within the advanced mind.

This is indeed a physical reality, which we must accept. We can use this to our advantage. When we understand this reality, we can create the specific Self-Aware Consciousness Clusters, for our specific desires. We will then ensure Complete Mastery over all of them.

Inserting Portions of Your Soul into the Self-Aware Characters

We are also able to insert portions of our souls into the self-aware consciousness clusters. This includes inserting our soul energies into the characters, that now exist in your mind.

Note that this process always begins with the Consciousness Clusters. These Consciousness Clusters exist whether or not there are soul energies. Thus, each of the Consciousness Clusters can exist as its own self-aware entity, with complex thought process; and yet without a soul.

At this point, the soul can be inserted. Remember that the soul exists as Soul Energies, which are essentially fluid. These soul energies can be moved around into any part of the body, and the brain. Therefore, after any of the Consciousness Clusters have been created, we can insert some of our soul energies into these Clusters. These self-aware entities will then have their own consciousness, and soul.

Real Beings, Residing in Your Own Mind

This is the reason why many of these characters in your mind, do seem to be independent beings. This is because…some of these characters really are… independent beings.

You have given them consciousness. You have given them soul energies. Therefore, you have indeed created a type of "life" within your own Being. It is a complex relationship, and yet it is reality.

You are essentially the God of their Existence. It is from your own large amounts of Consciousness Energies, that you create the separate Clusters. These clusters are themselves large enough to have their own complex thoughts and self-awareness. It is then also you, as a type of God, that added some of your Soul Energies into these Clusters.

Therefore, you created life. You created an actual existence, of separate being, with self-awareness and soul energies. These entities in your mind seem to act as separate beings, because essentially…they are.

You are God of this Realm; They are Subsets of You

However, always know that YOU are the God of this realm. You are the one who created each entity. There is no outside source. All of the characters that exist in your mind, were create by you.

This also means that every character is a subset of you, in some way. You may have put some imagination into a character; yet those traits from your imagination…are from you!

On a more physical level, all of the consciousness energies, which makes up each Consciousness Cluster, has come from your total consciousness. This means that knowledge and perspectives of each character…can only come from your own total consciousness.

Similarly, any soul traits that your characters have, were given to these entities from your total soul energies. They can only be given the soul energies that come from yourself.

It is important to remember this concept. You are the God and Master of this Realm; where the "realm" is your total mind and soul. All characters and staff you create, are created from your own consciousness and soul.

They only exist because you want them to exist. They have only what you gave them. They must conform to your desires. If you want to change something about any of these characters in your mind; you can do it.

Novelists Creating the Characters: Yes they are "Real"

Whenever you talk to a skilled novelist, there are three things the will tell you. The first is that creating their characters feels much like playing God. The second is…that their characters are very real.

We now understand why this must be the case. The authors did indeed create their characters. It is from total conscious mind of the author, including the thinking mind and the imagination, that each character is created. This character than actually…exists…as a separate cluster of consciousness, within the author's mind.

Therefore, yes…the author did create the characters; and the characters are indeed very real to the author. They are real because these self-aware entities, with some of his soul energies inserted, are now residing within his complex mind. The characters are indeed real.

Characters Have a Life of Their Own

The third truth that most novelists will tell you, is that the characters often have a "life of their own". The characters often have distinct mannerisms, way of speaking, and other traits.

Sometimes it feels as if the author is simply watching the events, and recording the events, rather than creating them. There is often a separate reality that exists, and the author is watching the events happen.

Again, we now understand why this is true. Each of these characters is so fully developed, that they are a distinct entity. These characters have their own self-aware consciousness; based on your own consciousness, and the "thoughts" as traits from your imagination. This creates realistic characters, as self-aware entities.

We combine this with the soul energies that we add, when creating the characters, and we have independent life. Once these characters are created, they have a life of their own. They may remain inactive until called upon, yet once you open the door, and start them up…these characters will behave in their own ways.

Furthermore, when you have multiple characters within the same mind, these characters can interact. This is seen most easily with the characters in the same novel setting. Yet it can occur for characters beyond as well.

The Realm of the Novel, as a Consciousness Cluster

When writing a novel, you will create a separate realm, in your mind, where the novel is taking place. This Novel Realm is created as a separate Consciousness Cluster.

This Consciousness Cluster becomes the setting of the novel. All the details of the location, and the events, are stored in this region. This is also the place where we create each of the characters.

Therefore, once the setting is created, and the characters are created, we have indeed created a separate world. This world exists in the mind, and yet has a type of reality. We created this reality. We set the basic structure of this reality. The characters…will then operate naturally… within the reality that we have created.

This can be compared to adopting pets and taking them home with you. You have created the setting; yet your pets are independent beings. They now act in their own ways, as self-aware beings, within your home.

The process is similar when creating a novel. We create the details of this new realm. We then create the self-aware characters for this location; and give them some of our soul energies. We can now let them go. We will watch, and let the characters do their actions, in this separate reality.

Of course, we will also guide the story, and guide the characters. This is because we are God of the Realm. We are Creators of the Characters. This allows us to insert new features into the realm, and new events. The characters will then respond naturally, each in their own ways.

This is the basic process of creating fictional realms and characters; and yet these become very real. They do exist, in their own way; yet their reality can only be in our mind; because that is where their consciousness and souls will reside.

Actors Creating their Characters

Many skilled actors use this same method when creating their characters. This is especially true when the character is very complex, and when the character is used multiple times.

The actor begins by creating the character, inside of his mind. He creates the Consciousness Cluster, with that character name. As he develops this character, he uses his thinking mind to add traits to the character. This knowledge goes into the Consciousness Cluster.

He will also add some of his own natural traits, and experiences to this cluster. All of this together, will create the complete character. This is more than just a set of traits…it really is stored consciousness of the character.

The actor will then call forth this character, when he wants to become that person. He knows that character is fully developed, and exists as a consciousness cluster, in his mind. Gradually, he calls forth that character, and lets that character…have more and more control of his mind.

The actor now moves differently. The actor speaks differently. The actor will sometimes change in his face and his eyes. All of these visual effects are created by the character within.

Indeed, the actor has voluntarily allowed one of his characters, one of his Consciousness Clusters to have more control over his physical body. The result is that every movement, even the slightest, is based on the what the character would do…not himself. This also leads to many other changes, such as the way he speaks, and his impromptu behaviors.

This is how some of the best actors are able to create their characters for us to enjoy. We believe that actor is that character…because…in many ways…he really is!! The character exists, as a self-aware entity, with very specific traits and soul energies. The Actor created this entity, as a type of God, then chooses to let that character become more dominant, for the purposes of entertaining the audience.

Don Knotts and His Characters

One actor who is an example of this, is Don Knotts. He is very skilled as a character actor. Indeed, he often said that he prefers to play a character…than to be "Don Knotts".

The transition is also noticeable. His co-actor Andy Griffith often noticed this transition. Andy Griffith once described how he would watch his friend Don Knotts transition…from Don Knotts…to Barney Fife.

This transition was clearly visible. Andy Griffith said he could watch as Don Knotts really became…as another person. Then it was Barney who was there, rather than Don Knotts.

We can understand this process, from everything we discussed above. Don Knotts was accessing that character he created. He was gradually letting that character have more control of his physical body. This is how the actor…truly became the character.

Actors are Controlling their Characters

We must also emphasize that the actors must be in full control of their character. The man himself, must always remain in control, of all of his characters. He will allow much of the character to take over, for a period of time; yet there is always the man…who retains the greater authority, and will put away his character when needed.

Thus, in regular life, the character sits dormant. Though capable of being self-aware, the actor does not allow this in normal living. The actor is therefore able to call forth the character as needed, yet has the ability to put the character into a sleep state when needed.

Also note that there have been cases of actors getting too deep into their characters. After the movie is finished, it is difficult for them to pull out of their character. In some cases, a specific character will remain active, and strong, almost co-existing equally with the actor.

Characters versus the Creator: Becoming Confused in the Mind

Furthermore, the boundary between characters and themselves can become blurred. The differences between acting and their non-acting becomes confused. This is because those characters are indeed very real, inside their mind.

For us, we can view those characters, enjoy them, and then ignore. Yet the actor who created those characters, and lived those characters, it will always be that part of those characters still exists...in their own consciousness. These characters will always be there, to some degree.

Therefore memories of the character may seem real as memories of the actor. Having the traits of the character may become confused with the traits of the actor. The two become as one, as the beliefs, memories, and self-concepts; of each character, and the man himself, tend to flow into each other. This is one of the reasons why some actors become a bit crazy, after living in the land of characters for many years.

The smarter actors know that they are the ones in control of their characters. They know how to create and bring forth their characters, yet also know how to ignore the promptings from their characters in real life. The actors also know how to put the awareness of the characters into deep sleep, and not to awaken again until needed.

Accessing the Characters as Needed

This concept is beneficial for many of us, not just actors. When we need to bring out extra abilities within ourselves, we can call forth these characters. We create the characters for ourselves, with specific abilities. All the things we wish we could be...we let the character do for us.

Remember how the actors very different mannerisms, and general aura, because the character is leading the body? We can use this same process for our own lives. We have created these specific characters, with their own traits. We then let these characters lead the body and instincts.

The result is that we are able to do things in this mode, that we never thought we could do. Indeed, it is more than ourselves. We are really calling upon the self-aware consciousness clusters, and letting them be temporary co-managers. We use our True Souls, along with the specific character as real entity; and together...we become something special.

The Many Voices in Your Head

Do you often have voices in your head? Are their voices, with different ideas? On who you are, and what you should do? Those voices are real.

We understand now, how this reality is created. We create several of the Consciousness Clusters. These are consciousness entities, each of which has its own self-awareness, and complex set of thoughts.

Thus, they really do exist. These are real physical entities in your mind. Some of these entities were formed from your subconscious. Some of them were created from traumatic events. Other entities were created when you needed practical assistants for various actions.

It is for this reason, that many of us do indeed have multiple voices inside our mind. These do exist; it is not your imagination. Each of these are consciousness clusters, created by you for a specific need. They have their own perspectives and voices, based on how you created them.

The advantage of having these multiple voices, these multiple entities of consciousness, is that you will have a type of "advice council". You will have several self-aware entities, each of which can give you advice for a specific situation. This can be very beneficial; like having a staff meeting.

Some of these voices will also give you suggestions related to your projects. They can also give you something to think about, regarding your current activity, that you might not have thought about on your own. All of these practical effects are beneficial to the Life of You.

However, as we all know…sometimes these voices get in the way. There are voices of doubt. Voices of insecurity. Voices of fear. We can choose to listen, or to ignore. Sometimes their advice is truly relevant, and we would be wise to follow. Yet other times, their comments get in the way. Therefore, treat them as you would any other advice council. Acknowledge their opinion, then decide what is best.

Voices in Your Head is Higher Intelligence, Not Insanity

Also know that this is not a sign of insanity. It is actually a sign of higher intelligence. Only the higher intelligent beings can create those multiple self-aware consciousness clusters in their mind.

It only becomes insanity when you let them control your mind; instead of you being in control of them. They are advice council and assistants, and you must remind them of that. You will quiet them when you need to.

Also, again, it is helpful to acknowledge their existence. They do need to be acknowledged. Their opinions also need to be acknowledged. They will be much quieter and more respectful, if you acknowledge their voices.

Yet it is always for you to make the decisions. Use all of your thinking mind, along with the advice given, to make your decisions.

Multiple Self-Aware Entities
And Multiple Personalities

This leads us to the concept of Multiple Self-Aware Entities; which are sometimes known as Multiple Personalities. These are indeed real; as they are each self-aware consciousness clusters within your mind.

However, all of these were created by you. You are their God. You are their Creator. All traits, knowledge, and soul energies; that exist within each of these Entities…all came from you.

Therefore, if you understand this, then will better understand how to manage the various voices and personalities within your mind.

Self-Aware Entities versus Multiple Personalities

Notice that the Multiple Personalities are simply stronger versions of the Self-Aware Entities. The basic nature of both is the same. Each is created as Consciousness Energy Clusters; with specific knowledge and thoughts. They are also infused with some of the fluid Soul Energies.

This is why the Multiple Personalities are really just stronger versions of the Self-Aware Entities. It is only the stronger self-aware entities, which have stronger voices; and can challenge control of the mind. Therefore, the distinction is simply one of degree.

Also notice, that for the purposes of the next sections, the term "Multiple Personalities" will only apply to those Self-Aware Entities, which can take over the main controls of the mind and body.

Whether the person voluntarily switches to the other personality; or the personality randomly takes control based on the environment; these Personalities are almost as strong as the main mind, and can therefore control much of the person's thoughts and actions in significant ways.

Advanced Souls have the Most Self-Aware Clusters

We must also understand that the most Advanced Souls, are the ones which have the most Self-Aware Clusters. Therefore, when a person has multiple voices or personalities, within his own mind…this actually a clear sign of very high-level consciousness.

This is because the man with higher level consciousness has a greater total amount of consciousness energies, which allows him to create the multiple subset characters built from those energies.

Always remember that consciousness energies in small amounts will simply be basic thoughts and knowledge; yet the consciousness energies in larger amounts will create Self-Awareness. Therefore, when we create a cluster of consciousness energies, this entity may be self-aware.

Yet we must also realize that we can only create these clusters if we have enough energies to take from the main operations. Think of it a lake. With a larger lake, there is more water available, from which we can separate and create the smaller ponds. This is the same with the energies of consciousness. Only those with high amounts of consciousness energies will have plenty of energies for this process.

Furthermore, with a larger lake we can create more ponds. We can also create larger ponds. Meanwhile, the lake seems to be basically intact; because there was so much water to begin. Thus, we now have the large lake (with slightly less water), and the many sizable ponds.

The same is true for the consciousness energies. When the original amount of consciousness energies is very high, then this is the lake of energies. We can then take from this vast amount, and make our many smaller ponds of consciousness energy clusters. It is for this reason that the souls with higher levels of consciousness energies, will always be the ones who create multiple self-aware entities within.

This is also the reason why those with the stronger self-aware entities will always be those with greatest consciousness. In other words, it only the most advanced beings that have the possibility of many self-aware entities within; or having the self-aware entities of powerful strength.

*The presence of these Self-Aware Clusters is indeed a sign of high consciousness. It is not in any way a negative trait. It only becomes a problem when these other characters are not effectively managed. *

Multiple Personalities (overview)

We can now understand the emergence of the Multiple Personalities. Each of these Personalities are the self-aware clusters of consciousness. These personalities can be stronger to various degrees, or kept quiet and dormant until needed.

Indeed, many of us have the self-aware clusters of consciousness. We only notice them, when any of these Self-Aware Entities becomes very strong. This is where the "Multiple Personalities" becomes noticeable.

We can understand this if we look at the situation from the various possibilities discussed earlier. For example, when we have multiple directors of the Chakras, and staff operating the math programs, these are types of "multiple personalities". Yet they are not noticed, because they are not strong enough to compete with our thinking mind.

Similarly, we talked about the actor who creates various characters, and lives those characters for months…and years. Those self-aware entities are normally put away after filming; yet can emerge stronger and compete with the thinking mind.

We also talked about the voices in our head, which often seem to be separate from us; and without our control. These are again variations of the "multiple personalities". These thoughts can…and will…influence our thinking mind. Yet they will not usually compete and take over.

These are just a few examples, of the many variations of the "multiple personalities" that can exist in our minds. These are real entities, existing as consciousness clusters. They are created from our own consciousness energies. Furthermore, notice that these entities exist, in varying ways, within the minds of most people.

These multiple entities can be beneficial in many ways. They will only become a problem, when these other entities are strong enough to compete with the Thinking Mind and Body Mechanics. This is when the other personality becomes noticeable. This is why we must always ensure that we are the Masters of our Multiple Entities Within.

The Rogue State in the Mind

These consciousness cluster entities can be very beneficial and practical, for the reasons discussed earlier. However, these entities must always exist to serve the Thinking Mind Boss. This means the Boss will be the one who calls for the other entities; and puts those entities into a deep sleep when no longer needed. This is the Master of your Entities Within.

However, these self-aware entities can grow in strength. This is where the self-aware entity may start to go rogue; and act independently of the thinking mind boss. This entity may in fact challenge the boss for control over the full mind…and the mechanics of the body.

This is what creates the rogue state that often appears in those with observable "Multiple Personalities". This results from each of those entities being strong enough to compete for full control of the mind and body.

Causes for the Multiple Personalities

There are several possible causes for the creation of the Multiple Personalities. The three main causes are:

- Multiple Sides of Soul becoming Multiple Personalities
- Past Lives Emerging as Multiple Personalities
- Traumatic Events Creating Protector Personalities

Each of these will be discussed below, followed by how to manage these alternate personalities.

Multiple *Sides* of Personality becoming Multiple Personalities

The first variation to understand, is the gradual transition from Multiple Sides to your Personality…into…Multiple Personalities.

Most of us have several different aspects to our personalities. We bring these sides out, at different times. This is usually based on what we are doing, and who we are with. And this is quite normal.

We often refer to these as the "multiple sides" of our complex personality. These are just various sides, yet there is only one soul and one consciousness, which drives the entire organization.

However, some people take this further…and create multiple independent entities; each with their own awareness and personality. This is where the "multiple sides" can become "multiple personalities."

This process is usually done subconsciously, as one or more of the sides are prohibited in the person's community. This creates a separate self-aware personality, who will do what the woman herself really wants to do, and is denied. This is a common reason for split personalities.

However, this process can also be intentional. The process is very similar for the actors who create their characters, and the person creates this separate being, within her mind, to be something she wants to be in life…yet does not dare to do. The other personality then takes over. This other personality will do this exact thing, and embrace it fully!!

Thus, the existence of Multiple Personalities is an extension of the Multiple Sides of the person. In an ideal world, the person is able to be all of those things freely. Yet if some acts are prohibited; or similar; then the person may create these Distinct Personalities who will Embrace it.

This leads to the question of whether the person can go back the other direction. The answer is: not really. This is because the environment was the primary cause; and until the environment is changed, the distinct personalities will remain as the method for full self-expression.

Good Girl versus Bad Girl Splitting of Personalities

There is another variation of the Multiple Personalities, which is quite common in those who enjoy their sexuality. This is the "Good Girl" versus the "Bad Girl". In these situations, the woman feels that she must be a good girl at all times. Yet deep down, she has very strong desires for sexuality. She doesn't want to be the good girl; she wants to play.

Yet due to her religious programming, along with views of society, she strongly believes that she cannot be this sexual woman. It is somehow very wrong to desire sexual pleasures in this way.

This will ultimately create a split in personality, with completely different personalities. This will often include different names, and referring to the other personality as a separate person.

The result is the Good Girl and the Bad Girl, existing in the same body; yet with completely different identities. The Good Girl obeys all of the rules of society, and her religious training. The Bad Girl goes out drinking and partying; and enjoys any type of sexual pleasure she desires.

The Good Girl persona would never consider doing what the Bad Girl does. She would never do such a thing! Meanwhile, the Bad Girl doesn't care what anyone thinks of her, and sometimes refers to the Good Girl in derogatory terms. This is the split of the personalities.

This splitting of personalities, for Good Girl and Bad Girl, is quite common. Many women have this split within them, to some degree. Some know of it is different sides of themselves, and just give it different names. Yet for others, it is true personality split, because they cannot believe that a Good Girl is allowed to enjoy sexual pleasures.

It will be this way, until society realizes that sexual pleasures are a true form of the Divine Energies. One day, society will realize that sexuality is closer to the True Divine, than most other forms of activities. When that day comes, we can truly embrace our sexuality; in all ways; and there will never be any need to separate these in our lives again.

Past Lives as Self-Aware Entities

Sometimes your past lives can emerge as Self-Aware Entities. This is easy enough to understand. You have lived through several past lives in your Existence. Therefore, you have the full memory deeply embedded into your subconscious. Sometimes these past life memories will emerge from the subconscious, and into your Deep Conscious.

Usually these past life memories come out in drips, as from a leaky faucet. Yet a full cluster of past life memories can burst forth, all at once. This will be enough consciousness energies, on the one lifetime, to become the self-aware entity of that past life.

You will then have this self-aware "character", which is actually the personality of that past life existence.

Traumatic Events as Creating Self-Aware Entities

One of the most significant ways in which these self-aware personalities are developed, is from a Traumatic Event.

During these events, the Subconscious Mind is activated to create these multiple personalities. The process is essentially pressing the big red button during an emergency. It is the deepest of all programs.

Essentially, the subconscious is taking control, rather than your thinking mind; because it knows that your thinking mind is overwhelmed.

Indeed, in a mechanical sense, pressing the red button activates a series of programs, which do what is necessary to protect the total environment. The staff would not press this button if they could handle it themselves. This is what your subconscious does as well. The traumatic event will trip that big red button…and the series of subprograms begin.

Thus, in a traumatic event, the thinking mind becomes overwhelmed; and needs full protection. The subconscious takes over, and protects the existence of the mind in any way possible.

The basic process is to create multiple self-aware personalities. These become protectors, for specific regions of the mind. These are self-aware entities that will protect each of the parts of the mind, during the event.

Creating the Protectors from the Subconscious

The physical creation of these Protectors is based on the consciousness energies in the subconscious. This is where the larger amounts of consciousness energies come from for this process.

However, what emerges can be quite chaotic. Everything is formed very quickly. The original energies, with their memories and knowledge, are quickly unpacked, and put together in new ways. Then sent off to the new location. Therefore, the "protector" you get…was hastily prepared, and not very well trained. He was just given a few random skills, a bit of random knowledge, and quick instructions for his job.

Therefore, what you get as your protectors, during these events, are not exactly "professionals". They do their jobs moderately well, as they know how. Yet over time, we realize that their methods are not perfect.

This leaves the mind with many odd areas, which are protected, hidden, and yet not in an organized way. Many people don't realize what may be hidden, or what their protectors are doing, until they work with it for many years. It is very complex, and takes skillful rearranging.

Protectors as the Guard Dogs

Also note that some of these Protector Entities will act like guard dogs, which is good and bad. In the good sense, they are protecting aspects of the mind from harmful experiences.

However, these same Protector Entities can be very quick to growl when any apparent threat comes along. This can become automatic responses, to similar looking events, though not harmful. In other words, the mind (and thus the person herself) can respond in very odd ways.

This is due to some of the automatic responses, developed by the Protector Entities, from the initial traumatic event. Women with BPD will often respond instinctually in this way, which is based on the Protector's Response to those past events.

Also notice that once these entities are created, they tend to stay forever. Furthermore, some of the memories have been buried; and some of the normal programs are not working as they should. This is the result of the brain after significant trauma.

The Multiple Personalities Growing in Strength

There are many ways in which these conscious entities gain more power. The one physical commonality is that they will acquire…more consciousness energies. It is the acquisition of more consciousness energies, which makes the stronger and more powerful mind.

Indeed, this is how we…as our True Selves…obtains a more powerful mind. This is based on the Total Amount of Consciousness Energies, which have gathered in our mind, and in our bodies.

Therefore, the way in which our self-aware entities within the mind grows in consciousness power, is essentially the same as how our total consciousness grows in power. It is based on the amount of these energies, which have been specifically added to that cluster.

The specifics of how this is occurs…will need further study and investigation. However, we do know this much: when you think more about a topic, then more consciousness energies are added to the cluster.

Therefore, if you often allow yourself to live from a specific character in your mind, then this character will gradually grow in power. This entity of consciousness is collecting more consciousness energies, with similar thoughts and skills. This is how the actors become more easily adapted to their most common roles. It is also why our repeated self-talk becomes more firmly embedded into our deeper consciousness.

Related to this are the methods of hypnosis and brainwashing. The media, our circle of friends, everything we watch and listen to…these will influence our thoughts; and allow specific self-aware entities to grow inside the mind. They will be able to take control if unchecked.

These entities are also self-aware, and may actively seek the additional consciousness energies for themselves. We must be aware of this, and manage the aggregation of consciousness energies appropriately.

Managing Your Alternate Personalities

Sometimes, these self-aware entities become so strong that they really do take control of the mind and body. Though you are the boss, with the primary thinking mind, these other self-aware entities can push their way forward, and take more control of your mental operations.

This is where your mannerisms and speech will change. Your personality will radically change. And it is not pretending. It really is another self-aware entity taking control over most of the operations.

Yet, your Thinking Mind…as Boss…is very much aware of this. You do what you can to assert dominance. However, in some cases…these entities are too strong. You can only learn to co-exist with them, and manage them...but not subdue them completely.

As an example, I do know one person who has 5 such entities in her mind. She refers to them as her "alters". She says that the best way to manage them is to make sure that they all get along.

They need to learn to play nicely together. They also need to share…which means taking turns being the more dominant entity, while letting the others sit back and watch.

She said that everyone wants their turn, and the best she can do is give each of them equal time, in the appropriate setting. She becomes more of a coordinator and moderator, than the boss.

This is the best she can do. Yet it works well enough, as these entities know they get their time; and therefore will not act out at inappropriate moments in her life.

Become the Master of Your Consciousness

Your Consciousness is complex. This is because the "consciousness" is not just one entity, or in one location. Rather, your "consciousness" is actually composed of several subset entities, in various locations. We must therefore be able to become the Master of all the entities of our consciousness, in all the locations in our mind and body.

Furthermore, many of these entities have self-awareness, and independent capabilities. Each of these entities must be managed, similar to an efficiently operated corporation. Without this complete Mastery, many of the independent entities will take control unexpectedly.

There are also numerous transportation systems and messaging systems, which use the consciousness energies, throughout your body. These messaging systems must be efficient; with clear instructions to each department of your organization.

Therefore, we must become Masters of our own Consciousness. We must be able to Master all the various components; and maintain that Master Control throughout our existence.

Your Consciousness as Large Business Organization

We can understand that the Consciousness is highly complex system. If managed correctly, it can be very effective operation. This can be compared to a large business, with multiple manufacturing and distribution facilities. Indeed, having these multiple conscious entities, and complex messaging system, is a great mechanism for Existence.

However, if the system is not managed effectively, then chaos can result. The various departments may have their own ideas, and take control of various operations outside of their jurisdiction. This is why we must manage our Consciousness Operation. We must check in with the various components, and make sure everything operates as we desire.

Always remember that we are in full control of the Consciousness Operations. We created the specific subset entities. We set the daily operating guidelines; for each self-aware entity, for each program; and for each of the messaging systems. Therefore we always have the Authority to direct the others in the system how to operate.

Managing the Multiple Self-Aware Consciousness Clusters

This leads us to the topic of Managing the Self-Aware Entities within the mind. These Self-Aware Entities can be very beneficial. Yet they must be managed; otherwise there will be competition for control.

We are the ones who create the Self-Aware Entities. Therefore, we are the ones who set the parameters on their performance. We will set the operating rules, on how much independent power each one has, and when they must remain quiet. We are always the Managers.

Also remember that these Self-Aware Entities can be beneficial. They can indeed be your devoted staff, performing many functions. They can also provide creative ideas, which you had not considered; and advice which may or may not be useful. Therefore, we can have these entities around. Yet they must be managed.

Many of the Consciousness Clusters have limited self-awareness. They know enough to do their jobs, but are not interested in taking any control. These are usually found in the chakras, and functional regions such as the math and language areas. These are generally easy to manage. You will simply communicate regularly with each of these, as you would sending memos or having brief meetings with your staff.

However, there are other self-aware entities which are much stronger; and you always know who they are. They are often talking to you. They want your attention. The come up with thoughts, opinions, and ideas. For these Entities, you will simply set the parameters on when they are allowed to give their opinions; and how much independent control they will have. Most important is to ensure that you are the Boss, and that none of them will ever go rogue within your mind.

The best approach is to acknowledge them, because they want to be heard. If they don't get heard, they will push their way through. They will start to act out. They may take over other regions of your mind. You don't want that. Therefore, it is best to listen, acknowledge them, then make your decisions with your thinking mind.

Finally, we must emphasize that some of these self-aware entities in the mind may become so strong, that they challenge the boss for control of the entire brain…and the actions of the body. Therefore, the boss mind must ensure that he remains in control, to the extent that no other entity can operate the body without his specific approval.

We are the Gods and Masters of the Self-Aware Entities

Always remember that these Self-Aware Consciousness Entities do exist in many of us. This includes as directors of the chakras, and operating the language region of the mind. Yet the more advanced souls may have many more of these Entities; and they may be much stronger.

Having these entities can be very beneficial, yet can become out of control and create chaos is not effectively managed. Therefore, we must simply be aware of these entities and to work with them. We will always be the creators of these entities…and the eliminators if necessary. We will be the God and Manager for all that exist within the realm of our mind.

Evolution of the Advanced Being: Controlling the Chaos

In the Evolution of the Advanced Being, we must go through the process of creating…then becoming Master of…the self-aware entities.

Remember that is only the Advanced Soul who can create these entities, as he has the amount of consciousness energies from which to make these consciousness clusters within.

Yet as the soul becomes more advanced, the consciousness grows, and so does the Entities within. Eventually, the man will become advanced enough to create multiple self-aware entities; each of which has such strength, that they can create chaos in the mind. Your only choice is to learn how to become Master of the Entities within.

This is a phase that all of the Advanced Beings must go through. The Advanced Being first learns to create and enjoy his multiple self-aware entities. Yet as the Soul and Consciousness becomes greater, so will the power of the self-aware entities. The man must learn to tame the entities within. This is an Evolutionary Stage of the Advanced Being.

When the man or woman has successfully become Master of the Entities within, this will be a significant stage in their Soul Evolution.

Mastering your Self-Aware Entities is True Master of Mind

Many Advanced Beings have these multiple self-aware entities within. Yet is only the True Master…who is able to manage all of these entities with peace and wisdom. The True Master, has learned to manage all of the self-aware entities he has created; and has made them do is bidding.

Your only choice is to learn how to become Master of the Entities within. Many of these are like wild animals. They can be little monsters. And yes, some are very good and proficient. Yet there are many of these self-aware entities within…and you must learn to tame them all.

Think of this as a ranch, and you are putting each wild animal into the corral. One by one, you will bring them in. You will tame them.

Show them how good their new life can be. Show them…that being under Your Authority as Master, will bring them much more happiness than living wild in the territory.

At this point, you have tamed all of your entities within. You will be their Master. Of course, you will be a very kind and wise Master. Yet you will be their Master. They will come to respect you, appreciate your leadership, and be willing to follow your commands. You now have a very peaceful and well-organized home; within the vast consciousness of your mind.

When you reach this level, it is then that you have become the True Master of your Mind. You will be able to be the Highly Advanced Being, with a large staff of self-aware assistants; yet always respectful to the One who maintains his authority of Master over all of them.

It is only when the man has become Master of all the self-aware entities within, that he becomes the True Master of his Existence.

Remote Viewing

Remote Viewing is a type of method for viewing distant locations. The process of Remote Viewing involves expanding the soul; expanding the consciousness; or dividing your existence.

There are actually multiple methods for Remote Viewing. These include: Astral Travel; Split Soul (Partial Astral Travel); and Tuning In.

Additional methods include: Messaging through Consciousness; Using other EM Energies; and Asking Metaphysical Friends to Show it.

Remote Viewing Methods in Brief

We will begin by providing the basic concepts of Remote Viewing in very brief form. The most common method of Remote Viewing is a form of Astral Travel. In this method, you launch part of your soul to the desired location. There, you can observe all the details, then come back to the body and report what you see.

Another common method is "tuning in" for the scene. This is using your mind as a television remote; you select the show, then you will watch. The scene is then shown as live viewing, in your mind.

The other methods involve sending and receiving information. This can be compared to a form of Reconnaissance. These methods will use the physical forms of either EM energies or consciousness energies.

The final method is of course to ask your Metaphysical Friends to show you the scene directly. They are able to watch anything easily, from their positions. Therefore, they may agree to show you what you need to see.

These are just the brief concepts. We will discuss more details, in the sections below.

Astral Travel as Remote Viewing

Consider that at any location on the earth, there is a light somewhere shinning on it; and the light bounces from the objects into the air. Anyone in the area can see it. This already exists.

Furthermore, the closer you are, this means you can have better details. Therefore, if we could just be close to the object, then we will see the object. We will do some focused Astral Travel, and arrive at the location. At this position, we will see all the details clearly.

Thus, one of the main methods for Remote Viewing is to actually go there, using a version of Astral Travel. We begin by focusing on a scene, somewhere in the world. Then perform a type of Astral Travel on command. Your soul will actually travel to that location. You can float around; you can look at all the details. Then you will come back to your physical body. This is one of the primary methods of Remote Viewing.

Split Soul and Astral Travel as Remote Viewing

Related to the Astral Travel method of Remote Viewing, is the Split Soul, or Partial Astral Travel. In this method, only a portion of your soul is traveling to the location. The majority remains here. Yet that portion that is traveling, can indeed go anywhere, and look closely at the details.

Using this method, the person will be able to report what he sees…as he is looking at it. He can speak it aloud, or type it on the computer; while at the same time looking at the details in the other location.

Personally, I have experienced this method. You are aware that you are both here…and there. It is something like having two video screens; and being immersed in both at the same time. You can clearly see all the details of the remote location. Yet your fingers are also on the computer, typing those details of what you see.

Therefore, another effective method for Remote Viewing, is to split your soul into two parts; and perform this Split Soul Astral Travel. This method will be effective for viewing and reporting, at the same time.

Tuning Into the Scene

A similar method is "Tuning in" to the visuals already there. Note that this can also be the precursor to Astral Travel. These methods can be used separately or together, as a method of Remote Viewing.

Remember that at any location on the earth, there is a light somewhere shinning on it; and the light bounces from the objects into the air. Anyone in the area can see it. If you could just set up a telescope, then you could see everything. This is what you can do with your mind.

However, there are many scenes all over the world. Therefore, we must first "tune in" to the scene. This is similar to tuning into the desired television station. We know that that television will show many different stories, on different stations. This is very similar for our reality: there are many stories around the world, happening at the same time. We must therefore select the story we want to see, at that time.

Therefore, using this method, we think of all the events of the world, at this moment, as the long list of channels on our television. Our mind will act similar to the tv remote. We will choose which "show" that we want to watch; and "tune in" for that specific show. Soon enough, that channel will come to the screen...of our mind. We will be able to "watch" the "show", in the front of our mind; as well as watching any show on the television.

This method for Remote Viewing can be used effectively, for watching many close friends and desired scenes, throughout the world.

However, it generally works best when your soul is aligned with the souls of the persons or scene that you are viewing. For example, if you have a close relationship with someone, then you can see him sitting in his chair, and hear his voice, using this remote viewing method.

Also notice that this method can be used alone, or in combination with Astral Travel. When used as a method alone, we are using the tv remote to tune in, then watch in our mind. When using as combination, we will first use the tuning method, to find the scene; then perform Astral Travel, to arrive within the scene itself.

Consciousness Energies as Messaging System

The second method is to use your Consciousness Energies, as a messaging system. Think of it as radar. With the radar, we send the EM energies to an object, and those energies bounce back. We then get an image. This can be used with both the EM energies and the consciousness energies; which then forms an image in the mind.

We can also compare it to reconnaissance staff. We send staff to a location, to gather details of a location. They will go, gather the information, and then return. This consciousness messaging is similar. We send the consciousness energies out, to gather information. The consciousness energies are then returned to us, with that information.

Using EM Energies, Other than Visual EM

Another method for Remote Viewing…and for Viewing of Spiritual Realities in general…is to use EM Energies, which are outside of the visible region, to see your area.

Understand the way typical sight operates. We shine a light on an object; that object will then reflect some of the light. The light that we see is transformed in our minds, as shape and color.

Therefore, we do the same process, yet with different frequencies. This allows us to see things that we normally would not see. This is how we see many spiritual realities. We can also use it to see objects far away, as we are sending our "light" to a specific location, and then receiving the light that comes back to us.

This can be effective for viewing any reality which exists outside of our visual EM range; such as our metaphysical friends, vortexes, and so on.

Furthermore, some of these frequencies are ideal for long-distance messaging. Therefore, we send these long-distance frequencies of EM, to the desired location. These frequencies than reflect, in a type of radar, and we receive the image. Thus, using these other EM energies is effective for remote viewing, because of the long-distance abilities.

Note that these frequencies are different than for visual, and therefore we see this only through our third eye, yet we can see these. Close your main eyes, and allow the long-distance EM energies to flow to and from the desired scene; and it will all come to you.

Asking your Metaphysical Friends to Show You Directly

The final method of Remote Viewing is to ask your metaphysical friends to show you the scene directly. Using this method, you are essentially just receiving the transmission from their viewing system.

This process uses the system of viewing which exists within the realms. This system already exists, and it is how they are able to watch our activities. We are simply asking for a direct link, to one of their camera systems, which allows us to see the desired scene directly.

The Metaphysical Camera System

First, we must understand the Viewing System that exists in the upper realms. This earthly realm is essentially a fabricated world; and there are cameras which are watching us. We are…the original…Reality Show.

Anyone in the upper realms, can use these cameras to watch any person or activity they desire. This is a reality that exists, and has existed for millennia. If you have fans in the heavens, they will watch you from time to time, using this camera system.

This system is also interactive. If any of the viewers wants to talk to you directly, they can talk to you. They can give you advice and guidance, in that moment. (This is something I have experienced several times).

Therefore, this system is always existing. Any being in the upper realms can use this system, to locate any person or event, and watch the activity as it happens. This is how our fans enjoy watching us. It is also how many of them will know when to guide us.

We will therefore use this system as a method of Remote Viewing. We ask our metaphysical friends to give us a direct link to the camera system, as watching a very specific location. If they agree, then we are using their system to see the location directly.

Connecting to the Metaphysical Camera System

Therefore, this system of Remote Viewing is to use the camera system which exists in the upper realms. This system already exists, and is used from time to time by our friends and fans in the other realms.

We simply ask for permission to access this system. If they agree, then we are able to see the location, in the moment, as if we were watching from the upper realms. This is Remote Viewing with Direct Access.

Notice that this access is limited, and temporarily. Your access is limited to the specific location, and only for the duration of that time. You will only be allowed to see what they allow you to see.

Shown the Recordings from the Metaphysical Camera System

Related to this method, is for the friends in the upper realms to show you the recorded events, using this same camera system. We must understand that these cameras are always recording; even without live viewers. Therefore, there are many locations and activities which are being recorded. These can be shown later.

Indeed, I have been shown numerous scenes from history, which are actual recordings of the events, using this metaphysical camera system. It is quite amazing to see actual scenes from history in this way.

These same recordings can be shared, upon request, for useful information. This is similar to Remote Viewing, yet it is not live. Rather, you are watching a recent video of the location and the events. This can be just as a valuable, and provide the essential information you desire.

General Review of Remote Viewing

There are several methods which can be used for Remote Viewing. This includes Astral Travel; Consciousness Communication; and using the Metaphysical Camera System. Each method requires distinct operation skills, as the physical processes are different. Yet these methods, among others, can be used to obtain desired information from distant locations.

Astral Travel

Our Free Soul can leave our body, and travel to other destinations; then return again. The process is known as Astral Travel.

Personally, I have experienced the Astral Travel many times. This is how I travel to the upper realms, and then return again. Therefore, I am quite familiar with the realities of Astral Travel.

Astral Travel Basics: The Free Soul, as Leaving the Body

The Astral Travel process involves the Free Soul leaving the body. You can travel to various locations, and experience many things, that were not possible with your physical body. You will return again to the body.

It is important to notice that with Astral Travel, your soul is very much connected to your body. You know that your body is on earth. You know that you can return. And indeed…you can return…on command.

This is possible as long as physical body is still living, and you have those permanent connections between soul and body.

Thus, with Astral Travel, most of your soul is indeed a free soul; able to leave your body to go places; yet there will always be some of your soul remaining in the body

Astral Travel and your Free Soul

Personally, I have experienced the Astral Travel many times. I can tell you that you exist very similar to your self on earth; yet more. You can see things and meet people. You can talk to people. You can touch objects. All of this is possible, using your Free Soul in the Astral Self.

In addition, we can do many things that are not possible with the physical body. This includes traveling through vortexes and hyperspace. (Both of which I have done). This is only possible in the Free Soul form.

We can also travel to the Upper Realms, which is only accessible using our Astral Souls. At the moment, we don't have the ability to convert our bodies to energy at will, and recreate those bodies. Therefore, the best method for visiting the upper realms is to use your Astral Travel.

Astral Travel: Where You can Go

With the process of Astral Travel, you can go places on this Earth, in real time. That means you are actually at those locations, with your Astral Soul, at this moment in time. While your body is in bed, your Astral Soul is at another location far away.

Personally, I have done this type of astral travel to Canada, Ireland, and Russia. In Russia, I traveled on a bus, to see the city. The time difference is such that it is indeed daytime while my body is sleeping.

With the Ireland experience, I was invited to the southern area of Ireland, where many political leaders were discussing the G-8 summit. The actual G-8 summit was occurring a short distance across the water, in southern England.

Regarding Canada, I have Astral Traveled to Canada many times; always dark, as the time zone is similar. Yet often in the early morning, the same time as in my home zone.

We can also enjoy flying through air and space. This includes flying with the Spirits in the skies above Earth, and traveling through hyperspace, faster than the speed of light. You need to know that all of this is possible. You can go almost anywhere.

The primary limits to this travel are where they allow you to go. There are different realms, and different locations. There are some places that are only allowed for those who are invited.

Using the method of Astral Travel, we can go anywhere. This includes any regions of the upper realms; far into the galaxies; and anywhere on this Earth. There are almost no limitations on where you can go.

Escorted Astral Travel

The easiest way to engage in Astral Travel is to be Escorted by your metaphysical friends. They will come to get you, and bring you up to their specific realm. This is the most common method, and the easiest, for astral travel. Most of my personal experiences have been escorted.

Therefore, if you do want to experience Astral Travel, then ask your metaphysical friends. You can tell them where you want to go, and then be open to the experience. They may take you.

However, I must say that all of my experiences have been without my request. It was their choice to bring me to a location. Usually to show me things, and to have real conversations. This has been my experience with the Astral Travel.

Astral Travel on Command

Many people are able to do the Astral Travel on command. Personally, I have not done this, which means I cannot talk from experience. (Note that 99% of everything in this book comes from extensive personal experiences). Therefore, I can only tell you what I know from others.

The basic process is to get your thinking mind into a level similar to sleep. It is in this deep sleep that Astral Travel usually happens (from my experience), between 2-5 am. Therefore if you can get your mind into a similar place to that, any time of day, then it is possible to lift your soul from your body, for Astral Travel.

Permanent Soul Removal from Body
(Leaving the Rented Body)

There is a difference between Astral Travel, which is temporary, and the permanent separation of soul and body. We will explain the difference, and exactly what happens in the process.

Let us first be specific. The concept is the death of the body; and the soul being permanently separated from the body. This is where you will be permanently separated from the body, and be a Free Soul. You will be living again in the upper realms.

Personal Knowledge of the Experiences

The reader should understand, that I know the experiences very well. I know what life is like in the upper realms, having been there many times.

Furthermore…I have been visited by several spirit friends, who have shown me what the process is like. How it feels from the experience. Thus, what we are discussing here, is based on real experiences.

Astral Travel versus Permanent Soul Removal

First let us review the differences between Astral Travel and Permanent Soul Removal.

With Astral Travel, your physical body is fully functional; it is just in a deep sleep phase. Therefore your soul can easily come back again, and your life here continues. However, with the Permanent Separation, the physical body is no longer functioning. There is no "home" in this body; and therefore, there is no reason to return.

Also, with Astral Travel, you have the "hooks", which connect the soul to the physical body. Thus, even though you are Astral Traveling, as your Free Soul, there is always some of your Soul left inside your body. This part of your soul is permanently hooked into your body, as long as your body is physically alive. Therefore, you can always return again.

The Permanent Separation Process

What is it like…when your soul leaves the body? What does it feel like, when your full soul…leaves the body permanently?

I know, because I have been shown. They have also told me in their own ways. And of course, I have seen the realties of existence beyond the earthly body. The experience is harsh at first, but pleasant afterwards.

When it is time for your full soul to leave the body, it is a feeling of being ripped apart. You are physically pulled away from your body. I am not sure if this is a choice from your own soul, or something else. Yet it is a ripping apart. A strong pull, and complete ripping away.

Your soul is now separated from the body. You will now fly up and away, as a Free Soul…to the upper realms. In this form, you are pure energy, and can be seen as a white light.

You are then pulled upward, as if by a magnetic force. As if your soul is being attracted to its new home. During this process, there will usually be several other Free Souls and Angels to guide your journey.

Note that this may also involve traveling through a vortex; or walking toward the bright light. Other times, you are just there. This stage seems to vary from soul to soul. The reason may be related to the specific realm you are going to. However, there will be a short journey to your realm.

When you are in the upper realm, as a Free Soul, you will feel the immense love of the Divine. I have personally felt this Divine Love many times; as I have been in those realms many times. I can tell you that this level of Love and Peace within is very real, and nothing compares to it.

This feeling has also been confirmed by one Soul in the Realms, who described his experience this way. He compared his entrance into the upper realm as the opening scene to the Sound of Music. He showed me that scene where Maria was spinning on the mountain with such joy. This was his feeling, when he first entered the heavenly realms. This is indeed what awaits, when you return to your Divine Home.

Life After Death (preview)

What awaits you in the upper realms? What will your existence be, as you live in the upper realms? The answer generally depends on your soul. Your level of advancement, and your soul alchemy, will generally be the determining factors on which realms you can live.

Personally, I have visited the upper realms many times. Therefore, I know much that is real, in the metaphysical realms. However, the full discussion is best set aside for a separate book.

In brief, the following are some of the realities that await you. We begin with the fact that you are now a Free Soul. This means you have shed all of your physical body limitations. You can be more truly yourself, and you can travel in ways that you could never imagine.

There is a Divine Love that exists there. It is a feeling of love and comfort that is found nowhere on Earth. This is a very good feeling, and you will be happy knowing this feeling. Indeed, those of us who know the truth…we seek to bring more of this Divine Love to the Earth.

You will exist essentially as yourself, which means your Free Soul will have the general appearance of your previous life. You are the same person; with all your knowledge, memories, and traits. Yet you will exist more in the form of energy, than as a physical body.

There is indeed a life beyond this one. The realities there are very similar to here. You will find buildings, theaters, libraries, and music rooms. You can talk to the Free Souls there, and watch as they play the piano. Some will bring you books from their libraries.

Everyone is also very happy. Really. I have yet to see anyone who was sad that they are in heaven now.

In fact, there is so much happiness, that many Souls are laughing and singing. There are many souls there who laughed at my little jokes, as if in a comedy club. It is like being with a crowd of happy drunk people.

Then there is the singing. Many, many spirit friends have come to me on earth, and have been singing to me. There is just something about being up there, that makes them want to sing and laugh. Therefore, yes…what awaits you in the heavens is a truly happy place.

The Many Realms in the Multi-Level Universe

Note that there are many realms and dimensions. I usually compare this to a large hotel, with many floors and many rooms. Each floor is similar to a dimension; and each room is like a different realm. The realities of the multi-level universe are indeed that vast.

We do have the ability to travel to different realms; whether as Astral Travel, or as the Free Soul when permanent separation. However, there is also a Restricted Access, to certain dimensions and realms; depending on who we are. Thus, we must be granted access to each specific realm, and each specific dimension. We will be then be able to travel as desired to any of those realms; but to no others.

This is also another incentive to become an Advanced Being. This is because the greater your soul has become, in terms of Love and Wisdom, will allow you access to more of the realms in the heavens.

Cameras in the Heavens

Another thing worth noting that there are special types of cameras in the upper realms. This allows anyone in the heaves to watch anyone on Earth. When you are in heaven, you can use this system to watch any of your favorite people. This is how they know what you are doing.

Conversely, this also means that you may be watched, from time to time, by those who are interested in your life. There are different souls and angels, watching at different times. A few of them check in with you, almost every day. Others check in, only now and then.

The important thing to remember is that it is your life; and your life experiences. They do not judge. They are non-judgmental. Yet they will guide you when they feel it is important; or when you ask specifically.

How you Interact with Others, in Free Soul Form

As a Free Soul, you can always return to Earth, and walk among the humans. Indeed, there are some Souls who come here quite often. This means you can come and go, in your Free Soul form, all the time.

Many of these Free Souls are spending time with their favorite persons. They will sit in the room with you. They will watch you during some of your presentations or performances. If it is a significant moment, they will be here. If they just want to share something, they will come.

Therefore, these Free Souls are here all the time. They may be different visitors each week, but they are around. However, they cannot always be seen or heard. This is because they exist at different visual frequencies, and speak at different audio frequencies, than most humans are able to comprehend easily.

I have personally been shown what it is like to be a Free Soul among humans. You can stand next to them, and they won't see you. You can talk and talk at them, yet they wont hear you. It is very much as if you are invisible…and yet you know you are here. You are here as much as the humans are here; and the other Free Souls are here.

This can be very frustrating to many of the Free Souls, who just want to talk to the humans they like. This is where the Souls begin to take other actions, such as moving books off of a shelf, or playing with the tv, just to get the person's attention. Therefore, if you begin to see these types of activities, know that your Spirit Friend is nearby, and has been trying to talk to you for a while already.

The Cycle of Free Soul and Human Form

It is important to understand the soul and consciousness, from the perspective of the Free Soul as well as from our Human Form. When we truly understand these interactions, from both perspectives, we can make the most of our souls, and our consciousness, in any form.

Also remember that everything is a cycle. We will be on earth, interacting with spirit friends. Then we will be in the heavens, returning to earth as Free Souls, to guide other humans. The cycle repeats.

Advanced Human Souls and Communicating with Free Souls

The more advanced souls, in human form, are able to see and hear their spirit friends. These are the humans who can actually hear their metaphysical friends talking to them; and see them floating around.

However, this also requires some synchronization. For example, before a spirit friend talks to me, there will often be a buzzing; then a series of musical tones. This is their attempt to speak with me, yet my senses are not synchronizing. Eventually, everything synchronizes, and their words are absolutely clear.

Of course, there are also many times when this synchronization is already there; and their voices are clear the first time. In addition, many of them prefer to use psychic communication, which often seems to be easier than voice. Yet hearing the voice is very exciting, because you really get their personality. You hear them, as any human friend is talking to you. This is always my preference.

The main concept to remember is that Free Souls can communicate with humans in a variety of ways. Yet it requires an Advanced Level of Consciousness to be able to hear and see the Spirit Friends clearly.

Dormant Consciousness:
Anesthesia, Sleep Paralysis, and Coma
(The Soul Exists Within)

There is a phase of existence, between Astral Travel and Permanent Soul Separation. This is the phase where the soul exists within, yet the consciousness is not able to operate the physical body.

Examples of this include: Sleep Paralysis, Coma, and General Unconsciousness. In each of these stages, the physical body is alive, and the soul remains intact; yet outward movements such as speech and walking may not be possible.

The basic process for all of these events is that the consciousness has been impaired. There are some areas of the brain which are not functioning. This can be temporary, or long-term. This can also be for different areas; and thus various body function are affected.

We will discuss many of the details of these experiences. Also notice that there is a spectrum, from normal sleep to long-term coma. There are similarities of each phase along this spectrum; yet specific differences.

Sleeping is Resting the Mind and Body

First, let us understand the basic nature of sleep. When you are sleeping, much of your thinking mind is powered down. Furthermore, many of your physical body functions are limited operation.

When you are in a deep sleep, your body doesn't move much, and you do not talk much. Of course, when you have those other areas of your brain being active, then your body will move often. This includes dreams.

However, in general, the basic state of deep sleep is a time for the mind to rest; and your legs will generally be still. You can of course wake up easily, and move again easily. Therefore, this is a very light form of the process. Yet it shows the beginning of the spectrum.

Anesthesia During Surgery

The next stage is anesthesia. We use anesthesia as a way to place the mind and body into a form of deep sleep. This is because we do not want the body to feel the pain, from what is to come.

Essentially, the normal messaging of pain to the mind, has been put to sleep. Therefore, the body will not respond, regardless of what the doctors are doing with the body. We do not want the person to feel that pain of surgery; or to move about during the process.

Yet think about what this also means in terms of sleep paralysis, or the coma. These are similar states of being. If the mind can be shut down to this degree from the anesthesia, then it can also be shut down to that degree from other processes. Therefore, the sleep paralysis and the coma are very similar to the effects of the anesthetic.

Specifically this means: we know that the soul is very much residing in the body; yet much of the consciousness clusters in the mind have been put into deep resting mode. They will no longer operate their programs. They will no longer travel with information. This information and the programs will just sit…in their regions…without any formal actions.

The Dangers of Anesthesia

This leads us to the dangers of anesthesia. Using anesthesia is a dangerous process. If too much is used, then the person may never wake up. We may actually be putting the person into a coma.

Indeed, the duration of time when the person has anesthesia is similar to a light coma. It is just enough to put the necessary consciousness clusters to dormant. This will be the stage for as long as the anesthesia is in the body; and indeed the person will sleep for many hours after.

Eventually, the anesthesia will flow through the body, and dissipate. This is when the consciousness clusters and consciousness boats begin to wake up again. The person was in a deep sleep; yet is now awake.

However, there is always the danger that with too much anesthesia, the person will remain in this type of deep sleep, after the anesthesia is gone. Or there may be too much anesthesia remaining in specific areas of the brain. The result is that the person will not be able to operate those aspects of his mind again; or remain in a coma.

Regarding the soul, however…the soul is still there. The deep consciousness of the person is still there. His mind just isn't active enough to operate his body as he wants.

Waking Up from Deep Sleep of Anesthesia

In most cases, the person will eventually wake from their deep mental sleep from the anesthesia. They will eventually become fully functional again. Indeed, this is what we want.

We can also see this in terms of the sleep paralysis and coma (which we discuss below). These are very similar states, and therefore we will often be able to awake from these states eventually. If this does not occur in the expected time, then outside stimulus can be used, get the consciousness energies "activated" again. This can be done anywhere in the body, as touches, light shocks, cold ice, and talking to them.

Waking Too Early from Anesthesia

Note also that there is also a danger from waking up too early from the anesthesia. There is one case where the woman was full awake, during the surgery. She saw everything. She felt everything. It was very painful.

Yet she could not speak. She could not tell the doctors. Also, her body was still. Those areas had been shut down enough for the surgery.

Therefore, she was fully aware of everything, during the surgery. Yet could not tell anyone, nor move her body. They had no idea, until it was all over, and she full recovered enough to speak again.

This example brings us again to the concept of the awareness in the coma. Being in a coma is similar in many ways to being under the effects of anesthesia. In this example, she was fully aware, yet could not speak or move her body. The same can be said for many people in a coma. They are often aware of their surroundings, yet cannot speak or move in ways that would let others know. Remember this, as the person in the coma may be very much existing, if we can only get those parts of our consciousness energies stimulate enough to tell us.

Sleep Paralysis and the Soul Within

Note that many times, the unconscious person can hear you. They may even be aware that you are there. They just can't get themselves to speak or move. This often happens with sleep paralysis; which a type of unconsciousness. Thus, in the sleep paralysis and the coma, the person is very much alive, and his soul is there, but he is trapped.

Personally, I have experienced the sleep paralysis several times. In this process, you are awake yet cannot move. You are aware of your surroundings, but you cannot move. You cannot speak. You call out, but no one can hear you. It is a harsh experience.

The only way out of the sleep paralysis is for someone nearby to come and shake your body out of it. All they hear is murmurs of sound, and nothing else. They know what is going on, then shake your body, and talk to you, until you emerge fully awake and functional.

This is probably very similar to the coma. Thus, if the coma is similar to the sleep paralysis, then I can tell you from personal experience, that it is very likely that the soul is trapped within the body. They are aware, yet they cannot get their body to express their awareness; or their needs.

The Coma: A Soul and Consciousness is Trapped Within

This leads us to the difference between Unconscious versus Permanent Soul Removal. This includes what we refer to as a "coma".

In the coma state, the body seems to be alive, yet there is very little outward response. The person usually does not walk, or speak. Yet the soul is often very much there.

This is always the question for those watching outside the person. Is she really there? Is the soul there? Will the physical body recover? These are difficult questions to answer. Yet we can provide some truths.

The soul may be fully within the body, and yet the operation of the body has malfunctioned. We know this from the stroke, where people have speech impairments. They are very much alive, and their soul is there, yet part of their brain has malfunctioned. This leads to problems with speech, and other areas of the mind unable to function.

The coma is a fuller extension of this process. The body is alive, and the soul is within the body. Yet much of the brain has malfunctioned, which results in many body functions unable to operate. Thus, the primary life systems are operational, yet walking and speaking are not possible.

Guiding the Person Out of the Coma, and What Emerges

There are indeed ways to guide a person out of their coma. We must first remember that most of their consciousness energies are stored within the subconscious region. Therefore, if the other regions of the body are not operational, and you get little response, then the person may have most of his soul and consciousness placed back into his subconscious mind.

This is also why it is difficult to reach the person in a coma. This means you have to reach deep into his subconscious mind. This can be done, as the person very likely can hear your voice; even if he cannot respond.

Similarly, many of the consciousness energies have become the independent clusters. These are self-aware clusters, with their own thoughts, and to a certain degree…specific aspects of our personality.

This is important to know, as we can access those specific areas of the mind. We talk not just to the person…but to those deep areas of the consciousness. We talk to the deep consciousness clusters, and to the subconscious itself. They will eventually respond.

Mel Blanc as Bugs Bunny

The most famous example is Mel Blanc. He was the voice of many characters, including Bugs Bunny. There was a time when he was in a coma, and was unresponsive for the longest time. The way out was when someone talked to him, as one of his characters. He responded, with the voice of Bugs Bunny. This was the first time he had spoken.

We can now understand this process. We now understand that the mind can create several independent clusters of consciousness. Each one of these clusters can have its own type of self-awareness; and a certain degree of independence. This is what allows us to have multiple voices in our minds. Yet it is also what allows novelists and actors to create their fully developed characters. This is what Mel Blanc had done.

Therefore, he had this multiple characters, as independent consciousness clusters within his mind. Furthermore, he had spent so much time as Bugs Bunny, that this character was…in many ways… closer to his soul than "himself" as Mel Blanc.

We can now understand what happened. His friends were at first talking to him as Mel Blanc. His ears heard, but this did not reach his brain. It was only when someone was joking around with his own version of the Buggs Bunny voice, that the body of Mel Blanc responded.

This means it was easier for the outside world to reach him through one of his primary characters (as the independent self-aware entities) than it was as the man without the characters.

This was the beginning, and after talking to him as with some of the characters he created…that the various characters in his mind began to fully emerge. They became "alive" in a way.

Thus, we could say that Bugs Bunny, and other characters he created I his life, were more in control of the Mel Blanc body, than the other Mel Blanc. Therefore, as they continue to talk to Bugs Bunny, and used their voices as his characters, those parts of him gradually woke up. These characters became more and more "alive". These characters were able to take command of the Mel Blanc body.

Soon enough, his body became fully awake, and fully functional. The Bugs Bunny identity was no longer needed, as Mel Blanc himself emerged. Yet it was essential to the process.

We can use this true story as an example, of how we may be able to access the deep consciousness, of anyone who is in a coma.

Past Lives and Coma Experiences

Related to the characters created by novelists and actors, are the actual past lives of a person. Remember that all of these past lives are stored as knowledge and memory, deep within the subconscious.

We may know of some of these past lives, and use the traits in our current life. Therefore, if the person is in a coma, and the outsiders know of his past lives, we can speak to him as in his past life. He may respond, if we address him as that person, and play videos from that era.

Also notice that the past lives may emerge, after the person has been brought out from the coma. This can include speaking different languages, or emerging with different character traits.

In one example, the woman woke up speaking with a British accent. This became her natural way of speaking. Yet she had never been to England, at least not in this lifetime. For the next several weeks, she could only speak with the British accent. We understand this because she had a past life in England, and this became her dominant personality.

The Soul Exists Within; He May Be Trapped Inside

As we finish this section, remember that the soul always exists within. The person may be unable to respond as he wants, yet he is there. Deep inside. He may be fully aware, or at least partially aware. And yet unable to speak clearly, or move his body as he wants.

The consciousness energies have become dormant. They are no longer moving. This means the programs are not operating. The boats of knowledge are not flowing. Nothing is operating.

It is as if an entire amusement park…has just shut down. All of the rides, all of the computer programs, all of the staff…shut down. Nothing is working, nothing is operating. This is essentially what is happening when the consciousness energies have become dormant.

Yet the soul still exists within the body. And many of the primary physical functions are still operating; as these programs are the deepest parts of the brain. However, those other programs, such as language and motor skills, are no longer operating. Those consciousness clusters have shut down. Therefore, some of the body is operating, but not all.

This is the state of the consciousness, when the mind has areas which are dormant. The person may also have some awareness, and thinking mind; yet inability to move or speak. This is a problem. The person does exist, his soul does reside in his body, and he most likely does have some awareness. And yet he cannot fully communicate this to those around him.

Notice also that this state of being is a spectrum. There can be several degrees of Dormant Consciousness Energies. There can also be varying locations of the dormant consciousness clusters. Therefore, we do find a variation of possibilities, in this general phase of dormant consciousness.

We refer to these stages of being, with terms such as "sleep paralysis"; "anesthesia induced"; "unconscious"; and "coma". All of these are variations of having some Dormant Consciousness Clusters, for periods of time which are longer than is standard.

When a person is in such a stage, always assume that his soul is there. Assume that he has some consciousness, some awareness, yet cannot communicate or move his body to show it. He wants you to know that he still exists. It therefore the responsibility of the friends outside his body, to find ways to prompt his body into response.

This primarily means finding methods to reawaken the dormant consciousness energies. Methods include: constant touch; shaking; hard physical touch; ice on skin; acupuncture needles; mild shocks; playing favorite music; and talking to him about his significant interests.

These are the main methods which will induce the consciousness energies to be stimulated enough to be fully operational. Also, sometimes the problem exists as neural damage; and methods such as mild shocks to the arm, or using acupuncture, and stimulate the electrical process.

*Always consider that the Soul remains within the body, during these times of dormant consciousness. He is alive and thinking, yet cannot do much else. Therefore, we must try everything we can, to reawaken the dormant consciousness in those other areas, and bring him back to life.

When Body is Self-Sufficient, the Person Exists

We must note that there is a variation of Dormant Consciousness. This is because the are many areas of the brain, as well as throughout the body, which have consciousness energies. Any one of these regions may have dormant consciousness energies, while other areas are functional.

We have been talking mostly about the partial dormant consciousness, which means the main functions of the body are operational. This is very important, because as long as there are self-sufficient physical functions, then we know that some of the physical body is still operational.

And if those functions are still operational, this means that the soul itself continues to reside in the body. The person still exists. And we must do everything we can to ensure that he wakes from this type of sleep.

Note on Full Dormant Consciousness: Physical Death

We must, however, mention the possible reality of physical death. This is from the Full Dormant Consciousness.

When all of the processes of the physical body have ceased to function, then this is Full Dormant Consciousness. There is the difference. As long as the person has self-sufficient body functions, then he has some of his consciousness operational; and this means that his soul still resides in the body. He still exists.

However, when the main body functions are no longer self-sufficient, it is then that we likely have Full Dormant Consciousness. This includes breathing and heart pumping. Those primary functions should always be self-sufficient. If these operations are not functioning, then it is very likely that the other areas of consciousness will not be operational either.

Therefore, no heart pulse; and no breathing; combined with no other body parts moving; and complete inability to speak; then it is likely that the consciousness has become fully dormant.

Alignment of Mind, Soul, and Body

Your Existence as a Free Soul is a combination of Soul and Mind. Then, while on earth, your Existence is a combination of Mind, Soul, and Body. Therefore, it is best if we can Align the three together.

The basic objective is to become the Master of each of those components; and then the Master of those Components in Combination.

This begins with Alignment of the Mind. This means the alignment of all areas of your consciousness energies. Become the master of those first, and you can generally become master of the others.

We can then align the various aspects of the soul, into one soul entity, yet able to flow in ways that we desire. We can call forth specific soul traits at various moments, and tame the others that become too strong.

Alignment of the body is in many ways the first…and the last. This is because most humans while on earth are more aware of their body than either their soul or consciousness. Therefore, those humans should learn to align all aspects of their physical body in good health. And remember, all body parts are connected together, and therefore what affects one area will often soon affect the other areas.

This alignment of the physical body mechanics will also lead to easier operation of the alignment of mind and soul; as your body will give you the physical vitality needed to perform the mind and soul operations. Yet, at the same time, the mastery of the mind and soul…will also create very real physical improvements in the physical body.

Therefore, again…we must learn to Align the Mind, Soul, and Body. We must maintain mastery over each component. We must also align all of these components, to work together for optimum existence of being.

Aligning and Maintaining your Self-Aware Clusters (overview)

We must first learn to align the Self-Aware Consciousness Clusters. There are many such entities in our mind, and in the body. Each of them has their own programs, knowledge, and desires. They also have different degrees of strength, and various desires for compliance vs independence.

Thus, it really is a large organization, with many directors and staff within. We created them, we desired them. Now it is time to align them and manage them. Manage the Entities within.

The Meaning of "Alignment"

For the purposes of this discussion, the term "alignment" means to have all aspects of the system working together.

The mind, soul, and body, are complex systems; individually and as one organization. Thus, we want everything to work together, as desired, in any moment. Whatever it is we desire, whether Core Desires or actions of the moment, these must be aligned effectively. All components will work together, as effectively as possible. This is your Alignment.

Thus, we refer to Alignment as having all systems to work together easily and effectively, without any complications arising unexpectedly.

We then provide three subset categories of Alignment. These are as follows: 1) alignment of organizational hierarchy; 2) Knowing the Roles; and 3) Understanding of the missions.

1) <u>Alignment of Organizational Hierarchy</u>

The first aspect of Alignment is for the Organizational Hierarchy. All large organizations need a clear system for roles and responsibilities. This must begin with making it clear that YOU are the BOSS.

Remember that YOU are GOD. This is your realm. You are the creator of each entity. Therefore, you…are…God. Always maintain your position of God over your realm. Make sure that all other entities know that you are their God, and they must comply with Your Desires.

You will then establish their roles, and maintain your God Authority.

2) <u>Knowing the Roles</u>

After you get all of your Entities to accept this, then it is for you to make their roles very clear. You will be clear on their specific functions.

You will give them the parameters for their independent operations, versus submitting to you. Remember that sometimes their independence is good, as they will provide services without you asking; and come up with some very creative ideas. Yet they must also know how far they can go, on their own, before asking their God first. They must also know when they should report their ideas, and their finished products.

Thus, the second aspect of Aligning the Consciousness Entities, is to be very clear on the specific functions and operating parameters, for each of these self-aware entities within.

3) Understanding their Missions

The third area of Alignment is for all areas to understand their Missions. This is similar to the roles, yet it is much grander scale.

Every department in an organization needs to have a clear mission statement. Every company needs an overall mission statement. (This can also be several mission statements, for different aspects of Existence).

These Missions must be clear. Notice that we must first be clear, in our own selves. For each major topic of our existence, we want to be very clear in our soul exactly what we desire. We must be clear exactly what we want in our lives, every day, in this topic area.

We must be very clear on these core desires first, before we can create the mission statements for any of our staff within. This, is often the most difficult process….and is usually refined through experience.

Yet once you are clear…absolutely clear…on your Core Desires for each topic area of life…it is then that you will write this down. You write it down for your thinking mind.

Then you repeat it, often, to your Entities within. You will also repeat these to your Deep Subconscious, and to your Subconscious. Repeat, repeat, repeat…these Mission Statements…these Core Desires of your Existence…until every Conscious Entity within your mind fully understands their primary goals for your existence.

Alignment of the Soul

The Advanced Being will naturally have a very complex Soul Alchemy. He is not just one trait. He is many traits. He is very complex.

As such, the Soul of the Advanced Being will naturally be a complex mixture of soul alchemy. Furthermore, the amount of these energies, will always be very strong, within this Advanced Being. Therefore, what we find in the Advanced Being is a highly complex soul alchemy, with multiple traits and desires, all of which are very strong.

Yet we must learn to manage these various soul energies. We must be able to allow these energies to flow as desired, yet also keep them in alignment as much as possible.

Note that the main complication is not from within, but from the environment. Where the environment allows complete freedom, as the Divine Intended, then this will be easy. It is only when the surrounding environment is managed by lesser beings, who do not understand Advanced Beings, or understand the true desires of Great Divine, that the Being who Knows…will develops fragmentation in the soul.

The best solution is for the Advanced Beings to take full command and control of their society. The policies and beliefs of the community should be set in place those who truly understand Divine; especially Freedom and the Life Force. We must then prohibit the lesser mortals from having control over our lives. They do not have the mental ability to understand.

Alignment of Soul and Mind

The next stage is to align the Soul and the Mind. This means aligning all aspects of the soul; and aligning all the aspects of the consciousness, in ways that work together. We want all systems to work together easily and effectively, without any complications arising unexpectedly.

The ideal is to have only One Soul, with One Main Consciousness. This is the best way to Exist. Therefore, our goal is always to have just one soul, fully integrated with all areas of consciousness energies.

If your subconscious forced a split of your soul, and created new characters; then you need to do the work to put them back together. This can be done by "encouraging" each character to merge with the others.

However, you must promise to let that character out and play, however. Otherwise this personality character will emerge on her own; and when you least expect it.

Another option is to harness these individual characters, and use them as desired. Remember, they are all you…just different versions of you.

Related to this, is deliberately creating different characters, and giving them job titles or names. This allows you to be the maximum of that aspect of your personality, without thinking about the others.

As a final note: It is not always necessary to have different self-aware souls within; you can simply have different aspects of yourself, which come out at different times.

Frequent Alignment Adjustments as We Advance

The best method for Alignment, is to make these adjustments as we experience life. Whenever we create a new self-aware entity, make sure it is aligned with the entire system. Whenever we develop strong emotions in a specific area, take some moments to align it with the system.

We are always learning and growing. We are acquiring consciousness energies and soul energies, throughout our Eternal Existence. We create self-aware entities, and gain knowledge. Therefore, we should often take the time…to focus on integrating and aligning these…as they arrive.

If we do this regularly, then we will be able to maintain our alignment more easily. These regular Alignment Adjustments will be the way to maintain inner peace and clarity, for our ongoing existence.

Master The Components of Your Existence

We must learn to become the Masters of our Existence. This means that we must be the Master of each of our components. We are the wise leaders, over ourselves. This is the only way to be content in our lives.

Learn to Control the Chaos Within

It is clear from our previous discussion that we have multiple components. The most important of these are Soul, Mind, and Body. We must therefore become Full Masters over each component.

Yet we also understand that there are often multiple Self-Aware Entities within the mind; each of which wants to control the system. We must therefore learn to manage all of these. It is when we do not fully control these Entities, that chaos is created in the mind. We must learn to manage all such entities, and control the chaos within.

The best method is to allow each component to enjoy its full existence, yet in the most effective ways. We allow each component to exist and express itself fully; yet only during the times and methods of our choosing.

In this way, we allow all aspects ourselves to be fully expressed, and to maintain full satisfaction, in the overall balance of our lives. We must be fully authentic, and be fully free, to be content and happy.

Managing Your Soul, Mind, and Body

Each component must be fully expressed and exercised. This is necessary for optimum health of all components. Yet these components can have their own whims, and take priority depending on the needs of the moment. We can sometimes allow this; if managed wisely.

We can indeed allow the free expression of each Entity, and each aspect of our Soul. We can also use our distinct components for specific purposes; which can be very beneficial. Yet ultimately…our CEO Mind will bring all the pieces together again. Our CEO Mind must set the rules.

We must always walk through our Existence, fully whole and content. Use each component as appropriate; yet ensure that all components work together in a peaceful way. This is the True Mastery over our Existence.

Chapter 4:
Emotions of Advanced Souls

Introduction

In addition to discussing the Intelligence of Advanced Beings, we must also discus the Emotions of Advanced Beings. In fact, the Emotional Development is often more important than the Intellectual Development.

Most of our discussions will clarify the distinctions between Emotions of the Soul, versus Emotions of the Body. These distinctions are very important, if we truly want to manage our various emotions properly.

Further note that there are two forms of Emotions of the body: the Chemical Responses, and the Subconscious Programmed Responses. We must learn to manage all forms of our emotions, and our thoughts, if we desire to become an Advanced Being.

Soul Emotions vs Body Emotions

Emotions can be categorized into two basic types: the Emotions of the Soul, and the Emotions of the Body.

The Emotions of the Soul exist as variations in our Soul Alchemy. In contrast, Emotions of the Soul exist as chemical reactions and our subconscious programming.

The Emotions of the Soul are far deeper, and much more stable. We must therefore develop the Emotions of the Soul; while carefully managing the chemical responses in the physical body.

The Soul as Existing in a Biological System

Always remember that we are a dual system. We are primarily a soul, and this soul exists for eternity. Yet our soul if often placed into a biological system, which we call the physical body.

These two systems exist at the same time. Therefore, it is natural that there are two systems of emotions, at the same time.

The emotions of the soul are created by the soul energies. These soul emotions are more deliberate and therefore long-term. In contrast, the emotions of the body are created by chemicals; and can therefore be driven by numerous uncontrolled factors.

Main Concepts of Each Emotional Source

Learn to understand the source of each of your emotions; at any moment; and manage accordingly. The following information will provide the main concepts, regarding each of the sources for emotions.

Soul Emotions

The Soul Emotions are part of your Soul Alchemy. These are the deepest emotions, and most stable. When you love from the soul, this love remains forever. When you find joy in your soul, for a specific activity, that form of pleasure is always a deep part of your identity.

Making adjustments in your Soul Alchemy requires more deliberate action; and this is usually based on profound experiences.

Chemical Emotions

The Chemical Emotions are the emotions which are created as chemical production inside the body. The effect is similar to taking large amounts of drugs. The effects can be instantaneous, and overwhelming.

The stimulation of these chemical emotions is usually from the various hormones emitted by other people in the area. This leads to passionate sexual attraction; head-over-heels type of love; and other emotions.

These chemical emotions are usually temporary; which means we can easily manage the unwanted chemical emotions with counter-actions.

Yet when these chemicals produce pleasure, we seek those same events which stimulate production of the drug again. This can be very good, or can cause long-term harm; choose wisely.

*Always know that your chemical emotions can be managed, whether to increase or decrease; each one as desires. It is your choice as to how to manage each chemical emotion.

Subconscious Emotions

The Subconscious Emotions are those produced based on deep programming. We have programmed our subconscious to automatically produce specific chemicals, based on certain cues. This is automatic, and our emotions will often ramp up based on a visual or spoken phrase.

This is often referred to as "trigger", and becoming "irrational". Therefore it is best if we do the work to eliminate such responses. Our minds will remain clear, and our responses will be more rational.

Soul Emotions

The Soul Emotions are the deepest, and will be most permanent. The emotions of the soul require the most effort to alter, and therefore any adjustments will be long-lasting.

Note that the truly Advanced Beings will place their emotions in their Soul Alchemy. It is from their deepest soul, that these Advanced Beings will operate their emotions. These Advanced Beings may also have their own subconscious emotions and chemical response emotions; yet the Soul Alchemy Emotions will always be their primary emotional base.

Alignment of Soul Alchemy Emotions

The Soul Emotions are influenced by external events, but only in the form of Alignment. When the emotions of another person are in alignment with your soul, then you will feel this emotional alignment. This is felt with the closest of friendships, and when listening to favorite music.

The Soul Emotions can also be out of sync with others. You can recognize this immediately. This can happen with your friends when you are not in alignment. More often, it happens when with a person or situation which is completely wrong for your soul alchemy.

Empaths and Soul Emotions

The Empath has difficulty with all of this, because the Empath feels everyone's soul emotions. Everything gets mixed in with his own soul. It is for this reason, he has a difficult time separating his own soul emotions from those of everyone in his environment.

Chemical Emotions

The Chemical Emotions are those emotions which are induced by chemicals in the body. Most of these chemicals are hormones of some type; which are automatically produced according to stimulus.

These chemicals can be influenced by many factors, including the chemicals in the environment. This is primarily due to the various hormones which are produced by others, and emitted into the air.

This often induces feeling of sexual attraction and a type of love. This can also induce variations of fear and anger. All of this is chemically induced, usually by chemicals emitted by other people.

The Subconscious and Glands as Producers of Chemicals

Also note that the production for many of these chemicals is directed by the subconscious, or one of the glands. Therefore, how we manage these areas can greatly influence our chemically induced emotions.

Chemical Emotions as Drug Stimulants

Large productions of these chemicals in the body can be equivalent to taking large amounts of drugs. Indeed, these chemicals are stimulants. And many times, the amount of chemical stimulants created in the body automatically…will overwhelm the mind.

This is what transforms the person into a type of drug addict; and who is hyper focused on just one activity. This is what results in the passionate sex; the deep desire to call your boyfriend; as well as irrational moments of insecurity. All of these situations are based on the large amounts of "drugs" in your body; as produced within your own body.

This is also what gets two people to become addicted to each other. This type of love is an addition. This type of desire for passionate sex, can be similar to a drug addiction. You crave that chemical high. You crave that euphoria of the pleasure drugs produced within the body. Therefore, you seek the same experiences, with the same partners, again and again.

*Note that this type of drug-like addiction is different from the desires in the soul. There is a difference when two people feel that deep love from their souls. The sexual pleasures are also different; as the sexual pleasures derive as much from the soul as from the stimulants in the body.

Reactionary Emotions and Responses

Notice that these emotional responses are reactionary. This means that your emotions at this moment, as based on your chemical stimulants, are in reaction to your immediate environment.

These emotions are not "you" in the deepest sense; though they can be enhanced versions of your natural self. This means…you always have the choice…on how you take actions based on your reactionary chemical emotions. Thus, your production of chemicals is automatic, but your next actions, based on those chemicals, is your own choice.

This may be something you desire, such as the sexual attraction. You will then give into the desires, and enjoy the pleasures. In this case, the chemical reaction to the environment is exactly what you wanted. Indeed, the external stimulus was encouraged specifically for this purpose.

However, if the chemical reaction is not desired, then you do not have to act on it. These examples include the chemical emotions of insecurity, jealousy, fear, and anger. These chemical emotions may be stimulated, yet you do not have to respond as those emotions. Instead, walk away, get some exercise, listen to music…and eventually those chemicals will pass away through the body. You are clean and peaceful once more.

Temporary versus Encouraged, for the Chemical Emotions

Notice also that these Chemical Emotions are naturally temporary. These are produced only based on certain external stimulus. It is your choice to encourage the continuous production of these chemical emotions, or to let these chemicals pass through your system.

For example, when you are feeling that fear and anger, there is no need to encourage it. Just get some exercise and let the chemicals pass through the system. The chemicals will soon be gone, and your emotions will be as clear as before. Yet if you continue to hold onto those emotions, and encourage your body to produce those chemicals, then will continue to get more of the same. This is always your choice.

Yet we can also encourage desired emotions. Those chemicals which give us feelings of joy, love, and pleasure…we can encourage those chemicals to be produced. When we eat well, play with friends, and enjoy our favorite pleasures; we are encouraging the daily production of the desired chemicals. In this case, also know that the good chemicals are temporary, and do our daily pleasures to encourage production.

Subconscious Emotions

There is a third area of emotions we must discuss, which is the subconscious programming of emotional response. The subconscious mind has many deep operating programs. Some of these deep programs are the Emotional Responses to specific stimulus.

This means, when a person hears a specific phrase, or sees a specific event, his subconscious mind automatically engages in the emotional response program. The person will feel strong emotions, which are very similar to previous experiences.

All of this happens automatically, without any active thinking. The program is embedded, and the response is automatic.

It is for this reason that we must be very careful to manage any of our automatic emotional responses. Indeed, we should do the work necessary to eliminate many of those automatic responses; as this removal of response programs will provide stability and clarity.

Consciousness Energies and Emotions

The Emotions of the Soul can be changed with a type of deliberate choice. This is not a choice in the mind, but it is indeed a "conscious" choice, as the consciousness energies flow between soul and body.

Remember that our consciousness energies can exist anywhere, and flow anywhere. These consciousness energies can flow into the soul, as well as into the mind.

Notice also that the consciousness energies can be not just ideas, but deep emotions. Therefore, the deeper consciousness energies, of a strong emotion, can enter the soul and alter the soul alchemy.

Also notice, at the same time, these consciousness energies of emotions will enter the subconscious, and alter the subconscious programming. This is how the deepest of emotional experiences can make permanent alterations in the soul and the subconscious.

Ride the Bronco of Emotions

Living with your emotions is similar to riding a wild bronco. Your emotions are wild; and for this reason, will often seem to throw your inner world completely into chaos. You are riding a wild bronco of emotions; and you are allowing this untamed beast throw you around.

This is no way to live. Having emotions is of course a large part of being human. However, you must manage your emotions, rather than letting your emotions control your destiny.

Separate from You, yet Under Your Control

Your Emotions are very similar to the Bronco. In both cases, there seems to be an entity, which is separate from you, and operating under its own control. This is why you can be thrown of the Bronco; as animal and as emotions. The bucking bronco seems to be independent of you, and acting in ways which are not under your full control.

Yet you can learn to ride the Bronco. And you can learn to ride your emotions. You can learn how to live with the beast within. You can also learn how to tame it; and only unleash the powers when desired.

Riding the Bronco: Adjusting to the Motions

You must learn to Ride the Bronco of Emotions. This means, you must learn to co-exist with your emotions; without letting your emotions throw you. This is very similar to riding the real Bronco.

Whether it is the real animal, or the Bronco of Emotions, the goal is ride smoothly, with the beast.

With the real bronco, the animal will have a variety of ways of moving. All of these motions are designed to throw you off and into the dirt. But you won't let that happen. You learn every nuance of the bronco's motions. You feel where those motions are going; and you learn to shift along with them. In this way, you learn to ride along with the motions of the bronco, rather than being surprised by them.

The Emotional Bronco is similar. As these powerful emotions come up, they will try to throw you from your stable position. Yet you will not let that happen. You will learn to ride with your bucking emotional bronco. Adjust with the nuances of the beast, and you will never be thrown again.

How to Ride the Bucking Bronco of Emotions

Learning to Ride your Emotional Bronco is one of the most important of practical skills you should acquire. This is because if you are unable to ride the beast within, you will always be thrown off your steady position. You will be at the mercy of your emotions. Yet when you learn to ride with your Emotional Bronco, you can now enjoy your human experience, with the variety of emotions; without being thrown from your path.

The process of riding the Emotional Bronco is to feel the nuances of your emotions. Learn every nuance of how the emotions will flow in your body. Learn the patterns of your automatic responses; in your mind and your body. Then make your conscious adjustments. Know how to move your physical body; and to change your thoughts.

This is how you will ride your Emotional Bronco. You will first learn the nuances of the emotional feelings and patterns. You will learn the automatic responses. Then you will adjust your own body and mind; in a very conscious way; to ride those emotions without being thrown.

With practice, you will learn to ride your emotions. It does not matter what emotions arise, or how strong they are, you will know how to feel the nuances, and adjust accordingly. Your mind and body will adjust to the bucking motions; and the beast will never throw you again.

Taming the Beast Within
Yet Using the Powers on Command

The ultimate mastery of emotions is to be able to Tame the Beast Within. This means you will experience more of the emotions you desire; and fewer of the emotions you do not want. Yet at the same time, we can learn to harness our darker emotions for powering desired actions.

Taming the Beast Within

The human experience is to have a Beast Within. This is the bucking bronco, as described above. This beast is wild and untamed. We must learn to ride with the beast, without being thrown. Then, we learn to tame the beast. The beast now works with us, and works for us.

Taming this Beast Within is an important practical skill. You must learn to tame this Beast, no matter how many lifetimes it takes. It is only through taming of your inner beast, that you will be on the path to Advanced Being.

There are many practical methods for Taming the Beast. However, these methods must all begin with you. It is your conscious choice, it is your desire to tame the beast, that is most important. When you are ready, then you can seek the mentors to guide you through the process.

The most effective methods include: Changing your Thoughts; Reprogramming the Subconscious; and Harnessing the Energies.

Harnessing the Darker Emotions

Note that taming of the beast within, does not always mean complete elimination of those unwanted emotions. Rather, we are learning how to harness those emotions.

We store those "negative emotions" as a type of fuel, which we will use later. This is like nuclear pellets; we can use for either great power or terrible destruction. This what we can do when we can do with our emotions. We can actually harness our darker emotions, for great powers.

This includes Physical Strength; Bravery; Risk-Taking; and Sexuality. All of these types of Powers require some amount of "Darker Emotions" as our fuel. Therefore, we want to keep those darker emotions. They can be useful. However, we will learn to harness those darker emotions in the best ways. We can store these energies, to use on command.

Personal Desires vs Rationality

We must note that there is a difference between Personal Desires and Rationality. The Personal Desires do not necessarily need to be rational. Your desires come from your soul. Your desires come also from your subconscious; and your physical needs. Therefore, your Personal Desires are acceptable, and yet do not need to be rational.

The basic rule of the universe here is simple. If your soul desires it, then you can have it. If it makes you happy and brings you pleasure, then you can do it. There is no need to put rationality into the process.

However, the "rationality" will come when deciding how to obtain those desires. You can be rational, when determining when and where to enjoy your desires. You can also be rational on best methods to obtain those desires, given your realities.

Note also that rationality comes into the process when involving others. This is the other part of the rule of the universe: Never harm another person, while obtaining your own personal desires. Therefore, we use our rationality (as well as empathy), to determine how to obtain and enjoy all of our personal desires; while harming the fewest people in the process.

Rationality to Over-Ride the Automated Systems

Rationality can also be used to over-ride your automated emotions. These automated systems come from either the chemicals in the body, or from the subconscious. You can over-ride both systems.

For the chemical emotions, the first step is to realize that these emotions (and physical effects) are the automatic responses to your environment. When your mind knows this, then you can use your rational mind to ignore the impulses. You will take actions which channel these chemical emotions in safer ways.

You can also do the same with your subconscious emotions. Many of your emotions are produced from subconscious programming. When you recognize this process is happening, you will use your Rational Mind to over-ride the system.

This over-ride process is similar to being the engineer in a control room. The automated systems may do one thing; but you always have the option to use your thinking mind, to over-ride the automated systems.

Zen and Stoicism

Always remember that your emotions and thoughts can be managed. Some of these may be automatic, and in response to the environment. Yet you can always learn to Ride or Channel the internal turmoil. You are in control. You always have been in control; and always will be.

However, this requires guidance and practice. This requires training and discipline. Eventually this will become very easy; yet in the beginning, this requires guidance and a type of spiritual path.

Two of the most effective paths, for being the Master of your thoughts and emotions, are Zen and Stoicism. Both are similar, in that they teach you how to live in this world while maintaining your clarity.

Learning to Experience Events with Composure

These paths do not deny the realities of the world, but rather provide methods for interacting with the world in a way that will not throw you. Using these teachings, you will be able to experience any unexpected event, and maintain a certain level of composure.

Note also that these teachings do not deny emotions; rather the teachings will train you to channel each emotion in optimum ways. You choose which emotions and thoughts to experience most, as well as your physical response. You will become calm and content, in any storm.

Follow the Paths of Zen and Stoicism for Self-Mastery

Therefore, if you know that you are often thrown by your emotions, then follow the teachings of Zen and Stoicism. Similarly, if you find yourself living in fear, jealousy, and anger; then follow the teachings of Zen and Stoicism. If you feel as if the Bronco is always throwing you around, instead of you riding with the beast...then Zen and Stoicism is the path you need. These methods will guide you, to become in full control, of all your thoughts, and all your emotions.

You will then be on your path...to becoming the True Master of your Existence.

Rule as a King of Your Own Self

We must always manage our thoughts and emotions. It is acceptable to have a range of emotions; and it is natural to have a variety of thoughts. However, we must rule over our emotions; we must never let our emotions rule over us. Always be the King of your emotions, never the slave.

Claim your Emotional Kingdom. Claim your Thoughts and your Mind. When you are able to do this, and you are the Supreme Emperor over your own thoughts and emotions, then you are on the path to True Mastery of your Existence.

Become the Ruler of your Inner Kingdom.

Chapter 5:
The Meaning of Life

Overview

What is the Meaning of Life? What is the Purpose of our Existence? These are the deepest questions for any man to ask. We will now answer these questions. In the following pages, the reader will discover the definitive answers, to all questions, related to the Meaning of Life.

Topics Within the Meaning of Life

Note that the phrase "Meaning of Life" has two distinct definitions. Both are essential to the fundamental understanding of our existence.

The first topic is "What does it mean to be alive?" There are four distinct categories of being alive, each of which are distinct from the others. We will discuss these categories in detail.

The second topic is "What is the Purpose of Life?" This is the classic question of why are we here on this earth? Why do we exist? How do I find focus and meaning in my life? There are definite answers to these questions, which we will explain in this chapter.

This leads us to the topic of Designing Our World. If we want to have the best experiences here on earth, then we must design our world for those experiences. We must design our societies, to be specifically based on the Universal Purpose of Existence. This topic is important, and will guide us into the next phase of human evolution.

Separate Book on the Meaning of Life

Before we discuss the answers to these profound questions, we must emphasize the importance of the separate book on this topic.

The answers provided in this chapter are concise, for the purposes of this book. However, the answers to these profound questions are more fully explored in the book "The Meaning of Life". We highly recommend reading that book. It is one of the few books you will ever need, as a practical guide for creating your best life.

Categories of Life

What does it mean to be Alive? Many of us believe we know the answer intuitively. But do we really know the answer? In truth, the reality of "being alive" are more complex than most people realize.

This is significant, because we must expand our understanding of what it means to be alive. We must realize that there are several ways to be alive, each of which are independent of the other meanings. Thus, an entity can be alive in one or two of the meanings, but not the others.

Complexity of Alive as Fundamental Categories

There are numerous aspects of being alive. However, most of these are actually specialized details of Fundamental Categories. These Fundamental Categories of Being Alive are as follows:

1. Divine Soul   (as Eternally Alive)
2. Self-Awareness   (as Mentally Alive)
3. Dynamic Physical Form   (as Physically Alive)
4. Inner Light   (as Joyfully Alive)

Therefore, we can define an entity as "being alive" based on these fundamental categories. Each of these fundamental categories is distinct, as an entity can be alive in one or more categories, and yet not in others.

Furthermore, all other "criteria" for "being alive" are actually just specific details within one of these fundamental categories.

*Note that the details of these categories are fully described in the book: "The Meaning of Life". In that book, we explain the specific physical details, for each of the categories.

Interactions of the Fundamental Categories

We can also appreciate the four fundamental categories of being alive, when we begin to see the possible interactions between the categories.

For example, the human has the potential for all four categories. He is an eternal soul; with self-aware consciousness; in a living physical body. He can also activate his Inner Light, and enjoy being joyfully alive. Thus, the human has the potential for being alive in all these ways.

However, these are distinct categories. It is possible to have some of the categories for being alive, yet not others.

For example, many people lack the inner light, and therefore are not joyfully alive. Yet they are physically alive. Their souls also remain in the physical body. Thus, they are alive in some ways, but not others.

We then have sleeping mental states, such as hypnosis, anesthesia, and coma. In these states, part of the mind is shut down; yet the main physical body is operational. The soul also remains in the body. Thus, again, the person is alive in some ways, but not others.

Then there are the metaphysical beings. These are beings of soul and consciousness, without the traditional physical body. These beings are fully alive in soul, mind, and inner light; yet their previous body is not living.

Therefore, we can begin to understand the interactions between the fundamental categories. Each of these fundamental categories for being alive is distinct; and must be considered independently.

The Universal Purpose of Life

Who am I? Why I am here? What is the meaning of life? These are the deepest questions of our existence. Many people spend their lives searching for the answers, with varying degrees of success.

Therefore, we will clearly explain the Purpose of Life. We will provide the answer to these important questions. It is important that you understand the answers early in life, as this will allow you make the most of your time.

Purpose of Life: Universal and Specific

We must first understand that the Purpose of Life is divided into two categories: Universal Purpose, and Specific Purpose.

The Universal Purpose of Life applies to all souls who come to this earth. The Specific Purposes apply to each specific soul. Yet the specific purposes, for each soul, will always exist within the Universal Purpose.

The Universal Purpose of Life

There is indeed a Universal Purpose of Life. There is indeed a Meaning of Life, which is the overall meaning for all souls. It is this Universal Purpose which we will focus on in this book.

The Universal Purpose of Life is to Explore, Experience, and Evolve. This is the purpose of life. This is the meaning of our existence, in any form. The Purpose is always to Explore, Experience, and Evolve.

Exploration

We begin with Exploration. This is exploration of ideas and activities; the exploration of places and possibilities. It is also the exploration of relationships…and of ourselves. We are meant to explore all things.

Notice also that our exploration never ends. There are infinite topics to learn, and many places to see. There are many possible activities to experience; and experience multiple times if desired. The world is large, and the universe is infinite. Therefore, we will always have something new to explore. We will always have something exciting to do or learn.

Experiences

We then have Experiences. We exist to experience; and it is through our experiences that we know we exist. We experience many things to know we are alive; and it is through these experiences we feel that we are truly living. Therefore, to be Experiencing is to be Living.

We experience our existence through each aspect of our Alive Categories. This means we experience with our Soul, Mind, and Body. We use each of these, individually and together, in each of our experiences.

Thus, as we are living and experience, we are interacting with the reality…using the Eternal Soul, the Consciousness, and the Physical Body. And if we are enjoying it, then we are also activating the Inner Light.

Life as Amusement Park

This life is very much an Amusement Park. We are here to explore the many rides, and experience each one. Yet the park is infinite, and we have limited time. Therefore, we must look around and make choices. We will choose the experiences we desire; and live those experiences.

This Amusement Park is also dynamic and interactive. This means that we can create some of the experiences ourselves. Furthermore, enjoying some experiences will lead to others…and to others…and to others.

Therefore, this life is a dynamic and interactive amusement park. There are infinite options of experiences. We choose the main desired experiences, which we co-create. We also allow the dynamic nature of the park to lead us to each future experience. It is an exciting journey!

Evolving: The Existential Transformation

The third aspect of the Universal Purpose of Existence…is to Evolve. This applies to our Eternal Soul and Mind, as well as our life here on earth. We are always evolving, to become better and wiser than before.

This process can be summarized as "Existential Transformation". With every experience and exploration, we are transformed.

Specifically, whenever we explore and experience, we also learn and evolve. It is therefore through the actual living fully our existence that we are transformed. This process occurs naturally. Furthermore, when we are transformed, our soul and mind exist at a completely different level.

This is the process of Existential Transformation; and it is essential to our eternal evolution. Indeed, this is one of the reasons that we are here on this earth: to choose the experiences which will help us transform most significantly. The wise man seeks those experiences which challenge him, precisely so that he can evolve to the greatest levels of existence.

Universal Purpose of Existence in Context of Eternal Being

Therefore, we can now understand the Universal Purpose of Existence. This Universal Purpose is to Explore, Experience, and Evolve. This Purpose applies not just to your specific life on earth, but to all forms of your Eternal Existence. As an Eternal Soul, you exist to explore and experience; which brings you great joy; and also transforms your being.

We must then see our life here on earth in this context. We will explore and experience as much as we can. We must be selective, as the options are infinite, yet our time here is limited. We choose our main desires, and are co-creator for most of our experiences. Yet we are also guided and led to other experiences and explorations.

In all aspects, we are to enjoy the experiences, and learn from our explorations. During these events, our souls and minds will be permanently transformed, to greater and greater levels. This is the Universal Purpose of Existence, in context of your specific life on earth.

Your Specific Purpose

The Specific Purpose is the Purpose for your individual life. This specific purpose is for you only. It is your soul which has this purpose. You will discover this Specific Purpose, and pursue it fully.

Notice that all souls on earth have the same Universal Purpose, yet each soul has its own specific purpose while on earth. Therefore, all of us are here to Explore, Experience, and Evolve. Yet each of us has our own specific purpose. This is yours alone, and you must dedicate yourself to it.

Specific Purpose as Motivation, Passion, and Fuel

There are many ways to know of your Specific Purpose. The best method is knowing your passions. When you are fully engaged in your Specific Purpose, you will become filled with Motivation and Fuel.

When you find this Specific Purpose, you are excited about it. You want to do it. Just thinking about gives you pleasure. And when you are doing it...you can be doing it for many hours...without losing interest.

You wake up in the morning fully excited! You are ready for all the fun pleasures that are coming today. You know you will be engaged in one of your most favorite activities. This becomes the motivation for your life.

You are motivated. You have anticipation. Your mind generates thoughts and ideas. Yes...this is your internal motivation. This is your pleasure. This is your passion. That is how you know that you have truly found your Life Purpose. You are excited and motivated for it.

Notice also that when you are in your purpose, the challenges are barely noticed. The physical and mental challenges, the scrapes and mistakes, the obstacles that appear...these have no effect on your soul.

Despite any obstacle or challenge, you want to be there. You want to continue. The pleasure you get from the project is far greater than any possible challenge. Indeed, you become better at your craft because of these challenges. When you feel this way, you are truly in your purpose.

The Focused Path

There are several practical aspects to this Path of Certainty. This includes choosing the path, and staying on this path.

Knowing your Specific Life Purpose provides you with the clear direction. This provides you with your identity, your self-concept. This also provides you with the life mission…who you are and what you do.

This knowing also keeps you focused. Instead of wandering down different paths, you will keep focused on your Life Purpose. You know that those other paths are not for you, and will only waste your energies. Thus, when there are choices in life, you know to align your decision with your life purpose. Knowing your purpose allows to make the clear choices.

Confidence in Your Life Purpose

When you know your true life purpose, deep in your soul and mind, it is then that you have absolute confidence. And when you have this level of confidence in yourself and in your path, then you will be the powerful creator of your destiny. You will be able to live fully, and be able to create anything you desire, as aligned with the path.

This confidence in the self and in the purpose is also extremely powerful. This confidence is very attractive. Indeed, when you know your purpose with this level of certainty, you will have such clarity and determination. It is who you are, and it is your destiny. You will always be fully confident in the life you create. Along the way, you will be able to attract enthusiastic partners, and create many wonders for the world.

One Life Purpose Above All

We can have more than one Life Purpose, with a maximum of 3 at any one time. This allows us to explore and express each aspect of our deepest soul. Our Life Purposes can also change in phases of life.

However, there is almost always the One Purpose Above All. This One Purpose provides the greatest clarity and the greatest joy. You will put your entire life…your entire being…into this purpose.

This becomes your One Life Purpose…Above All Others. It is your most powerful fuel for life, and your strongest desire in this world.

Designing Our World for the Universal Purpose

The Universal Purpose Life is to Explore, Experience, and Evolve. This is the reason for our Eternal Existence. It is also the reason for each of our specific lifetimes on this earth. Therefore, the societies and systems of the earth must be fully designed to encourage the Universal Purpose.

We must also design our societies for the specific life purposes of all people who come to earth. This means we must allow maximum freedom. This freedom is essential for each person to experience his unique life purpose, and therefore to evolve. This is the future of civilization.

The Divine Way for the New Societies

We must Design our Earthly Societies according to the Divine System. This includes Aligning our Societies with the Purpose of Life, as discussed above. This also includes establishing the Foundation of our Societies to be according to the Divine Way of Existence.

In simpler terms, this means we establish the "rules" and "norms" of our society to match the True Divine Way. It is essential that we design all aspects of our societies to be perfectly matched with the Divine Way of Being. This how we are meant to exist. This will bring the greatest joy, prosperity, and peace for all.

The 3 Rules of the Divine Way

The Divine Way has very simple rules. There are only 3 Rules to the Divine Way of Existence. These are few in number, yet must be adhered to with absolute devotion. These Rules of the Divine Way are:

1. Absolute Freedom
2. Kindness from the Soul
3. Open-Minded (Non-Judgmental)

Of these three rules, it is Freedom which is the foundation. We will therefore focus on the importance of freedom in our new societies. This freedom will align with our Universal Purpose of Existence. Such freedom will also bring the most practical benefits to the greatest number of people.

Existential Development through Free Expression

Freedom is essential for our Existential Development. The main reason we are here on this earth is to experience, learn, and develop. This process is only possible with absolute freedom.

Therefore, we must allow…and indeed encourage…all forms of expression and exploration. It is only through the freedom to explore, experience, and express ourselves, that we can learn more of ourselves. This is how we develop our souls, and develop our minds.

If we truly want to become the Advanced Souls that we truly can be, then we must have Absolute Freedom, in all areas. We must have this freedom to explore all possibilities, to experience what we desire, and to ultimately develop ourselves into more advanced versions of ourselves.

Wellness Through Free Expression of the Soul and Consciousness

It is our natural desire to express ourselves and to enjoy our chosen experiences. If we want our mind, soul, and body to be healthy, then we must freely express ourselves and enjoy our pleasures our souls as we desire. This free expression is essential for maintaining optimum wellness and vitality, in all areas. Therefore: we must freely express our souls and minds. This free expression is essential for optimum wellness of our Physical and Spiritual Existence.

Be Non-Judgmental of Other's Needs and Desires

We must always be Non-Judgmental of others. In combination with Absolute Freedom, we will never judge another person for his desires.

Remember, each person has a unique Soul Alchemy, which requires specific needs as nourishment. It is never for us to make judgements on the nourishment needs of another person. His soul requires these needs, and these needs must be obtained regularly. These nourishments are required for his wellness. That is all we need to know.

This applies to all components of the man (Soul, Mind, and Body). Each component, of each person, requires specific needs for wellness. It is not for us to make moral judgements, or prohibitions, for something which a man requires for his Existence. He was designed this way; and these are the nourishments he requires. That is all we need to know.

The Divine Does Not Judge

We must emphasize that the Divine does not judge man. It is only man who judges man. The Divine actually prefers that everyone pursue their desires, and live with joy.

As I have personally been with the angels and higher beings, multiple times, I can state with certainty…that the Divine wants us to be happy.

They really don't care about what we do, in any type of judging way. Just do what you like. Enjoy your life. The concepts of good and bad are far less on their thoughts than religious teachers have you believe.

The Divine Want to See in Humans: The Divine Perspective

However, there are some basic rules on Good versus Bad. There are some behaviors which the Divine values highly, and others which the Divine really doesn't want to see. Yet these are far simpler than most people are taught to believe.

What does the Divine want? The Divine wants you to have love in your soul, and bring that love to others. The Divine wants you to find your inner light, and live your life with joy each day. The Divine wants you to be true to your own soul, and express yourself freely, without compromising.

Yet the Divine also wants you to co-exist with others easily, and perhaps joyfully. Be true to yourself, yet be kind to others along the way.

The True "Sins" in the Divine Perspective

The inverse is the darkness that the Divine does not want to see in humans. The angels and divine beings want us to stay away from the spiritual darkness. It is really not that complicated.

Phrased another way: the only acts that displease the Divine are the following: Deliberate acts of cruelty. Being judgmental of others. And prohibiting the natural rights of innocent people. These are the only acts for which a man is judged by the Divine. For all other acts, anything that you want to personally experience is yours without shaming.

Subtleties: "What about…?"

Absolute freedom, in actual practice, is 99% freedom. There are a few prohibitions we can have, yet these are very few. We only restrict acts which are direct harm to others. All other acts are accepted. These details will be discussed in detail, in the separate book on "The Meaning of Life".

Amusement Park is Being Redesigned at Dual Levels

We must also emphasize that this is the moment for mankind to restructure all aspects of the earthly societies. There has never been any greater moment, in the history of man. It is our destiny.

Also remember that this Amusement Park is being renovated in the upper realms. They are doing their part to restructure the metaphysical operations. Yet there are many systems which are beyond their control.

We must therefore restructure our earthly societies and systems, to match the renovations in the upper realms. We must do our earthly actions; it cannot happen without our determination. And yet with the momentum from the upper realms, we can indeed create the new realities.

Review: Design Future Societies Based on Universal Purpose

A very important theme in this series of books, is to redesign our civilizations. We are living in the greatest transition period of human history, and it is our destiny to create the more evolved societies.

These new civilizations will be based on several important concepts. The general categories include: The Universal Purpose of Life, and the Divine Way. When we enact these principles, our future civilizations will be far more advanced, with greater happiness for all.

The Universal Purpose of Life is to explore, experience, and evolve. Similarly, we must always seek light, love, and wisdom. Therefore, our new civilizations must be designed for all souls to live in this purpose.

The Divine Way is the set of actual rules which the higher beings want for us. These rules are: Absolute Freedom; Kindness; and Not Judging Others. The higher beings know that these rules are essential for any advanced civilization to function. We must embrace these ideals fully.

Finally, we must always seek the Divine Love. This is the spiritual elixir which nourishes the soul, and brings out the best of ourselves. We must seek it, soak in it, and live it. When you have tasted the Divine Love, you know that nothing else compares. This is why our new civilizations must encourage the Divine Love, within each person and institution.

It is our destiny and our duty, to create the new civilizations on earth, based on these central concepts. This is our moment.

Chapter 6:
Greater Realities Beyond Earth

Overview: What Exists Beyond?

What exists beyond this earth? Are there other realms and other dimensions? If these places do exist, then what are these places? These are some of the most profound questions which humans can ask.

In this chapter, we will provide the factual answers. We will describe many of these other realms and distant locations beyond earth. Notice also that these descriptions are provided by someone who has personally traveled there. These are not speculations; they are experienced realities.

Personal Experiences and Travels

All of the descriptions provided here are absolute reality. The details are based on numerous personal experiences. I have been to the upper realms many times, where I have talked with various beings.

This must be emphasized. I have personally traveled to these locations, interacted with the environments, and talked with many souls. I have been in these other locations so often, that this earth barely seems like home anymore. Indeed, these other realties are more real in many ways, than anything we experience in this earthly environment.

Returning to the topic: Are there other realms? Yes, absolutely. Our souls are eternal, and we can choose many different realms to visit. This earthly realm is just one of infinite possibilities.

The Greater Reality

We will begin with the overall picture of physical reality. We can refer to this as the Greater Reality, or the Multi-Dimensional Universe. These phrases can be used to distinguish the Total Reality from the Universe that we are familiar with. We then proceed to describe the various types of locations within this Greater Reality.

Galactic Universes

The Galactic Universes are those large areas which contain numerous galaxies. Essentially, the "physical universe" that we are familiar with, is a Galactic Universe. It is a physical reality, with numerous galaxies and solar systems. We use this term to distinguish between this type of universe, and the Total Universe, which contains all realms.

The Galactic Universes are generally oval shaped; flat and elongated. They are types of bubbles with distinct yet elastic borders. These universes float along each other slowly, as two large ships, in a very large ocean. When the two are close, then it is easier to travel between them.

The other Galactic Universes are similar to ours, with the systems of stars and galaxies. However, the specific galaxies, stars, and planets are different. The constellations are different. This is as much as I know.

Spiritual Realms

There are many Spiritual Realms. These places do exist, and are as very real as any location on earth. The Greater Universe is composed of these spiritual realms, and it is the basis for many metaphysical realities.

The topic of Spiritual Realms is important enough to discuss in another section. For the moment, know that these realms do exist, and are almost infinite in number. However, which realms you are allowed to visit will depend on the evolution level of your soul.

Planets

We know of earth as our planet home. We also know that there are many other planets, in our solar system and beyond. Yet we can also know that such planets exist in other realms and other universes.

Consider that we have Our Universe, then Our Realm within that Universe. Then…we have our home planet…within that realm of that universe. This is the general physical structure, in many locations.

This means that there are many other planets, in other realms, and other universes. When you travel to other realms, this is usually traveling to a specific planet, within that realm. On this other planet, there are many similarities to the life we know of on earth.

This is also where we go, when we leave our earthly bodies. Most of the people who walked the earth, are now living on one of these other planets, in the other realms. The planets are similar in many ways to earth, yet have geographic differences. The societies also differ from those here, in many ways. We have options in where we live.

Analogy: Large Hotel with Many Floors and Rooms

The analogy I often use for these locations is the large hotel. Visualize a very large hotel, with multiple floors, and multiple rooms. This is our total universe. Each of the floors is then a Universe. Each of the rooms is a separate realm. Yet the realm is much more than a room, it is a place which may have multiple planets, and societies with many people.

Furthermore, consider the number of rooms in this large hotel. There thousands of separate rooms. This is also true for the spiritual realms. There are thousands of these realms, all of which are distinct.

Note also, as a reality experience, there have been times when I have been escorted to an upper realm where the experience begins by entering a type of room. It is very much like a hotel room or dressing room. Thus, the analogy has multiple meanings.

Meeting Locations

In addition to the main realms, there are smaller realms which are used for specific purposes. I refer to these smaller realms as Meeting Locations and Studio Realms. These may be sections of the main realms, or as separate realms just used for this purpose. Yet I do know these exist.

These Meeting Locations are similar to meeting locations on earth, where beings from different realms can meet in a common area. These locations are often a mid-way point between the earthly realm and the realm of the other beings; or a mid-way point between universes.

Of course, we can be escorted to any realm, and talk with anyone at those realms. Yet there are some places which are used specifically as common meeting areas between beings of different realms.

Studio Realms

Another type of specialized location is the Studio Realm. These realms are designed very much like movie studios. The purpose of these realms is to create an experience, which is designed to show us something.

This is why I refer to these places as the Studio Realms. These are physical locations. Yet the "reality" is a fabricated reality. It is a real place, and we are really there, interacting with the environment. Yet the objects are fabricated, with props holograms, and similar effects.

When everything is operating, you are essentially a character in a movie world. Yet the images change easily, and the objects are not always the actual objects. It is also common for some of your mentors and friends to be there with you, guiding you along the experience.

The entire purpose of the experience is to learn something important. They want you to have a visual and tactile experience. It will be realistic in many ways, for you to learn something. Your own observations, thoughts, and sensations, are combined with messages from your friends. You will then take this entire experience with you, for your journey on earth.

Metaphysical Dimensions as Larger Scales

In addition to the Universes and Realms, there seems to be a set of Dimensions. These dimensions are of larger scales. This is more of a perspective, than a separate physical reality.

For example, on the earthly level we can begin with an atom, then a stone, a mountain, and then the entire earth. What we can see depends on our size, relative to the size of the object. The atom and stone are smaller, and we can see many atoms and many stones at the same time. Yet the mountains and planets are larger, and we can only see one.

This is essentially the scale of metaphysical dimensions. As our soul becomes more evolved, we become larger beings. And when we are larger beings, we can see more of the realities, at the same time.

This scale of perspective seems to be a reality. This is why the Higher-Level Beings…those we call "Gods" …are capable of seeing and doing so much more. Their souls and minds exist at these larger dimensions.

The Actual Relationships Between Universes and Realms

Although I have personally traveled to many realms, and talked to many different beings from those realms, there are some things that I do not yet understand. This includes the exact physical relationships between realms; or exactly how the realms co-exist with the universes. I do not know these answers. Yet I know with absolute certainty that these other realms and universes do exist, because I have been there.

Spiritual Realms and Vortexes

The Greater Reality is composed of numerous Spiritual Realms. These realms are the main forms of physical environments. Therefore, we must understand the concepts of these realms, to understand our full reality.

Again, notice that these descriptions come from personal travels to these many realms. I have personally visited, seen, and experienced.

General Physical Realities of the Realms

Each of these spiritual realms is unique in its own ways, yet there are similarities. We begin with the physicality of the realms. These realms are physical locations, with physical objects. It is very much like our home.

When you are in these other realms, you can go to a library and read books. You can be with musicians and play along with them. There are various homes, entertainment centers, libraries, and research centers.

Indeed, the life in these other realms is very similar to life on earth, in many ways. We don't have the outer biological layer, yet we are the same in all other ways, and can interact with our environments easily.

Unusual Physical Realities of the Realms

However, there are many unusual physical realities in these realms. The laws of physics are often different. Holograms are often used. In many of these realms, they have abilities to create objects and interact with their environment, in ways not possible on this earth.

Therefore, these realms usually have many similarities to earth, and yet many physical laws of reality which differ from anything we know here.

Numbering System of the Realms

The realms seem to have a numbering system. The number for each realm is a long number, with several digits. I do not know the meaning of these numbers, but it does indicate that there are indeed many realms.

It seems that the realms are similar to radio frequencies. When you turn into the specific frequency, you can access that realm. Thus, the numbering seems to be the access channel, which allows you to see that realm or travel there.

Vortexes to Travel Between Realms

The method for traveling between realms is the Vortex. The vortex is the channel, through which our souls can travel from one realm to another.

These vortexes are very real, and come in several common forms. They are also temporary. These vortexes will open up, allow souls to travel through the other realm, then close out again. Vortexes can appear anywhere, yet are often reappearing in locations of high energy flow.

The vortex is essentially a whirlwind, through which anyone can travel. As with any whirlwind on earth, the center is hollow and calm. This area is the region through which anyone can enter, and travel the conduit between the realms. The travel time is almost instantaneous.

Notice also that this vortex is the conduit between any two realms, not just our realm and others. In fact, there are researchers in the upper realms who are experimenting with vortexes, to create the vortexes on demand, and to know which vortex will lead to each realm.

Traveling Through Vortexes in Different Forms

As pure soul, you can travel through almost any vortex, regardless of the size. This means you can compact the size of your soul to very small dimensions, and travel through the vortex to the other side.

Indeed, it is this compacting of the soul, which allows us to travel the vortex from upper realm to our new bodies during reincarnation process.

We can also take other forms, most commonly as a sphere or wisp. As a sphere, we can travel through the air as small orbs. Many people actually see these orbs in their daily life. These are spiritual friends, who are using their orb shape as easy travel.

The other common form is the wisp. These are small wisps of energy, appearing as a small cloud. In this form, they zip around through the air, in acrobatic style. These are also pure souls, who have traveled to be here.

Anyone can convert their pure soul into these smaller forms. This allows easy travel across the air…and through any vortex. Thus, we can enter these vortexes ourselves, at any time, when we know how.

Escorted and Invited to Realms

Although there are many realms, we are limited to the realms we can visit. We must be escorted to these realms. We must be invited. This is how it is, when we are living on this earth. The only way to enter these upper realms is to be specifically invited and escorted.

Further notice that when your soul is more advanced, and when you have reached a higher stage of existence, then you will be invited to the higher-level realms. You must be seen as worthy before being invited.

Options for Living in Other Realms

This brings us to the options for living in many other realms. One of the most common questions of man is regarding the afterlife. Do our souls live forever? Where to we go when we leave our bodies permanently?

The answer to the first question is yes, our souls do exist forever. The answer to the second question is more complex. In brief, you can go to live in one of several realms. However, you must be invited and allowed to be in those realms. It is like a passport. You can go anywhere that you have the authorization on your passport, but not anywhere else.

Also note that this is where the traditional religious view of being judged comes from. It is not judging in the sense of punishment. Rather, it is the evaluation of your stage of existence, and which of the many realms you can travel. All other realms are restricted to you, because your stage of existence is not ready. You wouldn't belong there.

Therefore, we have many possible realms to choose. We can also choose to come back here, after a period of time away. Yet instead of returning to earth, we can experience other lifetimes in other realms.

There are many options, for living in other realms. The options begin with the variety of realms themselves. Then we are evaluated for our stage of existence, which gives us a type of passport to a set of realms, yet restricted for the others. It is then our personal choice, which of these realms we have as our new home, as well as visit for other experiences.

Analogy of Access Cards for Hotel Elevator and Room

As an analogy, we again return to the large hotel with many rooms. If we want to access the elevator, we need the proper access card. The access card allows us to go to a specific set of levels in the hotel. We are prohibited from going higher. Only those people with the higher access will have the right access cards, and be able to take the elevator further.

This is essentially the reality with the many other realms. We can only access the set of realms which match our stage of existence. There is a range of realms, which correspond to the level of our own evolution. We can access this range of realms as desired, but not any higher.

We take the analogy further with the specific rooms, as the specific realms. We require the proper codes on the access card to enter each of the specific rooms. Thus, we must also be able to enter the specific realms, as well as the range of realms. This requires the access card, which is coded for our specific soul.

Again, the options of realms that exist is almost infinite, yet we can only access the realms for which we have been approved; and this approval is based on the evolution of our soul.

Divine Energies and Cultures in the Various Realms

Each of the realms also has its own culture. This is based primarily on the types of spiritual energies in that realm. This means there is an overall character of the realm.

Therefore, the souls who choose to live in this realm tend to have similar souls among themselves; which is also similar to the spiritual energy alchemy in the realm itself. You will want to live in the realms which are most aligned with your own soul. The energies will feel most nourishing, and you will meet the people who enjoy most.

Personal Invitations to Other Realms, and My Future

Many of my own personal guides have invited me to their realms. I have also been personally invited to live among other kings when my lifetime here is completed. More recently, I have been told to research the specific environments of other realms…for my future afterlife. There are many realms available to me, when my mission here has been completed.

Our Own Vast Galactic Universe

If we want to understand our greater reality, and what is beyond earth, then we must discuss our own galactic universe. We do indeed live in a vast universe, of many galaxies and star systems. Yet always remember that this is just one layer of the greater reality. There are other realms, and other galactic universes which do exist.

The Physical Structure of Our Galactic Universe

Our galactic universe is a vast oval, with elastic boundaries. Within this universe there are numerous galaxies and star systems. Everything moves according to the same laws of physics, just at different scales.

There are numerous planets, with different geologies and weather systems. They are also of different ages. This leads to a variety of planets which can be visited or become home for intelligent beings. This earth is not the only place for us to live in any incarnation. There are other locations within this vast universe for our next lifetime experience.

Traveling Through Hyperspace

There is a form of travel which I will refer to as hyperspace. Using this form of travel, our souls can travel across vast distances of the galactic universe, within a few seconds. I have personally experienced this, and it is quite an experience. It is a very wild trip.

If there is any one thing that can travel faster than light, it is our souls traveling through hyperspace. However, this is only possible with our souls. Our physical bodies are not capable of handling this intense speed.

Other Civilizations and Beings in the Galaxy

Given the number of galaxies and planets in this universe, there must clearly be other intelligent beings. Furthermore, considering that many of these star systems are much older than our own, these civilizations must be far older than our own, with beings who are far more advanced.

Indeed, this is the reality. There are many other advanced beings in this universe. Some of us know them quite well. We have very close relationships with these advanced beings. There are indeed advanced civilizations in many parts of the universe, and many species of beings which are far more evolved than humans.

Again remember that the purpose of life is to Explore, Experience, and Evolve. These intelligent beings have indeed been evolving for a long time. It is our destiny to become as advanced. We can do this, if we seek to evolve our souls, our minds…and our civilizations.

Private Lives of the Wise Beings

Many of these intelligent beings have chosen our solar system as their home. They have been here for many thousands of years. Yet they remain private and invisible. Generally, they want to live their own private lives, without interacting with the people of the earth. It is only when the humans are ready, will they show themselves.

They want to help us, they want to teach us. Indeed, many of them actually love us. They want the best for us. Yet humans are generally not that intelligent, and have a desire for cruelty. They watch, and wait. When our civilization is advanced enough, the Wise Beings will appear openly.

Starseeds as Advanced Souls from Distance Star Systems

The Advanced Beings assist humans by sending emissaries. These are beings from advanced civilizations, who come in human form. In this way, the soul appears to be human, yet is in fact an advanced being from a distant star system. These types of humans are known as Starseeds, and have been the guiding souls for humanity throughout the centuries.

I am such a starseed. Therefore, I understand this existence on a very personal level. My soul was created in the Rigel Star System. During my first visit to earth, I became a King of Atlantis. Many of my friends from Atlantis are communicating with me in this lifetime.

Over the next 12,000 years my soul has been to earth numerous times. Each incarnation visit, I came here with an assignment, to assist humanity in some way. This includes being an architect in Ancient Egypt, a knight in the medieval period, and a famous painter.

My current mission is perhaps the greatest of any lifetime. It is my mission in this lifetime to lead humanity in their next stage in evolution. Today, I am here to provide the foundations for the new civilizations.

It is my duty to teach the new truths; to lead humanity into Light, Love, and Wisdom. This is My Purpose. It is my Destiny.

And it is *your destiny* to put these new truths into practice. It is now your destiny to create the new societies. You will build the foundations of advanced civilizations on earth. Together, we will create the next stage of humanity. We will establish foundations for the next 20,000 years.

Chapter 7:
Welcome to Earth

You have arrived on earth. Everything seems new. And yet many things seem familiar. What do you do while you are here? In this chapter we will discuss the basic concepts for guiding you on your earthly journey.

Note that these sections will be brief summaries. You will find more detailed guides in other publications in the series.

Our Reality as a Subset of the Greater Reality

Always remember that our earthly reality is a subset of the Greater Reality. There are many other realms. We are living in just one realm of the many realms that exist around us. Furthermore, we are just one planet among many planets, which have civilizations. There is indeed much more beyond what we see and experience in this earthly home.

We must remember this perspective, if we desire to create the best experiences in this lifetime. This lifetime is just one of many lifetimes. This body is just one of many bodies we will inhabit. And we are never alone, as there are many unseen guides who assist on our journey.

Earthly Realm as Amusement Park

Earth is an amusement park. This is the design of the earthly realm. We are living in a giant amusement park. This means that we are here to experience as many rides and adventures as possible.

Again we return to the Universal Purpose of Existence: to explore, experience and evolve. We can do this in the Earthly Amusement Park.

This truth also has several practical implications. The first is to remember that this is not your permanent home, it is only a park to visit now and then. Yet, this also means that we can visit as often as we want.

Another implication is making the best use of your time. It is not possible to experience everything in one visit, therefore we must choose our most desired experiences. We are also responsible for co-creating the experiences we desire. Anything is possible, if you know how to do it.

Hidden Mechanizations of the Amusement Park

The Earth as Amusement Park is much more than an analogy. It is the reality. This is inherent in the design of the earthly realm. We can indeed create our own experiences, and transform our desires into reality. All of this is inherent within the deeper metaphysics of the designed system.

Hidden Mechanics of the Simulation

In any amusement park, there are many rides which are actually immersive experiences. We become immersed in an alternate reality, where there are hidden mechanics that operate the system. The entire experience is completely immersive, and we enjoy as a type of reality.

This is exactly how the earthly amusement park operates. Much of what we see and experience are simulations, which differ from absolute reality. There are many hidden mechanics, in the form of metaphysics, which create the simulations and our interactive environments.

Operators of the Earthly Amusement Park

These systems absolutely do exist, and are managed by operators in the upper realms. We often can collaborate with those operators to create the earthly experiences. We also have some control over the systems ourselves. The reality we see is only a small part of the simulation.

I have personally seen some of the control rooms, where these operators create the simulations. I have watched actual realities being overlayed with simulations, which then become real to the person.

They have also asked me from time to time if I wanted a specific type of experience. Therefore, I know very well that these hidden mechanisms and operators do exist. We can collaborate with them, to create the experiences we want…or don't want…during our earthly journey.

Remembering Your Purpose

We return again to your Life Purpose. Why are you here? What are the passions which will provide direction for your life? The answer to this question begins long before you arrived on earth.

Making the Arrangements Before We Arrive

This earthly realm is indeed a vast amusement park. We can create any experience we desire. Yet it is not possible to experience everything in one lifetime. Therefore we must plan before arrival.

When we are in the upper realms, we decide what experiences we desire most in our next visit. We will then tell all of our fellow guides, who will assist us on the journey. We also discuss our desires with the secret operators of the amusement park mechanics. Together, we have planned the important experiences of our next visit. The essentials are planned before we leave the other realms for our current visit.

Reincarnation, Knowledge, and Amnesia

When you arrive here on earth, you will retain all of your soul and knowledge from your previous eternal existence. However, you are also given a type of amnesia. There are many aspects of your previous lifetimes, and your time in the upper realms, which are hidden to you.

The reason for this is to allow you complete immersion in the earthly experiences. You are allowed to create a new life, without feeling the need to be what you were in any previous life. You are also allowed absolute free choice, to make all the new decisions you desire.

However, your core soul is always there. Your deeper memories are there. This is why you know…deep down…who and what you are. Follow your deepest soul, listen to your deepest mind. This is the wisdom that you need to guide you for who you are, and who you are meant to be.

Remembering Your Purpose

What is your Life Purpose? You know what it is. Deep down, in your deepest mind and soul…you know. You have always known. The only reason you don't remember is because of the amnesia and the new life.

Yet everything was planned before you arrived. You were the one who made the choices, before coming down here again. You arranged with your friends in the upper realms, to co-create these experiences.

Therefore, you just need to remember your purpose. You already decided what you wanted to see and experience, during this visit to the earthly amusement park. It is simply a matter of remembering again.

The most common method of finding your direction is to follow your pleasures and intuition. You are naturally attracted to certain activities. These experiences lead to other experiences (often guided by the hidden assistants). Then something happens inside. You must follow this path. It is not a question anymore. It is something you…must…do.

This is your path. It was your choice of life path before you arrived. You have now remembered it, and everything is clear. You are on your way.

You Can Have These Successes and Pleasures

Always know that you are meant to have your deepest desires. Those desires that you want, that you crave, that you must have…they can be yours. All of your fantasies and dreams can become reality.

We must understand how this works. You deeply desire this lifestyle and experience, because it is what you came here for. Everything was arranged in the heavens before you came here. Your deep desire is simply the reminder that this is the path you came here to experience.

Further notice that this desire may be impossible for many people, yet it will be yours. You can be a famous rock star or actor quite easily, if that is your destiny. Again: we must always follow our own life purpose.

You can easily have what is impossible for others, because you are here for that experience. Conversely, if we attempt to follow the path of others, we will rarely succeed; because it is not what we arranged. Your deepest desires are always meant for you, and easy to obtain.

Soul Contracts

In addition to our primary desires for this lifetime, many of us also have Soul Contracts. The soul contracts are agreements for pre-arranged activities before coming to earth. These soul contracts are generally between several souls, who will be doing activities and relationships.

These soul contracts can be a variety of activities and purposes. Most of these are pre-arranged relationships, which will benefit both people. The partners will be brought together at the best time for everyone.

There are also contracts for the Mission on earth. There are some special souls, who have been given special assignments to assist humanity. The special soul knows well of his mission while in the upper realms. He signs the contract, then commit his lifetime to the special missions. This type of contract becomes his Divine Mission, and becomes the over-riding agreement for his life path. It is a special devotion.

Therefore, our Life Purpose may also be related to the special soul contracts we signed before arrival. Our most profound relationships, those which affect our lives the most, are also often agreed to in these contracts.

Of course, there are many people we meet without soul contracts, and we have free will regarding our choices. Yet our most significant relationships and experiences are often a result of these soul contracts.

Personal Guides and Assistants

We are also given Personal Guides and Assistants on our journey. They remain invisible and quiet most of the time, yet they are always nearby. They watch us and guide us on our lifetime journey.

These personal guides and assistants are metaphysical friends. They remain in their pure soul form, while we are immersed in our physical bodies. They listen to us, and guide us when needed. Some of these guides came with us, as soon as we arrived. Others come on their own, throughout your lifetime. Your guides are always watching, listening, and guiding. And other assistants will do work on your behalf in this reality.

Note that when you return to the upper realms, you will be asked to do the same type of guiding and assistance; for those who helped you; who are on their next lifetime journey.

Co-Creation of Our Experiences

Always remember that we are co-creators of our life experiences. The lifetime journey is yours, yet there are many others involved. Before we embark to the earthly amusement park, we make arrangements with the park operators and fellow travelers, in addition to the devoted spiritual assistants on our journey. We develop the desires together.

However, every desired experience is yet to exist. Nothing is created until the moment. There are of course some plans and chess moves in action, yet the fully formed experience does not exist until the moment.

This means that we can change the desired experiences before they occur. We can revise our desires along the way. We can also make our own choices during our journey, which deviates from the original plan. Thus, we are always co-creating our experiences as we proceed.

Further note that we can always talk with our Ride Operators, for them to make permanent adjustments in our path. We can establish that some activities are very important; and other experiences never to be seen. The operators will generally follow your new desires.

Also note that you must be absolutely certain in your soul, and show your commitment through your own actions. This is the only way that the assistants are willing to move the chess pieces around for your desires.

Reincarnation as Infinite Visits to the Amusement Park

The final important aspect of this earth being an amusement park, is knowing that we can always return again. As with any amusement park, it is a place to visit, then return home. Yet you can always return again.

The same is true of the physical form in this lifetime. You are visiting this earthly amusement park for a lifetime, and you make the most of it. Yet this is not your home. Eventually you will return home, in the upper realms. Your soul is eternal, and there are many other realms to enjoy.

Yet you can always return to this amusement park again. Indeed, most of us have returned here dozens of times; and will return again.

Chapter 8:
The Greatest Moment in Human Evolution

Overview:
This is Our Transition Moment

We are currently living in the era, of the greatest transition moment in the history of mankind. This is truly a significant era, and it is our destiny to make the practical changes during this transition period.

This truth must be emphasized. It must be emphasized again and again and again. All good people of the world must realize the moment that is upon us, and have the deep conviction to create new realities.

Therefore, in this chapter we will discuss the realities of human evolution, as guided by the Higher-Level Beings. We will also explain how this moment was created by the higher beings, and it is with their support that we are asked to create the new civilizations.

The Long-Term Plan for Human Evolution

We begin with the general plan for the evolution of humanity. This is a long-term plan, which has been guided over many thousands of years. We are currently in one of the most significant jumps in all of earth history.

Humanity's Place in the Greater Reality

Know this truth and know it well. Humans are the lowest form of intelligent species in the universe. They are also among the least evolved souls among the entire set of metaphysical realms.

Humans must understand their place. Compared to other civilizations in our universe, and in other realms, humanity is barely on the growth ladder. This means that humanity must learn from others, if they are to advance. We must seek the guidance of the advanced beings, in all realms and galaxies, if we truly want to become evolved.

Guiding Humanity Over Centuries

However, also know that the higher-level beings want to teach us. They want to help us evolve. There are many advanced beings, who see our potential, and devote themselves to teaching us. Although they know humans are far inferior, the higher beings hold out their hand, and offer their guidance. All we need to do is be willing to learn.

Of course, most humans are very slow learners, and this takes centuries. Yet the higher beings have amazing patience. They watch and wait. When we are ready for a new step, they send another set of starseeds to guide humanity forward. This is how it always has been.

Higher Councils and Other Celestial Beings

Who are the Higher Beings? Who are these beings that are far wiser than humans, who desire to teach humanity? There are several groups, each of which lives in a different location, and has different goals.

Very few humans are able to know of these beings, and interact with these higher beings directly. I am one of those who has the privilege.

However, most of humanity is not yet ready to know of their existence. Or know the specific details of their personalities. What I can tell you is that there are several Higher Councils, and each of these Higher Councils has Advanced Beings. These beings are celestial beings, which exist in several different forms; most of which are very similar to human form.

Some exist as very bright lights. Others are tall and slender. Some are councils of ancient kings, and others are councils of galactic beings. Thus, there are several different types of Advanced Beings, and several versions of Higher Councils. All of these are very wise and loving souls.

They only want the best for humanity. All seek love and wisdom, for themselves, and for all beings in the greater multi-level universe.

Angels as Messengers, Healers, and Protectors

We should discuss Angels as a special type of spiritual being. These angels are messengers. They are also healers and protectors. All angels are translucent, with brightly colored wings. When an angel touches you, the effects are profound. They can fill you with Divine Love, and transmit Great Wisdom, all with a few moments of touching your body.

Societies Must be Based on Higher Consciousness and Divine Love

All societies, in any location, must be based on Higher Consciousness and Divine Love. This is the ideal. This is the goal. This is how it must be, for all civilizations on earth; as it is on any other planet and in any realm.

Therefore, we must redesign our civilizations for these ideals. If we want to evolve, if we want to achieve the better societies that we desire, then we must redesign for the new ways of existing.

Creating Advanced Civilizations is Possible when Changing Beliefs

Can we really create a society based on higher consciousness and divine love? Is this really possible? Yes it is. Humans are not as limited as many people think. Much of what humans do is not actually "human nature". Rather, most of what humans do is based on the society in which they live. It is their culture, their beliefs, and their programming, which drives the behaviors and emotions of most humans.

Therefore, we can change the society, change the culture, change the programming of the people, and their behaviors will change. We change the systems and beliefs, and the humans will adapt. This is how we achieve the new societies. It is not inherent in humans; it can be changed.

Mastering Your Existence

If we want to redesign the world, then we must first become Masters of our own Existence. It is only when we fully master ourselves, that we can create the world we want to see.

What does it mean to Master Your Existence? This means that you live thoughtfully and strategically. It means that you operate from your soul and your mind, rather than from your emotions. Mastering Your Existence is becoming in full control over all aspects of yourself, and your life.

The Four Components of Existence

There are Four Distinct Components of Existence. These are your Soul, your Consciousness, your Body…and Divine Love. We have mostly been discussing the first three components, yet it is Divine Love which is the basis for all other realities.

If you want to Master your Existence, then you must claim full control over all three aspects of yourself. You must also place Divine Love as the absolute center of your existence. This is the only way to truly Master your Existence, in any lifetime or any location.

Purpose of Life: To Explore, Experience, and Grow

Always remember that the primary purpose, for any life on earth, is to experience and to grow. It is our purpose to explore and experience as much as we can while living here. It is then from these experiences that we develop ourselves. We improve our souls, and we expand our consciousness. We become more advanced souls and minds.

This is the purpose of life. This is always the main purpose of life. There is no other goal that compares to this. Always remember that our primary purpose in life is to develop ourselves. We exist here, for the purposes of experiences, pleasures, and developing ourselves.

Thus, always remember to seek experiences and personal development in your life. You must always become better each day.

Divine Love is the Core of Existence

As we experience life, and develop ourselves, we must always place the Divine Love as the Core of our Existence. In all of our choices, in all of our actions, we must have Divine Love as the Core. When we have this Divine Love in our soul, we will then have everything we desire.

With Divine Love as our Core, we can create joy and pleasure in the world. We will also attract all the friends and material success into our lives. This all begins with knowing and being that Divine Love.

This is most important when interacting with other people. Each person must be treated with kindness and courtesy. We must see all other people as equal value to ourselves. We must know how to love others, to serve others, and to find solutions which benefit all people involved.

Therefore, we must always place the Divine Love as the core of our existence. Regardless of anything that is happening around us, we must return to the Divine Love. This is the way to Master ourselves; and to ultimately create the new civilizations on earth.

Mastering the Soul: Knowledge and Freedom

The first step to Mastering Your Existence is to become Master of your Soul. Your soul your primary being; it is an Eternal Existence. You soul is your combination of personality traits. Therefore, if you want to master your existence, then you must become Master of your Soul.

This mastery requires three stages: Knowing; Exploration; and Freedom. We begin with Knowing Ourselves. This is knowing our personality traits and desires. The second stage is Exploration of New Experiences. We explore and experience based on what our soul desires most. This is how we experience pleasure and develop our soul.

The third stage is Absolute Freedom. We must have an environment of absolute freedom, where we can express our true soul, as desired, in every moment of every day. This is where we let our soul out to play, and our Divine Light will shine for all the world to enjoy.

Notice also that this is an-ongoing process, which continues throughout our existence. We are always exploring, we are always refining the knowledge of ourselves. This is what we do, as our Free Existence.

Mastering the Consciousness Within

We must then Master our Consciousness. This is more complex, as the culture has corrupted the mind for most people. However, we must do the work to remove the corrupted programing, and fully reclaim the mind.

We must learn to see the false teachings of society. We must realize the many ways in which the media and peers have corrupted our thinking. We believe many things to be true, which are false. We see the world not as it is, but as they have programmed us to believe it is.

This is known as indoctrination or brainwashing. The indoctrination has been pervasive and intense, for 20 years. Therefore, the minds of most humans have been soaking in these false thoughts for years. It is our job to recognize this brainwashing, and remove the corrupted programing from the consciousness clusters of the mind.

This is a necessary step to reclaiming fully Mastery over the Mind. This is also essential for rebuilding our world, into the advanced society that is our true destiny. Eliminate the propaganda, and begin to see clearly. This the first step, to reclaiming your mind, and our world.

Mastering the Self-Aware Entities

We must also manage the multiple Self-Aware Entities in the mind. All humans have at least two, and often more. The Self-Aware Entities are Clusters of Consciousness, which are large enough to become Self-Aware. These are fully natural, and most common in those with advanced minds. Therefore we must learn to manage these effectively.

Each of these Self-Aware Entities has its own personality, its own desires, and its own voice. They are indeed independent of your Thinking Mind; though created from your own Encoded Consciousness Energies.

These Self-Entities will attempt to take over the mind. They will voice their opinions, and sometimes take full control if you let them. Therefore, we must establish the Thinking Mind as the CEO of all others. We will allow their opinions, and self-expression, yet always be in control. This is the first job of Mastering your Consciousness.

Mastering the Emotions

Mastering yourself also includes Mastering your Emotions. You will only become an Advanced Being, when you learn to become full master of your emotions. This means you allow your emotions to exist, but you choose to act based on your intellect.

Many people let their emotions control them, like a wild bronco. They let the bronco of emotions jump all over, while the person himself is thrown about in all directions. This is not how to live. Rather, we must become master of our emotions. We control the bronco, we ride with the bronco; yet we never let the bronco throw us around.

If you want to have the best life, and the best relationships, then you must become Master of your Emotions. You must always place your Intellect, and your Divine Love, above your Emotions.

You can allow your emotions to exist, but only act based on the civilized and loving responses.

Mastering the Body

The final component we must Master is the Body. This means we provide what the body desires, yet in the healthiest ways. We learn to listen to what the body needs, and give the body what it needs, yet always in the ways which are most beneficial.

Notice also that each body is different, and has its own special nourishment requirements. We are also the ones who live in this body. Therefore, we have absolute primary authority to provide what our body requires, and to reject anything which may be harmful.

Furthermore, notice that it is never for any of us to judge the physical nourishment needs of another person. We are not living in their body; and therefore we cannot fully understand the physical requirements of the other person. It is for this reason that we must allow each person to enjoy his nourishment needs, freely and without interference. They will allow the same for you. This is our Absolute Right as Diving Beings.

Relationships Based on
Soul, Consciousness, and Spirituality

In the Future of Relationships, all relationships will be based on Soul, Consciousness, and Spirituality. This is how all relationships should be, and it is the way in which all relationships shall be.

Divine Love and Compassion

We begin all relationships with Divine Love and Compassion. When we have Divine Love in our souls, we know the highest levels of existence. We feel the greatest joy, and we understand life at the most fundamental levels. It is therefore from this knowing of Divine Love from which all relationships must be based.

When you enter into any relationship, you must always begin from the perspective of Divine Love. If you do not feel it at the moment, then you must gradually reclaim it and develop it. The success of the relationship, and your own personal happiness depend on this knowing of Divine Love.

Compassion and Empathy

Relationships must also be based on Compassion and Empathy. We must have deep compassion and empathy for all other beings. We must value the lives of other people, as much as we value our own.

Compassion and Empathy are Divine Laws. These are the prime moral codes for all beings of the universe. Therefore, we must always have this kindness, compassion, and empathy in our daily lives.

Having Compassion and Empathy is to know, deep in your soul, that all other people and animals have as much right to living as you. We must see that each person is a Divine Being, with full Right to Exist. He has the Right to be treated with courtesy, to express himself fully, and have every opportunity to enjoy his full pleasures without interference.

This is what it means to have Compassion and Empathy. We must realize that we are not the only being in the universe. There are others. And all beings have just as much right to life, pleasure, expression as yourself. Be good to all. Never hurt or take advantage of another. This is the basis for all relationships, of any form.

Soul Alignment

Relationships are the connections between two or more people. The best relationships are based on Alignment of the Souls. Remember that each person is a Divine Soul Alchemy, which is a mixture of core traits and desires. Therefore, when two souls have a similar Soul Alchemy, they will be able to enjoy being together very easily.

This is why you should always be fully free with your soul. It is when you are fully free with your soul, that others can see and feel your soul energies. They know your soul very well. The right people will be very attracted to this. The relationship will be easy and pleasurable.

Consciousness Energies in Relationships

When two souls are aligned, their consciousness will also be aligned. They will develop a type of telepathic connection, that exists far beyond the connections with other people. This can only happen when the two souls are very strongly aligned.

We can use this to our advantage. We can think very clear thoughts, which will then reach the mind of our closest friends. The same will also happen when they think specific thoughts directed toward us. In this way, we can have telepathic communication across the miles. We can share thoughts, remind each other how much we like them, and other messages, regardless of the distance.

The combination of minds, working together…and yet below our Thinking Mind Awareness…can produce some of the most creative and profound results. Therefore, we should always develop the connection of consciousness energies, between those we have Soul Alignments. The things we can do with each other, and for each other can be profound.

Practical Aspects of Relationships

Relationships will require many practical considerations. We always begin with empathy, kindness, and intelligence. Yet we must also consider practical aspects of negotiations and discussions.

Therefore, we will be providing a series of books on Relationships. These books will be practical guides, for the most effective and mutually pleasurable relationships; based on each type of relationship. Look for these publications, especially in the series on Dispute Resolution.

Review of Consciousness and Soul

We will now review the main truths of Consciousness and Soul. These are the most fundamental concepts. It is from this understanding that we will master our own existence, and build our civilizations of the future.

Of course, there are many practical details regarding consciousness and soul; and indeed the entire series exists to describe the details. Yet there are some fundamentals which are the foundation. These are the concepts which we will now review and emphasize.

Soul Alchemy

The Soul exists as an Alchemy of Soul Energies. These are energies of traits and desires, which make the soul exactly who he is. This Soul Alchemy has a general size; yet can be expanded; and is very fluid.

The Soul exists for Eternity; it is only the physical form which changes. Also, the core mixture remains essentially the same, and yet we have the ability to transform our soul alchemy through our significant experiences.

For practical applications, the Soul can be considered fluid, able to change size and shape. We can also move some energies to different places; both in our body, and in regions of space.

The Soul Extends far beyond the region of the physical body; which allows us to feel the soul energies of those nearby. When our Souls are Aligned, we feel refreshed; and when separated again we feel empty.

Your Inner Light

One aspect of being "alive" is to be emotionally and spiritually joyful. This state of being can be reality, when we let our Soul out to Play. Thus, it is essential that we express our souls fully and freely, at all times. We must always let our Soul out to Play; doing whatever gives us joy.

This becomes the Inner Light. Your Inner Light is your personal fuel, it is your shining star within. This Inner Light gives you the internal energy to fully enjoy your existence. This Light also brings people and pleasures to you. The way to access this Inner Light…is letting the Soul out to Play.

Consciousness in General

Consciousness exists as small energies. These energies are encoded with information. When these Encoded Energies are aggregated together, we then have complex thoughts. As we further aggregate these Encoded Energies, we build Clusters of Consciousness. These Clusters are the processing programs, databases, and Self-Aware Entities in the mind.

Consciousness Energies are always being Encoded, Processed, Duplicated, and Emitted. Therefore, the entire world has consciousness. Specifically, these thoughts are being emitted and absorbed; then later duplicated, added to, and emitted again. It is for this reason that these Consciousness Energies, as thought streams and thought clouds, are floating around everywhere.

Notice also that the small Encoded Consciousness Energies can be absorbed into any material; and will often exist within the atoms. The larger clusters will be located in specific regions of the body.

Consciousness Energies as Drops of Water

Consciousness energy can be compared to drops of water. When we gather larger amounts of conscious energy, as similar to gathering drops of water in a container, then we will have greater consciousness power.

Each drop of Consciousness is essentially a small entity of information. When we aggregate these drops of information together, the concepts become more complex. Therefore, the larger aggregations of the drops of consciousness energy will become larger databases; more complex ideas; and complex processing programs.

These Consciousness Energies are also similar to water drops in other ways. These drops are emitted as streams of thoughts. They also exist as thought clouds. These can also be built up as balls of snow.

Thus, the physical reality of consciousness energies is very similar to drops of water. Understand this, including the aggregation and flow, and you will truly understand the reality of consciousness.

Aggregated Consciousness Energies

Aggregated boats/drops of consciousness energies becomes a flowing mechanism of knowledge; as an intricate set of gears. Yet it is far more complex, as the "gears" can move in multiple directions as needed. This is how we obtain mental processing programs.

Self-Aware Entities

Larger amounts of aggregated consciousness energies will then become a self-aware entity. Furthermore, with more of the aggregated consciousness energies, the self-aware entity becomes mentally stronger.

Each person has two Self-Aware Entities: the Thinking Mind and the Subconscious. Many advanced beings have more Self-Aware Entities. These multiple entities within can be very useful, as devoted staff and providing insights. However, we must manage them effectively.

Encoded Consciousness Energies

These Consciousness Energies can also be compared to boats. These boats can hold cargo of codes; which is essentially knowledge. Thus, the empty boats can receive information; and the filled boats can be sent to their destination for processing. These boats are the Encoded Consciousness Energies; and are the basis for all complex thoughts.

Inter-Connected Consciousness

Also remember that these Consciousness Energies exist everywhere. This includes the plants, trees, rocks…and all physical objects. The amount of consciousness energies is small; yet does exist. Thus, trees and plants do have some consciousness. Some larger objects also have their own levels of consciousness.

These consciousness energies, in the trees, rocks and larger physical objects, can be accessed if the person is trained properly. This becomes the inter-connected consciousness.

Physical Reality of the Inter-Connected Consciousness

We also understand the physical reality of the Inter-Connected Consciousness. Although many people believe that we are existing in a sea of consciousness, this is not exactly true. It is more precise to say that each being emits consciousness energies. These are groupings of energies, which are transmitted by each being, and received by others.

These consciousness energies are sent out as streams of consciousness energies, and clusters of consciousness. The receiving mind will then be able to absorb these energies, which becomes the known information to the thinking mind.

Thus, it is true that we can be inter-connected with consciousness. We can indeed create wonderful futures with our aligned consciousness energies. Yet it is slightly different than typically understood.

We can further connect our consciousness energies to the many sprit friends in the various realms of the universe. Similarly, the Advanced Beings in the Universe will guide us; often using these methods.

Remember that all beings have some consciousness energies. Our conscious thoughts can then extend across space, in all directions. In this way, our thoughts can influence the thoughts of others.

Changing our Physical Environment with Consciousness

The most highly advanced method of using our Consciousness is to create our physical realities through our consciousness. Using our understanding of conscious energies, and other forms of Divine Energies, we can indeed create new physical realities.

The realities we see in front of us are not permanent. We can influence the realities we see, using our consciousness energies.

This is because all objects have some conscious energies. Therefore, we can use our minds, along with our deepest soul, to send instructions to all other objects and beings in the universe. Many of these other objects and people will then adapt to our desires. This allows our physical realities to change. We have then created a new reality. The most advanced beings know of this ability; and use it to their advantage.

Changing our Societies with Consciousness

This leads us to the importance of changing our societies, using our consciousness. The more Advanced Beings know that this is possible. Indeed, we know that much of our realities are not based on the actions we see…but rather based on the beliefs of millions around the world.

Therefore, we change our beliefs about how our societies should be, and our societies will change. We will believe…deep in our souls…that we can indeed have these realities as a new society; and these realities can become true. Of course there will be specific actions, yet the beliefs alone, by the majority of people, will cause shifts in the actual reality.

Many People with the Same Intention Will Indeed Change Realities

A greater application is to use many Advanced Beings, together, to create the same changes in physical reality. When we align the desires of many higher level beings….the True Power of using the Consciousness Energies to change reality becomes significant.

This is the concept behind prayer meetings, and large spiritual gatherings. When many people are aligned with the same intention, then this becomes a large Power Burst of Consciousness. When there are 500 people with the same thoughts, this becomes a power burst. And as these same thoughts are repeated in their minds, or out loud, we have repeated intention of the same desire. The physical reality will change. It must change. And this change will happen much sooner.

This is indeed a primary method for humanity to change their world. When everyone believes in peace and freedom, then the world must conform to this belief. When humanity truly believes that their specific views of a better society can be reality, it is then that the actual reality must change. We will, of course, take certain practical actions. Yet the strong belief, alone, from millions of people will change realities.

The Great Transition Moment in History

We are living in a transition period. We are, in fact, living in the greatest transition moment in all of human history. Such is the significance of the era we are in. It is therefore our duty to make the most of it.

Everyone must understand the significance of this era, and to take diligent actions in creating the new civilizations. This is the time. This is the moment. All of the factors are aligned in our favor. We must act now.

Moments of Evolution in History

Throughout history, there have been significant moments of evolution in humanity. These eras include the intellectual periods of Ancient Greece, the Renaissance, the Enlightenment, and most recently the 1960s-1970s.

Each of these periods of time was a great advancement in human development. These moments brought significant advancements in the individual consciousness and cultural beliefs; in the philosophies and in the technologies. We are now in such an era again; the greatest such evolution in all of human history.

Restructuring Entire Civilizations, Across the Entire Earth

The difference between those eras and today is one of scale. Those previous eras of advancement were regional, only for specific topics, and were building on previous systems.

Our moment is vastly different. The moment today is for the entire earth, and is an entire restructuring of civilizations. These are not simply advancements in philosophy or science, this is a complete restructuring of all aspects of civilization, and for the entire earth.

We are tearing down all of the old systems and beliefs, then replacing with the new foundations. There will be very few similarities between the past 10,000 years and what we are about to create.

Changes at Metaphysical Level and Earthly Level

Furthermore, our realm is being completely redesigned at the metaphysical levels. The hidden mechanics are being modified. The higher beings are sending emissaries with grand blueprints. At no other time in history has there been such a major restructuring, at all levels of reality, and guided by the wisest beings in the universe. The time is here.

The Next Stage in Human Evolution

We are here at this moment, to create the next stage in human evolution. Everything we do in the next few decades, will establish the future of humanity for the next 20,000 years. We must embrace this.

Society Falls Apart for the People to Rebuild

Why do you think it is that we are living in such chaotic times? The reason is that the old systems are falling apart, for us to create new systems. We must let these old systems fall apart naturally. Let them decay and disappear. From the clearing, we will create the new systems.

The existing society can be compared to a set of old buildings. Their foundations are rotting, their walls are falling apart. There is no point in attempting to fix these structures. They are beyond any type of repair.

The best solution is to completely tear down these structures. We will actively and purposely tear the systems down, for the purposes of creating new systems which are much better. Therefore, it is best to let the rotten structures of society fall apart. We need these eliminated and cleared away, for us to rebuild the new and much better systems.

Growth Can be Painful, but Necessary

Transitions can always be difficult, yet the existence after the transition is always much better. This is greater truth when we are growing in some way. Growth always requires letting go of something old, to create something new and better. The process is difficult, but the result is so much better, and very much worth the pains of the process.

This is where we are in the history of mankind. We are going the most significant growth period in the past 10,000 years. This means that there will be some difficulties during the transition years. Yet we must do it. We must eliminate the old, and create the new, for our evolution.

Reincarnation: Creating for Our Own Future

Always remember the reality of reincarnation. We will be coming back here, again and again. What kind of world do you want to be living in, the next time you come? If you want that world, then you must create it.

This means that you will be doing the difficult work, in this lifetime, to create the better world. Yet when you come back, the better world will be functioning, and you will be able to simply enjoy the experience.

The Practical Details of the New Civilizations

How should these new civilizations be designed? What are the new systems which will replace the previous systems? These are complex questions, yet we have prepared answers.

The new societies will essentially be the best of Western Civilization, with significant modifications. The civilizations will operate on absolute freedom. This also includes the natural flow of goods and energies, which is the actual method for all humans to obtain their desires.

There are of course many practical details. These details are described in many books by this author. The practical details of the new systems, for government, economics, dispute resolution, media, and other areas of life, are explained in great detail in these books.

Practical Transitions from Existing to New Systems

There are also many practical concepts for transition from the chaos of the moment, into the new civilizations of our future. These practical details of transition are also discussed in many books by this author.

We must remember that change occurs through evolution, not revolution. It is important that we change gradually, not abruptly.

We must also build the new systems as independent and co-exiting with the old systems. We must have both operating, gradually shifting the percentage of operations from old to the new. Only when the new systems are fully operational and effective, do we completely tear down the old.

We can evolve, for our entire structure of human civilization, but we must be intelligent and compassionate as we proceed. The practical steps for transitions are discussed in other books by this author.

The Great Spiritual Battle for Humanity's Future

We are living in a great spiritual battle, between good and evil, for the future of humanity. And the winner takes it all.

Let us repeat, because this truth is extremely important. We are currently living in a powerful spiritual war between the forces of good and evil. These evil beings are very real, and they have a long-term plan to enslave humanity in their darkness. They have increased in recent years, at an almost exponential rate. This is their moment for full global darkness.

However, the good forces actually are greater in number. And despite appearances, the good forces do have the upper hand. If we understand this, and seize the opportunities, we can defeat the darkness permanently.

This truth must be understood. It is far more than allegory. This is real, very real. It is real in ways that most humans cannot comprehend. We must defeat the darkness, for the future freedom and light of humanity.

The Darker Spiritual Beings

The darker spiritual beings do exist. They are very real. This truth is extremely important to understand, and therefore we will discuss in detail later in this chapter. For the moment, know these important concepts.

Spiritual beings come in many forms, with a variety of soul alchemies. This means that many of these spiritual beings are composed of absolute darkness. Their desire is to destroy society, to enslave others, and to cause the greatest suffering. These beings are very, very real.

Also know that these darker beings can enter the bodies of humans. They enter through your anger and fear, and then begin to darken your soul. It is similar to blackening the lungs from smoking, but now your entire soul is gradually becoming fully dark. It is worse than any cancer.

They can also take over bodies completely, and subjugate the mind. The person is no longer the man or woman you knew, the mind and body are taken over by the darker being, who uses you for spreading darkness.

This is the absolute reality of the darker spirits. Indeed, many of the elite and the street mobs have been infected by these darker spirits. We must know that we are fighting evil spirits, not fellow humans.

The Long-Term Plan of the Darker Spiritual Beings

The darker spiritual beings have always had a long-term plan. Their plan is to spread total darkness over the entire earth. They want to destroy all freedom and all kindness. They seek to enslave the people, and take perverse pleasure in watching others suffer.

In many ways, this long-term plan runs parallel to the long-term plans of the Higher Beings of Goodness. The higher beings of goodness seek to advance humanity, bringing the divine live and the greater good for all. Yet the forces of darkness despise all that is joyful and loving. Therefore, these darker beings work in secret, to destroy what good is created.

Although there have always been some evil beings here on earth, the current situation is much more extensive. Their long-term plan for world domination started around 1800. They have been planning, making their moves gradually, and mostly in secret. Their goals have always been to enslave the world, and eliminate joy from humanity.

We must realize that the events of today did not just happen. It was long-term strategy, with gradual steps. This is why few people noticed. Yet after 200 years…the beings of darkness are ready for global domination.

The New Global War between Good and Evil

This battle between good and evil has been going on for centuries. Indeed, since the very beginning of human civilization, the two spiritual sides of good and evil have been influencing the paths of humanity.

However, what we are experiencing today is at a completely new level. In the previous centuries, the battles were localized. There were a few people, a few incidents, and some physical battles regionally. Today we are experiencing this war on a global scale. This battle is for the entire earth, and for the entire future of humanity.

This is the biggest war in all of human history. And it is being fought on the spiritual level, as well as the physical level. We will either enter the New Age of Light, or Complete Darkness; for the next 10,000 years.

The winner takes it all. The stakes are for the entire earth, the entire population of humans, and the future of humanity for thousands of years.

Beware of the Darker Beings

Dark spirits do exist. This is a reality, and everyone should be aware of their existence in our world. The two most important concepts to emphasize are the following: they are very real, and very dangerous.

There are three main reasons for discussing these darker beings in this book. These reasons correspond to three main layers of the book.

We begin with the intellectual knowledge, where we learn the truth about these entities and what they do. Then we reach the personal level, where we understand how these dark forces can harm our souls, and destroy our existence. This leads to the society level, where we can see the harm that such dark beings have created in our world.

Therefore, if we desire to understand our realities, and to make the most of our time, then we must understand the influence of the darker beings. Their influence is far more pervasive than most people know.

The Terrifying Reality of the Darker Beings

The darker beings are very real, and extremely terrifying. We must be absolutely clear on this. Most people are unaware of their existence, and yet under their influence every day. Meanwhile, some of us have actually seen some of these darker beings. Trust me when I say, that there is nothing more terrifying than seeing a truly dark spiritual being.

These darker spirits come in many forms, which we will describe later. Yet all of them have the souls of darkness. You can feel their energies. The energies of darkness, anger, suffering, and evil.

It is very important that you understand the reality of such beings. You must understand that they are darkness and evil, with complete absence of all love and empathy. They feed off anger and hate. They take pleasure in causing suffering, destruction, and enslavement.

And the energies who feel when near them, will make you want to seek the light, and hold onto your own soul, as tightly as possible.

These beings do exist. They are here, as spirit form and in the bodies of many humans. They are the prime cause of all evil in this world.

Secretive and Stealth

These darker beings operate very much in stealth. They remain hidden. They lurk in secret. They rarely make their presence known in an obvious way. This is one of the reasons that many people can be infected, and yet never realize it. The true cause remains invisible.

Furthermore, the infection is very gradual. The darker beings know very well how to infect just a bit of darkness into you. Then a bit more. And a bit more. You will never feel it as a sudden darkness. Rather, you will feel just a bit more anger, a bit more irrational fear, and act on those feelings. This builds the power of darkness within you, and makes you easily susceptible for more injection of the dark energies.

Thus, the entire operation of being corrupted by darkness is always subtle. It is gradual. Those who are infected gradually develop more and more darkness, until they become irrational with anger and cruelty.

Feeding on Fear and Anger

The darker beings feed on fear and anger. This is how they feed themselves. It is also how they gain entry into your own soul. This is why you should never give into the fear and anger; you are only making yourself vulnerable to infection from the darker beings.

Always remember that these darker beings are energy feeders. They feed off energies. They will consume your soul energies. They will absorb the energies of light, but they prefer energies of darkness. Never give them what they want. They will only grow in power, and return again for another energy feeding. Do not let them see your soul as another meal.

Entering Your Soul and Converting to Black

These darker beings also want to enter the bodies of humans, for feeding and for transformation. The process is very similar to smoking tobacco. With each day of smoking, your lungs become darker. In a similar way, with each day of anger and cruelty, your soul becomes darker. The darker beings attach themselves easily during these times, and covert the soul within.

The result is far worse than any type of cancer. A normal cancer just affects the physical body, yet the soul is eternal. However, if your soul becomes blackened…your darkened soul is now also eternal. This is a fate you never want. It is far worse than any physical pain.

Taking Over Your Mind and Body

These dark beings can also take over your mind and body. If you are vulnerable, the darker beings can enter your body, and live there.

They can set up permanent home inside your mind. They can gradually take over the programming of your consciousness clusters. They can over-ride your self-aware entities. Of course, you will have some battles in the mind, but if you have a weak mind, they will take over.

Always remember that is very possible for any darker being to enter a human body. It is possible for any darker being to set up a permanent home in the mind. It is possible for any darker being to fill the body with his own darker soul energies. The darker beings can take over any part of a human, from within. They can also come and go as desired.

Note that actually any metaphysical being can do this. Any of the good beings in the upper realms can do this also. It is just that they respect your autonomy, and would never do such a thing. They may enter your body or mind for healing purposes, but they will leave when completed.

It is important, therefore, to be of a very strong soul and strong mind. You must have such strength within, that there is no being, of any type, which can enter your body without your permission.

Dark Beings as Born into Human Bodies

There is another reality that we must emphasize. There are many dark souls which are born into human bodies. This is a reality.

Remember that all humans are eternal souls, which enter the human body for a temporary life experience. Also remember that each soul, is a specific soul alchemy, with combination of soul traits and consciousness.

Therefore, we can easily understand that many darker souls of the realms can enter into human bodies. The process is the same, and they generally arrive in the same way. Thus, there are indeed many humans who are actually born with dark souls. This is very much a reality.

Furthermore, the souls in the upper realms will often choose families and environments which align with their desires. For the darker souls, this means that they will often choose bodies in families and cultures where evil already exists. It is for this reason, that many of the elite are true families of dark souls. The dark souls incarnate into those dynasties, where their natural darkness will flourish.

What are the Dark Beings, and Where do they Exist?

These darker beings do exist. Many of us have seen them. And most humans have been infected by them. So what are they? Where do they come from? The answer is complex, as there are many types.

In general, the variety of darker souls is comparable to the variety of divine souls. Furthermore, as there are numerous spiritual realms, there are many permanent homes for these darker beings. If you are a person who seeks the love and light, you will rarely see them; but if you are a person who lives with anger and fear, then they will live with you.

However, those of us who are of a very bright soul, who have a mission for the good of humanity, we are also visited by the dark souls from time to time. They want to steal our light, and prevent us from doing the good that we are here to do. As such, we have seen these beings.

I will give you the names of two such beings. The first is the "reaper". This is their real name. They came to me recently and attempted to steal my light, but my soul was too strong and I beat them. What I learned later is that they believe that they should have more control over humanity. They are growing in their power, and are seeking more control.

The second type I will name is the Lizard Being. Yes, they are real. This is not conspiracy theory. They are absolutely real. They are also the most frightening sight. It not because of their appearance, it is their soul. You can feel their darkness, their energies, which makes them terrifying.

There are other dark beings, seen by other spiritualist friends that I know. Most come in various shapes, like small animals or wisps. If you see one of these, just maintain your strength, and command them to leave. They will usually leave if you command them with enough force.

Resisting the Darker Beings

We must resist the influence of these darker beings. There are many practical methods for doing this. The first is simply to live a happy joyful life. They feed off anger and fear, and if you have none, then they have no reason to be there. They will also find you boring, and leave you alone.

We can also resist by ignoring all media and groups which are violent and cruel. They may be infected with darkness, and have dark beings nearby. But you don't have to absorb it. Avoid the anger, never live in fear, and you will not be susceptible to any darker spirits.

The Influence of True Dark Souls on Civilization

We now return to the third theme of this book: the practical effects of the profound mysteries on our civilization. Specifically, we will discuss the influence of the dark souls on our society. We will understand how we have come to be where we are in this chaotic world.

Of course, this is a complex topic and therefore we can only describe the highlights. Further details will be provided in other publications.

The Existence of True Darkness in Human Form

We must first acknowledge the existence of truly dark souls in human form. As described above, there are dark souls who reside in human bodies. They have the appearance of human on the outside, but a soul which is truly darkness and evil within. This is very much a reality.

Throughout history, there have always been humans with these truly dark souls. These are the ones who create darkness and suffering in their region. They also obtain personal power using any means necessary.

When we understand that such dark souls do exist, and are not like other humans, then we can more accurately understand the motives and operations of those darker beings on earth. They have no limits on what they will do for power, control, and creating suffering in the world.

Operating in Secret

These darker souls also operate in secret. It is the same whether in their spirit form or in human bodies, they choose to operate in the most secret ways. They have money, power, and influence; and yet are mostly unknown. The true leaders of darkness on earth have always been hidden to the public. They can only be found within layers upon layers of secret societies and institutions. They are the true players in modern civilization.

The Dark Soul Dynasties

We therefore have these dynasties of hidden power. These are true dark souls, born into human bodies, among the families of wealth and influence. This is very much reality. Their long-term motives are for ultimate power and global suffering of the people.

The Long-Term Secret Agenda

The long-term agenda of the dark souls was set into place centuries ago. The agenda is simply to maintain in the long-term, as the dark souls from the realms will choose to arrive in these same families. And with the reincarnation, the same dark souls continue their plans, every few years.

We therefore have an elite group of dark soul dynasties. These are truly dark souls, born into families of wealth and influence. The dark souls know what they are doing, long before they arrive on earth. And because reincarnation is also a reality, the same dark souls will return every few generations, and perpetuate the original plan for global domination.

Obtaining Power and Spreading Darkness

The dark souls have been operating in secret, yet with power and influence, for a very long time. It is in this way, that they gradually took control of every institution. All banking, media, governments, and food production are now within the control of a few dynasties worldwide.

Furthermore, using their total control of media and education, they have been able to spread the darkness to millions of people. This is why many people are also always with anger, fear, and cruelty.

Most of these people are also infected with the dark souls (in spirit form) who are eager to take control of the willing humans. Essentially, an entire world-wide army of dark souls has been created; who are eager to follow the agenda of darkness from their media leaders.

We must understand this reality, and know it well. We must know the deeper reality of what we are fighting, if we want to change our world.

True Dark Beings versus Influenced Humans

This leads us toa very complex topic. How do we recognize the true dark souls, versus the average person who has been influenced by darkness? Furthermore, how do we distinguish the human who is simply at a lower stage of existence, versus those who are truly dark souls?

We can provide guidelines, however these details will require a separate publication. The defining factor is energy. When you are a pure soul, you can feel the true darkness in others. It is very clear.

Aside from the energies, we look at the lack of empathy; or their delight in causing suffering. When they enjoy cruelty, this is a darker soul.

Our Destiny is to Create the Advanced Societies

The ultimate truth of our current era, is that it is our destiny to create the new civilizations. It is our purpose, our duty to follow the blueprints for building the societies and new institutions. This is our destiny.

This moment in history is the greatest moment in all of man-kind. It is from this era of change and confusion, that we will build the foundations for the new age of man. Everything is truly aligned in our favor.

Chaos is Opportunity

Many people see the current reality as chaos. However, the wise man knows that chaos is another form of opportunity. When there is chaos, there is dynamic flow. This dynamic flow is the perfect opportunity to create all that we desire. It is simply a matter of moving everything into place. We create new systems as we rearrange the components.

Consider the craft of metallurgy. We begin with solid metals such as steel and brass. As solid objects they are fixed in their form. Yet we melt these, and everything becomes dynamic. We mix all the liquid metals together, in the exact compositions we desire. Then we pour into the molds; the molds of our design. We create exactly what we desire.

The same is true for our current society in chaos. We harness the chaos. This is because all of the solid institutions and systems are now changing form. As with the metals, everything that was once solid and permanent in society is broken and melted. We can move everything around, and mix together in our own combinations. It is an opportunity!

Therefore, as we watch the traditional systems fall apart, and our previous beliefs being challenged, we study the pieces carefully. We know that from this chaos we can create the new age of mankind.

We must simply follow the Divine Blueprints, and create the new alchemy to our desires.

Battle for Global Domination

Also remember that the darker souls have been planning their agenda for global domination. This is also the era when the darkest souls are fully implementing their plans for global control and endless suffering.

This is why we must be vigilant in fighting, and defeating, all aspect of evil on earth at this time. If we do not rise together and defeat the evil today, they will enclose the entire earth in their darkness. It is very much a spiritual war, and a war for the future of the entire earth.

Yet also have much hope, because the good souls do have the greater power. We do have the upper hand. Despite the appearances, the darker forces are being defeated in many areas. We have them on the defense, and they know that we are the stronger force. All we have to do is keep strong, and bring the light to more regions of society. We will win this war.

This is the Moment to Defeat Evil….Permanently

This is also the moment to defeat evil on this earth…permanently. In all of human history, there has never been a greater moment to actually defeat the evil on this earth…permanently and completely.

Although the darker forces seem to have all the power, and impossible to defeat, we actually have the greater powers. We are in the majority, and we have the higher beings in the upper realms behind us. As long as we maintain our strength, and follow strategies, we will defeat the darkness.

Again, this is the best moment in all of human history to actually defeat the darkness on the earth. We could not do this 50 years ago, or 150 years ago. The time was not right. Today…is…that time. Everything has been aligned, for the good people of the earth to rise together, and defeat the entire force of darkness. Seize the opportunity. It is our destiny.

The Divine Beings are Working With Us

We are also fortunate in that the Divine Beings are working with us during this moment. The entire design of the earthly realm, as managed from the upper realm, is being completely renovated. Within a few years, the metaphysical mechanics of the earthly realm will be very different.

Therefore, the earth systems are being renovated from the upper realms as well as on the earth itself. This is a grand plan, to completely renovate all aspects of the earthly realm and human civilization.

Furthermore, many of humans on earth today are actually volunteers from the heavens; sent here specifically to enact the great transition. These volunteers are guided by the higher beings and angels, to make the new age of man into a practical reality.

The time is here. The time is now. In all of human history, there has never been a greater moment in the renovations and redesign of human civilization. It is our duty, and our destiny, to make this a reality.

The Blueprints and Truths in Several Publications

This series of books, along with other publications, will provide the detailed blueprints for our new civilizations. It is our duty to create these new civilizations as our reality. Always remember that is from the chaos we create the opportunities. Your future self will be happy.

Made in the USA
Columbia, SC
03 December 2023